FUTURE 3

English for Work, Life, and Academic Success

Second Edition

Series Consultants
Sarah Lynn
Ronna Magy
Federico Salas-Isnardi

Authors
Irene Schoenberg
Margot Gramer
with Jamie Greene,
Julie Schmidt,
and Geneva Tesh

 Pearson

Future 3
English for Work, Life, and Academic Success
Copyright © 2019 by Pearson Education, Inc.

Pearson Education, 221 River Street, Hoboken, NJ 07030 USA

Staff credits: The people who made up the *Future* team, representing content development, design, manufacturing, marketing, multimedia, project management, publishing, rights management, and testing, are Pietro Alongi, Jennifer Castro, Dave Dickey, Gina DiLillo, Warren Fischbach, Pamela Fishman, Gosia Jaros-White, Joanna Konieczna, Michael Mone, Mary Perrotta Rich, Katarzyna Starzyńska-Kościuszko, Claire Van Poperin, Joseph Vella, Gabby Wu

Text composition: ElectraGraphics, Inc.
Cover Design: EMC Design Ltd
Illustration credits: See Credits page 282.
Photo credits: See Credits page 282.
Audio: CityVox
Development: Blue Crab Editorial Services

Library of Congress Cataloging-in-Publication Data
A catalog record for the print edition is available from the Library of Congress.

ISBN-13: 978-0-13-527833-8 (Student Book with App and MyEnglishLab)
ISBN-10: 0-13-527833-3 (Student Book with App and MyEnglishLab)

ISBN-13: 978-0-13-453791-7 (Student Book with App)
ISBN-10: 0-13-453791-2 (Student Book with App)

Printed in the United States of America

www.pearesoneltusa.com/future2e

CONTENTS

Welcome to *Future: English for Work, Life, and Academic Success*

Future is a six-level, standards-based English language course for adult and young adult students. *Future* provides students with the contextualized academic language, strategies, and critical thinking skills needed for success in workplace, life, and academic settings. *Future* is aligned with the requirements of the Workforce Innovation and Opportunity Act (WIOA), the English Language Proficiency (ELP) and College and Career Readiness (CCR) standards, and the National Reporting System (NRS) level descriptors. The 21st century curriculum in *Future*'s second edition helps students acquire the basic literacy, language, and employability skills needed to meet the requirements set by the standards.

Future develops students' academic and critical thinking skills, digital literacy and numeracy, workplace and civic skills, and prepares students for taking standardized tests. Competency and skills incorporating standards are in the curriculum at every level, providing a foundation for academic rigor, research-based teaching strategies, corpus-informed language, and the best of digital tools.

In revising the course, we listened to hundreds of *Future* teachers and learners and studied the standards for guidance. *Future* continues to be the most comprehensive English communication course for adults, with its signature scaffolded lessons and multiple practice activities throughout. *Future*'s second edition provides enhanced content, rigorous academic language practice, and cooperative learning through individual and collaborative practice. Every lesson teaches the interpretive, interactive, and productive skills highlighted in the standards.

Future's Instructional Design

Learner Centered and Outcome Oriented

The student is at the center of *Future*. Lessons start by connecting to student experience and knowledge, and then present targeted skills in meaningful contexts. Varied and dynamic skill practice progresses from controlled to independent in a meticulously scaffolded sequence.

Headers highlighting Depth of Knowledge (DOK) terms are used throughout *Future* to illuminate the skills being practiced. Every lesson culminates in an activity in which students apply their learning, demonstrate their knowledge, and express themselves orally or in writing. A DOK glossary for teachers includes specific suggestions on how to help students activate these cognitive skills.

Varied Practice

Cognitive science has proven what *Future* always knew: Students learn new skills through varied practice over time. Content-rich units that contextualize academic and employability skills naturally recycle concepts, language, and targeted skills. Individual and collaborative practice activities engage learners and lead to lasting outcomes. Lessons support both student collaboration and individual self-mastery. Students develop the interpretative, productive, and interactive skills identified in the NRS guidelines, while using the four language skills of reading, writing, listening, and speaking.

Goal Setting and Learning Assessment

For optimal learning to take place, students need to be involved in setting goals and in monitoring their own progress. *Future* addresses goal setting in numerous ways. In the Student Book, Unit Goals are identified on the unit opener page. Checkboxes at the end of lessons invite students to evaluate their mastery of the material, and suggest additional online practice.

High-quality assessment aligned to the standards checks student progress and helps students prepare to take standardized tests. The course-based assessment program is available in print and digital formats and includes a bank of customizable test items. Digital tests are assigned by the teacher and reported back in the LMS online gradebook. All levels include a midterm and final test. Test items are aligned with unit learning objectives and standards. The course Placement Test is available in print and digital formats. Test-prep materials are also provided for specific standardized tests.

One Integrated Program

Future provides everything adult English language learners need in one integrated program using the latest digital tools and time-tested print resources.

Integrated Skills Contextualized with Rich Content

Future contextualizes grammar, listening, speaking, pronunciation, reading, writing, and vocabulary in meaningful activities that simulate real workplace, educational, and community settings. A special lesson at the end of each unit highlights soft skills at work. While providing relevant content, *Future* helps build learner knowledge and equips adults for their many roles.

Meeting Work, Life, and Education Goals

Future recognizes that every adult learner brings a unique set of work, life, and academic experiences, as well as a distinct skill set. With its diverse array of print and digital resources, *Future* provides learners with multiple opportunities to practice with contextualized materials to build skill mastery. Specialized lessons for academic and workplace skill development are part of *Future*'s broad array of print and digital resources.

In addition to two units on employment in each level, every unit contains a Workplace, Life, and Community Skills lesson as well as a Soft Skills at Work lesson.

Workplace, Life, and Community Skills Lessons

In the second edition, the Life Skills lesson has been revised to focus on workplace, life, and community skills and to develop the real-life language and civic literacy skills required today. Lessons integrate and contextualize workplace content. In addition, every lesson includes practice with digital skills on a mobile device.

Soft Skills at Work Lessons

Future has further enhanced its development of workplace skills by adding a Soft Skills at Work lesson to each unit. Soft skills are the critical interpersonal communication skills needed to succeed in any workplace. Students begin each lesson by discussing a common challenge in the workplace. Then, while applying the lesson-focused soft skill, they work collaboratively to find socially appropriate solutions to the problem. The log at the back of the Student Book encourages students to track their own application of the soft skill, which they can use in job interviews.

Academic Rigor

Rigor and respect for the ability and experiences of the adult learner have always been central to *Future*. The standards provide the foundation for academic rigor. The reading, writing, listening, and speaking practice require learners to analyze, use context clues, interpret, cite evidence, build knowledge, support a claim, and summarize from a variety of text formats. Regular practice with complex and content-rich materials develop academic language and build knowledge. Interactive activities allow for collaboration and exchange of ideas in workplace and in academic contexts. *Future* emphasizes rigor by highlighting the critical thinking and problem solving skills required in each activity.

Writing Lessons

In addition to the increased focus on writing in Show What You Know! activities, *Future* has added a cumulative writing lesson to every unit, a lesson that requires students to synthesize and apply their learning in a written outcome. Through a highly scaffolded approach, students begin by analyzing writing models before planning and finally producing written work of their own. Writing frameworks, Writing Skills, and a checklist help guide students through the writing process.

Reading lessons

All reading lessons have new, information-rich texts and a revised pedagogical approach in line with the CCR and ELP standards and the NRS descriptors. These informational texts are level appropriate, use high-frequency vocabulary, and focus on interpretation of graphic information. The readings build students' knowledge and develop their higher-order reading skills by teaching citation of evidence, summarizing, and interpretation of complex information from a variety of text formats.

Future Grows with Your Student

Future takes learners from absolute beginner level through low-advanced English proficiency, addressing students' abilities and learning priorities at each level. As the levels progress, the curricular content and unit structure change accordingly, with the upper levels incorporating more advanced academic language and skills in the text and in the readings.

Future Intro	Future Level 1	Future Level 2	Future Level 3	Future Level 4	Future Advanced
NRS Beginning ESL Literacy	NRS Low Beginning ESL	NRS High Beginning ESL	NRS Low Intermediate ESL	NRS High Intermediate ESL	NRS Advanced ESL
ELPS Level 1	**ELPS** Level 1	**ELPS** Level 2	**ELPS** Level 3	**ELPS** Level 4	**ELPS** Level 5
CCRS Level A	**CCRS** Level A	**CCRS** Level A	**CCRS** Level B	**CCRS** Level C	**CCRS** Level D
CASAS 180 and below	**CASAS** 181–190	**CASAS** 191–200	**CASAS** 201–210	**CASAS** 211–220	**CASAS** 221–235

The **Pearson Practice English App** provides easy mobile access to all of the audio files, plus Grammar Coach videos and activities. Listen and study on the go—anywhere, any time!

Abundant Opportunities for Student Practice

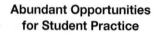
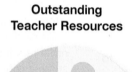

Student

Student books are a complete student resource, including lessons in grammar, listening and speaking, pronunciation, reading, writing, vocabulary, and Soft Skills at Work, taught and practiced in contextual activities.

Workbook—with audio for lower levels—provides additional practice for each lesson in the student book, with new readings and practice in writing, grammar, listening and speaking, plus activities for new Soft Skills at Work lessons.

MyEnglishLab allows online independent self study and interactive practice in pronunciation, grammar, vocabulary, reading, writing, and listening. The MEL includes the popular Grammar Coach videos and new Pronunciation Coach videos and activities.

Teacher Edition and Lesson Planner includes culture notes, teaching tips, and numerous optional and extension activities, with lesson-by-lesson correlations to CCR and ELP standards. Rubrics are provided for evaluation of students written and oral communication.

Outstanding Teacher Resources

Teacher

ActiveTeach for front-of-classroom projection of the student book, includes audio at point of use and pop-up activities, including grammar examples, academic conversation stems, and reader's anticipation guide.

College and Career Readiness Plus Lessons supplement the student book with challenging reading and writing lessons for every level above Intro.

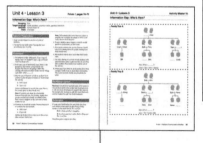

Assessment Program, accessed online with interactive and printable tests and rubrics, includes a Placement Test, multi-level unit, mid-term and final exams, and computer-based ExamView with additional ready-to-use and customizable tests. In addition, sample high-stakes test practice is included with CASAS test prep for listening and reading.

Multilevel Communicative Activities provide an array of reproducible communication activities and games that engage students through different modalities. Teachers' notes provide multilevel options for pre-level and above-level students, as well as extension activities for additional speaking and writing practice.

Go to the Teacher website for easy reference, correlations to federal and state standards, and course updates. www.pearsonelt.com/future2e

Preview questions activate student background knowledge and help the teacher assess how much students know about the unit theme.

4 Getting a Job

PREVIEW
Do you have a job now?
Are you looking for a job?
What experience and skills do you have?

A full-page photo introduces the **unit theme** and provides opportunities for interactive classroom discussion.

UNIT GOALS

☐ Identify qualities of good employees
☐ Talk about work experience
☐ Read a job application
☐ Describe your work history

☐ Talk about the past and the present
☐ **Academic skill:** Make inferences
☐ **Writing skill:** Add specific details
☐ **Workplace soft skill:** Be positive

65

Unit goals introduce the competencies taught in the unit and allow students to track and reflect on their progress.

UNIT TOUR

> Key **vocabulary** is contextualized and practiced in connection to the unit theme.

> **Study tips** introduce the learning skills and strategies students need to meet the rigor required by the CCRS.

Vocabulary

Qualities of good employees

A LABEL. Use the words in the box to complete the descriptions of the pictures. Use the word that has the same meaning as the first sentence.

Qualities of good employees

cooperative	flexible	organized
dependable	hardworking	pleasant
efficient	motivated	punctual

B ▶ LISTEN AND POINT. Then listen and repeat.

1. Carmella comes to work every day and helps her patients. She is _____.

2. John is very fast. He is an _____ worker.

3. Alisa is neat and knows where everything is. She is always

4. Bill always comes to work on time. He's very _____.

5. Carlo smiles a lot and is always friendly to customers. He is _____

6. May and her co-workers work well together. They are

7. These men want to do a good job and finish the project soon. They are _____.

8. Yusef works hard at the fabric store. He is very _____, so he might get a promotion.

9. Rana can do many different things at work. She is _____.

Vocabulary

C PRACTICE. Sometimes former employers write a letter of recommendation. This letter tells a new employer good things about the employee. Read the letter and the statements. Write *T* (true) or *F* (false).

Study Tip

Make Connections

Make cards for five new words. Write a quality on the front of the card. Write a job that needs that quality on the back.

To Whom It May Concern:

I would like to recommend Omar Ramos as a sales associate for your car dealership. Omar worked at my car dealership for five years. We'll miss him when he moves to Los Angeles.

Omar is a very good salesperson. He is always friendly and pleasant. He knows how to talk to customers and make them comfortable. Omar is sincere. Customers feel like they can buy a good car from him. He's also hardworking and almost never misses work. Please call me at 312-555-6571 if you have any questions.

Sincerely,
Sam Banks
Sam Banks
Manager

_____ 1. Omar is leaving his current job.

_____ 2. Customers feel that Omar is honest.

_____ 3. Omar's manager thinks Omar needs to work harder.

_____ 4. Omar's manager thinks Omar is a good salesperson.

Show what you know!

1. COLLABORATE. Look at the list of qualities. Which qualities do you have? Which qualities do you need to work on?

A: Which qualities do you have?
B: I like to work fast, so I'm really efficient. I'm also punctual and dependable. I arrive at work on time every day. How about you? Which qualities do you have?
A: I'm very organized.

2. WRITE. Write a letter of recommendation you would like to receive from an employer.

To Whom It May Concern:

I am happy to write this reference for Yi Wang. Yi worked at my restaurant for over a year. She is hardworking and efficient. She is also punctual and dependable. Yi is very friendly and enjoys meeting new people. She has my highest recommendation.

Sincerely,
Kevin Clement

I can identify qualities of good employees. ☐   I need more practice. ☐

For more practice, go to MyEnglishLab.

> In **Show what you know!**, students apply the target vocabulary in meaningful conversations and in writing.

Three **Listening and Speaking** lessons provide students opportunities for realistic conversations in work, community, and educational settings.

Pronunciation activities help students learn, practice, and internalize the patterns of spoken English and relate them to their own lives.

Listening and Speaking

Lesson 2 Make small talk

1 BEFORE YOU LISTEN

A MATCH. Look at the pictures. Write the correct letters.

_____ 1. go to a park

_____ 2. walk a dog

_____ 3. take an exercise class

_____ 4. watch a soccer game

B MAKE CONNECTIONS. How do you meet people in your neighborhood?

A: I meet new people when I walk my dog.
B: I talk to my neighbors when I go to the park with my children.

2 LISTEN

Edwin and Marco are watching a soccer game. They meet and introduce themselves.

A ▶ LISTEN FOR MAIN IDEA. Circle the answer.

Edwin and Marco are _____.
  a. teammates   **b.** old friends   **c.** new friends

B ▶ LISTEN FOR DETAILS. Circle the answers.

1. When does the Atlas soccer league meet?
   a. Saturdays
   b. Sundays
   c. Saturdays and Sundays

2. What happens when it rains?
   a. They play indoors.
   b. They still play.
   c. They don't play.

C ▶ EXPAND. Listen to the rest of the conversation. Write _T_ (true) or _F_ (false).

_____ 1. Marco knows many players in Edwin's soccer league.

_____ 2. Marco and Hector are both from Brazil but from different towns.

_____ 3. Hector is surprised to see Marco.

8   Unit 1, Lesson 2

Listening and Speaking

3 PRONUNCIATION

A ▶ PRACTICE. Listen. Then listen and repeat.

Po land   Bra **zil**   Cam **bo** di a   **Chi** na   U **ni** ted **States**

B ▶ APPLY. Listen. Mark (•) the stressed syllable.

1. La os   2. Ko re a

3. Mex i co   4. Russ ia

5. Vi et nam   6. Co lom bi a

4 CONVERSATION

A ▶ LISTEN AND READ. Then practice the conversation with a partner.

A: Great game. Is this the Atlas soccer league? I've heard about them.

B: Yes. I love to come here and watch them.

A: Do they play every Saturday?

B: Yes, unless it rains. By the way, my name's Edwin.

A: Hi, I'm Marco. Nice to meet you.

B: Nice to meet you, too. Do you live around here?

A: Nearby. I live in Southside. I'm originally from Brazil.

B INTERVIEW. Get to know your partner. Introduce yourself. Ask questions.

Are you a new student in this school?
Do you live far from school? How do you get to school?
Why do you want to learn English?

> **Syllables**
>
> Words are made up of syllables. In English, one syllable in a word has the strongest stress. It is longer and louder than other syllables.

I can make small talk. ☐   I need more practice. ☐

For more practice, go to MyEnglishLab.

Unit 1, Lesson 2   9

Multiple listening opportunities progress from listening for general understanding, to listening for details, to listening to an extended version of the conversation.

Conversations carefully scaffold student learning and build language fluency.

Checkpoints at the end of lessons provide students an opportunity to reflect on their progress and identify further resources for more practice.

Before You Listen activities let students make connections between the topic and their own experience.

UNIT TOUR

Each unit presents three **Grammar** lessons in a systematic grammar progression. Every Grammar lesson focuses on language introduced in the preceding Listening and Speaking lesson. Additional grammar practice is available in the Grammar Review and online.

Images provide scaffolding for meaningful grammar practice.

Lesson 3 Grammar
Articles

A, An, The

The car needs a battery and **an** air filter.

The battery is weak, and **the** air filter is dirty.

Today is a sunny day, and **the** sun is shining.

Grammar Watch

- Use the article *a* or *an* the first time you talk about something. Use *a* before consonant sounds. Use *an* before vowel sounds.
- Use the article *the* when you talk about something for the second time.
- Use *the* for things that are known to both you and the listener.
- Use *the* when there is only one of something.

A INVESTIGATE. Read sentence (a) and underline the articles. Then cross out the incorrect article in sentence (b).

1. (a) Alex told Claudia about a used car he liked.
   (b) Claudia asked Alex if he bought **a / the** car.

2. (a) Alex told Claudia that he bought the car.
   (b) Claudia asked if it had a / **the** warranty.

3. (a) Claudia asked if the car needed repairs.
   (b) Alex said it didn't, but **a / the** turn signal wasn't working.

4. (a) Claudia asked Alex if he fixed the turn signal.
   (b) He told her that he bought **a / the** new light bulb and installed it.

B PRACTICE. Use *a*, *an*, or *the* to complete the paragraph.

Two months ago, I bought ___an___ old car for very little money. _____ car had problems. _____ air conditioner and _____ heater didn't work well. I also had to buy _____ air filter. There was _____ noise coming from _____ engine. There was also _____ hole on _____ floor of _____ car. I covered _____ hole and got used to _____ noise. _____ car gets me to work, and that saves me time. I hope _____ car lasts until _____ summer. Then I'll have enough money for _____ better car.

130 Unit 7, Lesson 3

Grammar

C ▶ APPLY. Complete the conversations with *a*, *an*, or *the*. Then listen and check your answers.

1. **A:** My car won't start. ___The___ battery must be dead.
   B: Let me jump-start your car. I have jumper cables in my car.

2. **A:** I think there's _____ oil leak under _____ car.
   B: I'll take _____ look.

3. **A:** After the accident, he called for _____ tow truck.
   B: Did it take long for _____ tow truck to come?
   A: It finally came after _____ hour.

4. **A:** We have _____ flat tire.
   B: Oh, no. I hope we have _____ spare tire in the trunk.

5. **A:** Is there _____ good auto repair shop nearby?
   B: I always go to _____ garage on East 4th Street. _____ mechanics there are excellent, and _____ prices are fair.

6. **A:** What's _____ problem with your car?
   B: There's _____ noise in the engine.
   A: Is it _____ same noise you complained about last month?
   B: No. It's _____ different noise.

D COLLABORATE. Practice the conversations.

jumper cables

oil leak

flat tire

spare tire

Show what you know!

1. DISCUSS. Talk about an experience or problem you have had with a car, a mechanic, or getting to work or school.

2. WRITE. Explain how to fix or take care of a car. Choose a specific topic. Use articles.
   - How to change a flat tire
   - How to change the oil
   - How to wash a car
   - How to jump-start a car
   - How to choose a good mechanic

I can use the articles *a*, *an*, and *the*. ■   I need more practice. ■

For more practice, go to MyEnglishLab.

Unit 7, Lesson 3 **131**

Grammar activities progress from controlled to open practice, leading students from understanding to mastery of the target grammar.

Grammar charts present the target grammar point in a clear and simple format.

Every **Show what you know!** integrates an interactive exchange and a writing task so students demonstrate their mastery of the grammar point using a range of language skills.

Workplace, Life, and Community Skills lessons develop real-life language and civic literacy, prepare students for the workplace, and encourage community participation.

Interactive activities develop real-life communication and collaboration skills.

Workplace, Life, and Community Skills

Workplace, Life, and Community Skills

Lesson **4**

Read a job application

1 READ A JOB APPLICATION

A READ. Look at the job application. Talk about any words you don't understand.

Caruso's Application For Employment

We are an Equal Opportunity Employer and committed to excellence through diversity.
Please print or type. The application must be fully completed to be considered. Please complete each section, even if you attach a resume.

Personal Information

Name	Address	City	State	ZIP
Chu, Li	342 Sycamore Street	Alhambra	CA	91803

Phone Number	Mobile Number	Email Address
(520) 555-9832		Li.Chu@email.com

Are you a U.S. citizen? ● Yes ○ No   Have you ever been fired from a job? ○ Yes ● No
Can you legally work in the U.S.? (If hired, verification within 3 days is required.) ● Yes ○ No

Position

Position	Available Start Date	Desired Pay
Inventory Supervisor	Immediately	$20.00/hr.

Employment desired ● Full Time ○ Part Time ○ Seasonal/Temporary

Education

School Name	Location	Years Attended	Degree Received	Major
East Los Angeles College	Los Angeles, CA	2011–2012	no	Business
Caballero High School	Los Angeles, CA	2006–2010	yes	n/a

B INTERPRET. Read the statements. Write *T* (true) or *F* (false).

_____ 1. Li is looking for a part-time job.
_____ 2. Li wants to be a store manager.
_____ 3. If Li gets the job, he needs to prove that he can work in the U.S.
_____ 4. Li was fired from his last job.
_____ 5. Li graduated from high school.

C READ. Look at the next screen of the job application.

Employment History

Employer (1)	Job Title	Dates Employed		
IWS	Inventory Associate	8/2017–Present		
Work Phone	**Starting Pay Rate**	**Ending Pay Rate**		
(520) 555-8100	$15.00/hr	$17.50/hr		
Job Duties	**Reason for Leaving**	**Supervisor**		**May we contact?**
Count stock, help organize warehouse inventory	Want promotion and better salary	Hector Borado		● Yes ○ No
Address	**City**	**State**	**Zip**	
3500 E. Sunrise Drive	Monterey Park	CA	91754	

Employer (2)	Job Title	Dates Employed		
Koll's	Clerk	8/2013–7/2017		
Work Phone	**Starting Pay Rate**	**Ending Pay Rate**		
(520) 555-9875	$12.00/hr	$15.00/hr		
Job Duties	**Reason for Leaving**	**Supervisor**		**May we contact?**
Worked cash register, customer service	Wanted more hours	Victor Santoro		● Yes ○ No
Address	**City**	**State**	**Zip**	
2200 E. Elm Street	Monterey Park	CA	91754	

Signature Disclaimer

I certify that my answers are true and complete to the best of my knowledge.

Li Chu	October 14, 2020	Li Chu
Name (Please Print)	Date	Signature

D CONNECT. Answer the questions.

Where does Li work now? Where did he work before?
Why does he want to leave his job?
Is it OK for Caruso's to call Li's supervisor at Koll's?

E ROLE-PLAY. Practice a conversation between an applicant and the supervisor at Caruso's.

F GO ONLINE. Search for a company you want to work for. Do they have an online application?

I can read a job application. ☐	I need more practice. ☐
	For more practice, go to MyEnglishLab.

Unit 4, Lesson 4   73

In **Go Online activities,** students use their devices to practice concrete online tasks, such as researching information or inputting data.

UNIT TOUR

All-new informational **Reading** lessons develop academic language and build content knowledge to meet the rigorous requirements of the CCRS.

Informational readings containing level-appropriate complex text introduce academic language and build content knowledge.

Students develop **numeracy** skills by interpreting numeric information in charts and graphs.

Lesson 7 — Reading
Read about interview questions

1 BEFORE YOU READ

RECALL. Have you ever had a job interview? What questions did the interviewer ask you?

2 READ

▶ Listen and read.

Academic Skill: Make inferences

In an article, some ideas are not stated directly. Readers must guess or infer these ideas as they read.

Legal and Illegal Interview Questions

The interview is an important part of a job search. Most employers conduct an interview before they offer someone a job. During an interview, employers can ask many questions. But they are not allowed to
5 ask certain kinds of questions.

Legal Questions
What questions can interviewers ask? They can ask questions about an applicant's qualifications. This means they can ask about his or her skills and work
10 experience. Different jobs need different kinds of employees. For example, nursing assistants need to be patient and kind. They also need to be strong. The interviewer needs to know if an applicant can do the job well. He or she is allowed to ask questions
15 to figure that out.

Illegal Questions
What kinds of questions are not allowed? Interviewers may not discriminate against applicants. They can't treat them unfairly. Some kinds of questions might
20 do this, so these questions are illegal. For example, in the U.S., some people have certain ideas about old people. They think that old people aren't good workers. They don't have much energy. They can't

learn new things. Some employers don't want to
25 hire them. However, many older people *are* good workers. That is why interviewers may not ask about an applicant's age.
Some employers don't want to hire people with young children. They think these workers will call
30 in sick or come in late too much. Some employers may also not want to hire people of certain races or religions. This is unfair to these people. That's why questions about an applicant's family, race, and religion are all illegal.
35 Remember, in an interview, legal questions ask for information about your qualifications. Illegal questions could help employers discriminate against you.

Interview Questions	Legal	Illegal
What job skills do you have?	✓	
What work experience do you have?	✓	
How old are you?		✓
Do you have children?		✓
Where were you born?		✓
Are you a patient person?	✓	✓
What is your religion?		✓

3 CLOSE READING

A IDENTIFY. What is the main idea of the article?

a. Most employers conduct an interview before they offer someone a job.
b. Interviewers can ask questions about an applicant's skills and experience.
c. Some interview questions are legal, but other questions are illegal.

Reading

B CITE EVIDENCE. Complete the sentences. Where is the information? Write the line numbers.

Lines

1. Job applicants _____ answer illegal interview questions.
   a. have to   b. don't have to   _____

2. An interviewer _____ ask, "Do you know how to use a computer?"
   a. can   b. can't   _____

3. Interviewers are _____ to ask, "How old are you?"
   a. allowed   b. not allowed   _____

4. It is often _____ for an older worker to find a job.
   a. easy   b. hard   _____

5. The question "Are you married?" is _____.
   a. legal   b. illegal   _____

C INTERPRET GRAPHICS. Complete the sentences about the chart.

1. The chart includes examples of _____ during an interview.
   a. questions that can be asked
   b. questions that cannot be asked
   c. questions that both can and cannot be asked

2. According to the chart, asking about an applicant's age _____.
   a. is legal
   b. is illegal
   c. can be legal or illegal, depending on the situation

4 SUMMARIZE

What are the most important ideas in the article? Write three sentences in your notebook.

Show what you know!

1. COLLABORATE. List the legal and illegal interview questions from the reading. Then think of one more example of each.

2. WRITE. Explain why some interview questions are legal and some are illegal. Give examples.

   It is legal to ask the question "Where did you work last year?" This is because the employer needs to know about the applicant's work experience. It is illegal to ask...

I can make inferences while reading. ☐	I need more practice. ☐

To read more, go to MyEnglishLab.

Close-reading activities require that students return to the reading to find textual evidence of detail, to summarize for general understanding, and to make inferences.

Graphs and charts introduce students to information in a variety of formats, developing their visual literacy.

Academic tasks, such as summarizing, help students develop academic skills.

Writing lessons follow a robust and scaffolded writing-process approach, engaging students in analyzing writing models, planning, and producing a final product.

A **Writing Skill** explains and models appropriate writing. Later in the lesson, students apply the skill to their own writing.

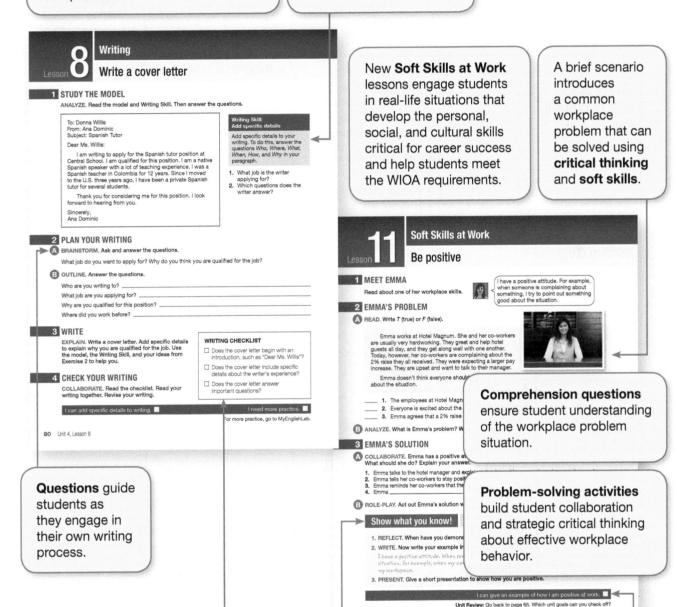

New **Soft Skills at Work** lessons engage students in real-life situations that develop the personal, social, and cultural skills critical for career success and help students meet the WIOA requirements.

A brief scenario introduces a common workplace problem that can be solved using **critical thinking** and **soft skills**.

Comprehension questions ensure student understanding of the workplace problem situation.

Problem-solving activities build student collaboration and strategic critical thinking about effective workplace behavior.

Questions guide students as they engage in their own writing process.

The **Writing Checklist** at the end of each Writing lesson reinforces the lesson's writing objective and allows students to review and revise their work.

Show what you know! invites students to talk and write about the soft skills they bring to the job.

My Soft Skills Log in the back of the student book is a personal resource for students as they apply for jobs or undergo performance reviews.

SCOPE AND SEQUENCE

Unit	Vocabulary	Listening and Speaking	Reading	Grammar
Pre-Unit **Getting Started** *page 2*	Clarification questions	• Meet your classmates • Talk about things you have in common with your classmates • Ask for and give clarification	• Locate information in your book.	• *Wh-* questions • *Yes / No* questions • Introduction to noun clauses • Introduction to reported speech
1 **Living in a Neighborhood** *page 5*	Countries	• Make small talk • Talk about places in the neighborhood • Talk about holidays and celebrations **Pronunciation skills:** • Syllables • Pronunciation of *do you*	• Read an article about where Americans live **Academic skill:** • Understand the main idea	• Simple present • Adverbs of frequency • Quantifiers
2 **Setting Goals** *page 25*	Goals	• Identify steps to a better job • Look for a new job • Identify community services **Pronunciation skills:** • Contraction of *will* • Pronunciation of *going to*	• Read an article about immigrant entrepreneurs **Academic skill:** • Predict	• The future with *will* and *might* • The future with *going to* • The future with present continuous
3 **Going to School** *page 45*	School activities	• Help children with school • Ask for time off work • Deal with bullies **Pronunciation skills:** • Phrasal verbs • Past-tense verb endings	• Read an article about effective study habits **Academic skill:** • Use what you know	• *Should* and *have to* • Adjective or noun phrase + infinitive • Simple past
4 **Getting a Job** *page 65*	Qualities of good employees	• Talk about work experience • Describe your work history • Talk about the past and the present **Pronunciation skills:** • Plural pronunciation • Syllable stress	• Read an article about interview questions **Academic skill:** • Make inferences	• Present perfect: Questions with *ever* and *never* • Present perfect: Statements with *for* and *since* • The past with *used to*

Writing	Document Literacy and Numeracy	Workplace, Life, and Community Skills	Soft Skills at Work
• Complete statements about things you like	• Use unit and page numbers	• Introduce yourself • Greet people	
• Write about a move **Writing skill:** • Write a topic sentence	• Locate countries and regions on a world map • Understand a recipe • Interpret a bar graph	• Follow written instructions **Digital skill:** • Go online and look up other recipes you can use when making tacos.	• Be inclusive
• Write about your goal **Writing skill:** • Write supporting sentences	• Read a calendar	• Set goals • Talk about obstacles and supports **Digital skill:** • Go online and identify a certificate, license, or associate's degree. Find out how long it takes to get.	• Take responsibility for professional growth
• Give your opinion about a school issue **Writing skill:** • Support an opinion with reasons	• Understand the grading system in the U.S. • Interpret a report card	• Communicate with your child's teacher **Digital skill:** • Go online and find a video that shows a meeting between a parent and a teacher.	• Separate work life and family life
• Write a cover letter **Writing skill:** • Add specific details	• Understand a job application form • Read a job advertisement • Interpret a chart	• Read a job application **Digital skill:** • Go online and search for a company you want to work for. Find out if they have an online application.	• Be positive

SCOPE AND SEQUENCE

Unit	Vocabulary	Listening and Speaking	Reading	Grammar
5 **Traveling** *page 85*	Air travel	• Follow instructions at an airport • Make travel arrangements • Talk about travel delays and cancellations **Pronunciation skills:** • *Can* and *can't* • Stressed words	• Read an article about airport safety **Academic skill:** • Get meaning from context	• *Can / Could* for possibility and ability • *Be able to* for ability • Possessive adjectives and possessive pronouns • Making polite requests
6 **Getting a Good Deal** *page 105*	Problems with purchases	• Identify product defects • Discuss problems with cell phone service • Make an exchange at a store **Pronunciation skills:** • Sound of *th* • Linking words	• Read an article about warranties and service agreements **Academic skill:** • Understand formatting clues	• Additions with *too* and *either* • Comparing with adjectives • Comparing with *as . . . as*
7 **Getting There Safely** *page 125*	Driving and traffic	• Talk about car maintenance • Discuss traffic accidents • Identify steps to take after an accident **Pronunciation skills:** • Articles • Stressed syllables	• Read an article about safety on the road **Academic skill:** • Interpret charts	• Articles • Past continuous • Time clauses
8 **Staying Healthy** *page 145*	Eating habits	• Identify healthy eating habits • Talk about family health • Talk about dental health **Pronunciation skills:** • Stress with superlatives • Tone in questions	• Read an article about school lunches **Academic skill:** • Understand facts and opinions	• Superlatives • Verb + gerund as object • Gerunds as subjects

Writing	Document Literacy and Numeracy	Workplace, Life, and Community Skills	Soft Skills at Work
• Explain how to use a transportation app **Writing skill:** • Use time-order words	• Read a boarding pass • Understand instructions on a ticket machine • Interpret a map of a train station	• Read instructions and maps **Digital skill:** • Go online and find an app for buying train or bus tickets in your area.	• Find creative solutions
• Compare two stores **Writing skill:** • Use details to compare and contrast	• Read product advertisements • Compare product prices • Analyze a rebate application	• Read about rebates • Analyze a rebate application **Digital skill:** • Search for special offers and rebates. Search by ZIP code to see what is available in your area.	• Respond to customer needs
• Write about an accident **Writing skill:** • Prepare two different opinions when arguing	• Interpret a bar graph	• Identify car parts • Identify dashboard icons **Digital skill:** • Look up different types of cars, such as sedans, SUVs, crossovers, and hybrids. Learn about the differences.	• Be flexible
• Write about a food **Writing skill:** • Support an opinion with facts	• Use a Venn diagram • Interpret nutritional labels • Compare nutritional value	• Read nutritional labels • Talk about diets and food allergies **Digital skill:** • Go online and find the nutritional information for two foods you like to eat. Compare the ingredients.	• Take initiative

SCOPE AND SEQUENCE

Unit	Vocabulary	Listening and Speaking	Reading	Grammar
9 **Doing Your Job** *page 165*	On the job	• Ask for clarification • Identify expectations on the job • Respond appropriately to correction **Pronunciation skills:** • Stress for clarification	• Read an article about working the late shift **Academic skill:** • Skim	• *One / Ones* • Verb + object + infinitive • Reported speech
10 **Going to the Doctor** *page 185*	Places in a hospital	• Reschedule a doctor's appointment • Talk about symptoms • Discuss medical procedures and concerns **Pronunciation skills:** • *-ed* endings • Stressed and unstressed syllables	• Read an article about vaccinations **Academic skill:** • Interpret graphics	• Participial adjectives • Present perfect continuous • Preposition + gerund
11 **Spending and Saving Money** *page 205*	Money and banking	• Use bank services wisely • Budget expenses • Ask about appliances and utilities **Pronunciation skills:** • Pausing at punctuation • Pronunciation of *want to*	• Read an article about credit card debt **Academic skill:** • Identify author's purpose	• Present real conditional • Future real conditional • Gerunds and infinitives as objects
12 **Visiting Washington, D.C.** *page 225*	Washington, D.C.	• Identify and discuss favorite places • Talk about the U.S. government • Identify famous places in Washington, D.C. **Pronunciation skills:** • Pronunciation of *did you* • Compound nouns	• Read an article about rights and freedoms **Academic skill:** • Summarize	• Simple present and simple past: Additions • Simple present passive • Past passive

Writing	Document Literacy and Numeracy	Workplace, Life, and Community Skills	Soft Skills at Work
• Describe a job **Writing skill:** • Define new words and acronyms	• Understand safety signs	• Identify safety hazards at work **Digital skill:** • Go online and look up safety hazards for machinery you use at work or at home.	• Listen actively
• Write about a healthy habit **Writing skill:** • Write a concluding sentence	• Interpret a medical history form • Interpret a vaccination schedule	• Read and complete a medical history form **Digital skill:** • Go online and find information about one of the conditions listed on the medical history form. Find out the symptoms of the condition.	• Prioritize
• Write about ways to save money **Writing skill:** • Add specific examples	• Interpret a budget form • Calculate income tax • Calculate expenses • Interpret a utility bill • Understand classified ads for apartments	• Read a utility bill • Save money on utilities **Digital skill:** • Go online and find other ways you can save energy.	• Think critically
• Describe a place **Writing skill:** • Use sensory words to describe	• Interpret a subway map	• Read a subway map • Ask for and give directions **Digital skill:** • Go online and find an app for the Washington, D.C. Metro System. Find an app for the subway system where you live.	• Locate information

CORRELATIONS

Unit	CASAS Reading Standards (correlated to CASAS Reading Standards 2016)	CASAS Listening Standards (correlated to CASAS Listening Basic Skills Content Standards)
1	L1: RDG 1.7, 2.3, 3.4; L2: RDG 1.5, 1.7, 2.2, 2.3; L3: RDG 1.7, 2.1, 2.2, 2.3; L4: RDG 1.7, 1.8, 2.8, 3.2, 3.4, 3.8, 3.11, 3.12, 4.2; L5: RDG 1.7, 1.8, 2.10; L6: RDG 1.7, 2.9; L7: RDG 1.7, 1.8, 2.2, 2.3, 3.1, 3.2, 3.6, 3.7, 4.2; L8: RDG 1.7, 3.4; L9: RDG 2.9; L10: RDG 1.7, 1.8; L11: RDG 1.7, 1.8, 3.2;	L1: 2.1, 2.3, 2.9; L2: 1.3, 1.4, 1.6, 2.1, 2.3, 4.1, 4.2; L3: 1.3, 2.1, 2.3, 3.1, 4.1, 4.2; L4: 4.2, 6.1, 6.2, 6.10; L5: 1.5, 2.1, 2.3, 4.1, 4.2, 4.7, 6.1, 6.2; L6: 2.1. 2.3. 3.9. 4.1. 4.2; L7: 4.2; L8: 2.1, 2.3, 4.1, 4.2, 4.7, 6.1; L10: 2.1, 2.3; L11: 2.1, 2.3, 4.1, 4.2;
2	L1: RDG 1.7, 2.2, 2.3; L2: RDG 1.7, 2.2, 2.3; L3: RDG 1.7, 2.2, 2.9, 4.3; L4: RDG 1.7, 1.8, 2.2, 2.3, 3.2, 3.7, 3.8, 3.11, 4.2; L5: RDG 1.7, 2.2, 2.3, 2.10; L6: RDG 1.7, 2.9; L7: RDG 1.7, 1.8, 2.2, 2.3, 3.2; L8: RDG 1.7, 2.2, 2.3; L10: RDG 1.7, 2.9, 3.4; L11: RDG 1.7, 1.8, 3.2;	L1: 2.1, 2.3, 2.9, 4.1, 4.2; L2: 2.1, 2.3, 3.3, 4.1, 4.2, 6.1, 6.2; L3: 2.1, 2.3, 3.3, 3.9, 4.1, 4.2; L4: 2.1, 2.3, 4.1, 4.2, 5.8, 6.1; L5: 1.5, 2.1, 2.3, 4.1, 4.2, 5.8, 6.1, 6.2; L6: 2.1, 2.3, 3.3, 3.9, 4.1, 4.2; L7: 2.1, 2.3, 4.2; L8: 2.1, 2.3, 4.2; L9: 4.11. 5.8. 6.1; L10: 2.1, 2.3, 3.6, 3.13, 4.1, 4.2; L11: 2.1, 2.3, 4.1, 4.2;
3	L1: RDG 1.7, 2.2, 2.3, 2.7; L2: RDG 1.7, 2.2, 2.3; L3: RDG 1.7, 2.9; L4: RDG 1.7, 1.8, 2.2, 2.3, 3.2, 3.7, 3.11, 4.2; L5: RDG 1.7, 2.2, 2.3; L6: RDG 1.7, 2.2, 2.3; L7: RDG 1.7, 2.9; L8: RDG 1.7, 2.2, 2.3, 3.4, 3.5; L9: RDG 1.7, 2.2, 2.3, 2.6; L10: RDG 1.7, 1.8, 2.1; L11: RDG 1.7, 1.8, 3.2;	L1: 2.1, 2.3, 2.9, 4.1, 4.2; L2: 1.4, 2.1, 2.3, 2.8, 4.1, 4.2, 6.1, 6.2; L3: 2.1, 2.3, 3.9, 4.1, 4.2; L4: 2.1, 2.3, 4.1, 4.2, 5.8, 6.1; L5: 2.1, 4.1, 4.2; L6: 2.1, 2.3, 4.1, 4.2, 6.1, 6.2; L7: 2.1, 2.3, 3.9, 4.1, 4.2; L8: 2.1, 2.3, 4.1, 4.2, 6.1, 6.2; L9: 2.1, 3.9, 4.1, 4.2, 6.1, 6.2; L10: 2.1, 3.9, 4.1, 4.2; L11: 2.1, 4.1, 4.2;
4	L1: RDG 1.7, 2.2, 2.3; L2: RDG 1.7, 2.2, 2.3; L3: RDG 1.7, 2.9; L4: RDG 1.7, 1.8, 2.2, 2.3, 3.2, 4.9; L5: RDG 1.7, 2.2, 2.3; L6: RDG 1.7, 2.9; L7: RDG 1.7, 1.8, 2.2, 2.3, 3.2, 3.11, 4.2, 4.3; L8: RDG 1.7, 2.2, 2.3; L10: RDG 1.7, 1.8, 2.1, 2.10; L11: RDG 1.7, 1.8, 3.2;	L1: 2.1, 2.3, 2.9, 4.1, 4.2; L2: 1.2, 1.4, 2.1, 3.7, 4.1, 4.2, 4.11, 6.1; L3: 2.1, 2.3, 3.6, 3.13, 4.1, 4.2; L4: 2.1, 2.3, 4.1, 4.2, 5.8, 6.1, 6.2; L6: 2.1, 2.3, 3.9, 4.1, 4.2; L7: 2.1, 2.3, 4.2, 5.8, 6.1, 6.2; L8: 2.1, 2.3, 4.1, 4.2; L9: 2.1, 2.3, 3.1, 4.11, 6.1, 6.2; L10: 1.5, 2.1, 2.3, 3.9; L11: 2.1, 2.3, 4.1, 4.2;
5	L1: RDG 1.7, 2.2, 2.3; L2: RDG 1.7, 2.2, 2.3; L3: RDG 1.7, 2.9; L4: RDG 1.7, 1.8, 2.2, 3.4, 4.9; L5: RDG 1.7, 2.2, 2.3; L6: RDG 1.7, 2.6, 2.9; L7: RDG 1.7, 1.8, 2.3, 2.8, 3.2, 3.11, 4.2; L8: RDG 1.7, 2.2, 2.3; L10: RDG 1.7, 1.8, 2.9; L11: RDG 1.7, 1.8, 3.2;	L1: 2.1, 2.3, 2.9, 4.2; L2: 1.4, 2.1, 2.3, 3.3, 4.1, 4.2, 6.1, 6.2; L3: 1.3, 2.1, 2.3, 3.1, 3.9, 4.1, 4.2; L4: 2.1, 2.3, 4.2; L5: 2.1, 2.3, 4.2, 6.1, 6.2; L6: 2.1, 2.3, 3.2, 4.2; L7: 2.1, 2.3, 4.2, 5.8, 6.1, 6.2; L8: 2.1, 2.3, 4.2; L9: 1.4, 2.1, 2.3, 6.1, 6.2; L10: 2.1, 2.3, 3.9; L11: 2.1, 2.3, 4.1, 4.2;
6	L1: RDG 1.7, 2.3; L2: RDG 1.7, 2.2, 2.3; L3: RDG 1.7, 2.9; L4: RDG 1.7, 1.8, 2.3, 3.2, 3.10, 3.11, 4.2; L5: RDG 1.7, 2.2, 2.3; L6: RDG 1.7, 2.2, 2.9; L7: RDG 1.7, 1.8, 2.3, 3.2, 3.10; L8: RDG 1.7, 2.2, 2.3; L9: RDG 2.6; L10: RDG 1.7, 1.8; L11: RDG 1.7, 1.8, 3.2;	L1: 2.1, 2.3, 2.9, 4.2; L2: 1.1, 2.1, 2.3, 4.2, 6.1, 6.2; L3: 2.1, 2.3, 3.9, 4.2; L4: 2.1, 2.3, 4.2; L5: 2.1, 2.3, 4.2, 6.1, 6.2; L6: 2.1, 2.3, 3.10, 4.2; L7: 2.1, 2.3, 4.2; L8: 2.1, 2.3, 4.1, 4.2, 6.1, 6.2; L9: 3.10, 4.1, 4.2; L10: 2.1, 2.3; L11: 2.1, 2.3, 4.1, 4.2;
7	L1: RDG 1.7, 2.3; L2: RDG 2.2, 2.3, 2.9; L3: RDG 1.7, 2.9; L4: RDG 1.7, 1.8, 2.3, 4.9; L5: RDG 1.7, 2.3; L6: RDG 1.7, 2.9; L7: RDG 1.7, 1.8, 2.3, 3.2, 3.4, 3.11, 4.2, 4.9; L8: RDG 1.7, 2.3, 4.7; L10: RDG 1.7, 2.1, 2.9; L11: RDG 1.7, 1.8, 3.2;	L1: 2.1, 2.3, 2.9, 4.2; L2: 1.4, 2.1, 2.3, 4.2, 6.1; L3: 2.1, 2.3, 4.1, 4.2; L4: 2.1, 2.3, 4.2; L5: 1.4, 2.1, 2.3, 4.2, 6.1, 6.2; L6: 2.1, 2.3, 3.3, 3.13, 4.2; L7: 2.1, 2.3, 4.2, 5.8, 6.1; L8: 2.1, 2.3, 4.2; L9: 2.1, 2.3, 4.2, 6.1, 6.2; L10: 2.1, 2.3, 3.3, 3.13, 4.2; L11: 2.1, 4.1, 4.2;
8	L1: RDG 1.7, 2.3; L2: RDG 1.7, 2.3; L3: RDG 1.7, 2.3, 2.6; L4: RDG 1.7, 1.8, 2.2, 2.3; L5: RDG 1.7, 2.3; L6: RDG 1.7, 2.6, 2.9; L7: RDG 1.7, 1.8, 2.3, 3.2, 3.7, 3.11, 4.2, 4.7; L8: RDG 1.7, 2.3; L9: RDG 1.7, 2.3; L10: RDG 1.7, 1.8, 4.7; L11: RDG 1.7, 1.8, 3.2;	L1: 2.1, 2.3, 2.9, 4.2; L2: 1.4, 2.1, 2.3, 4.2, 4.11, 6.1; L3: 2.1, 2.3, 4.1, 4.2, 6.1, 6.2; L4: 2.1, 2.3, 4.2, 5.4, 5.5; L5: 2.1, 2.3, 4.2, 4.11, 6.1; L6: 2.1, 2.3, 4.2; L7: 2.1, 2.3, 4.2, 5.8, 6.1, 6.2; L8: 1.4, 2.1, 2.3, 4.1, 4.2, 6.1; L9: 3.13, 4.1, 4.2; L10: 2.1, 2.3, 3.9; L11: 2.1, 2.3, 4.1, 4.2;
9	L1: RDG 1.7, 2.3; L2: RDG 1.7, 2.3; L3: RDG 1.7, 2.6; L4: RDG 1.7, 1.8, 2.3, 3.2, 3.9, 3.11, 4.2; L5: RDG 1.7, 1.8, 2.2; L7: RDG 1.7, 1.8, 2.3, 2.6, 2.9; L8: RDG 1.7, 1.8, 2.2, 2.3, 3.6, 3.11; L9: RDG 1.7, 2.3; L10: RDG 1.7, 2.6, 2.9; L11: RDG 1.7, 1.8, 3.2	L1: 2.1, 2.3, 2.9, 4.2; L2: 1.4, 2.1, 2.3, 4.2, 6.1, 6.2; L3: 1.3, 2.1, 2.3, 3.7, 4.1, 4.2; L4: 2.1, 2.3, 4.2, 6.1; L5: 2.1, 2.3; L6: 2.1, 2.3, 4.1, 4.2, 6.1; L7: 3.1, 4.1, 4.2; L8: 4.1, 4.2; L9: 2.1, 2.3, 4.2, 6.1, 6.2; L10: 2.1, 2.3, 3.13, 4.1, 4.2; L11: 2.1, 2.3, 4.1, 4.2;
10	L1: RDG 1.7, 2.3; L2: RDG 1.7, 2.3; L3: RDG 1.7, 2.6, 2.9; L4: RDG 1.7, 1.8, 2.3, 3.2; L5: RDG 1.7, 2.3; L6: RDG 1.7, 2.2, 2.6, 2.9; L7: RDG 1.7, 1.8, 2.3, 3.2, 3.4, 3.8, 3.11, 4.2, 4.9; L8: RDG 1.7, 1.8, 2.1; L10: RDG 1.7, 2.6; L11: RDG 1.7, 1.8, 3.2;	L1: 2.1, 2.3, 2.9; L2: 1.2, 1.4, 2.1, 2.3, 4.2, 6.1; L3: 1.3, 2.1, 2.3, 4.1, 4.2; L4: 2.1, 2.3, 4.2, 6.8; L5: 1.4, 2.1, 2.3, 4.2, 6.1, 6.2; L6: 2.1, 2.3, 3.9; L7: 2.1, 2.3, 4.2, 5.8, 6.1; L8: 2.1, 2.3, 3.11; L9: 2.1, 2.3, 4.2, 6.1, 6.2; L10: 2.1, 2.3, 3.9, 4.1, 4.2; L11: 2.1, 2.3, 4.1, 4.2;
11	L1: RDG 1.7, 2.3, 2.8; L2: RDG 1.7, 2.2, 2.3; L3: RDG 1.7, 2.6, 2.9; L4: RDG 1.7, 1.8, 2.3, 3.2, 3.11, 3.14, 4.2, 4.6; L5: RDG 1.7, 1.8, 2.4, 3.2; L6: RDG 3.4, 4.9; L7: RDG 1.7, 2.6, 2.9; L8: RDG 1.7, 2.3, 4.9; L9: RDG 1.7, 2.2, 2.3, 2.10, 3.6; L10: RDG 1.7, 1.8, 2.9; L11: RDG 1.7, 1.8, 3.2;	L1: 2.1, 2.3, 2.9, 4.2; L2: 1.4, 2.1, 2.3, 4.2, 4.11, 6.1; L3: 2.1, 2.3, 3.9, 4.1, 4.2; L4: 2.1, 2.3, 4.2, 6.1, 6.2; L5: 2.1, 2.3, 3.11; L6: 2.1, 2.3, 4.1, 4.2, 6.1, 6.2; L7: 2.1, 2.3, 3.9; L8: 2.1, 2.3, 4.1, 4.2; L9: 1.4, 1.5, 2.1, 2.3, 4.2, 6.1, 6.2; L10: 2.1, 2.3, 3.9; L11: 2.1, 2.3, 4.1, 4.2;
12	L1: RDG 1.7, 2.3; L2: RDG 1.7, 2.3, 2.10; L3: RDG 1.7, 1.8, 2.3, 2.9, 3.2; L4: RDG 1.7, 1.8, 2.3, 3.4; L5: RDG 1.7, 2.3; L6: RDG 1.7, 2.9; L7: RDG 1.7, 1.8, 2.3, 3.2, 3.11, 4.2; L8: RDG 1.7, 2.3, 4.1, 4.2, 6.1, 6.2; L9: RDG 1.7, 2.9; L10: RDG 1.7, 1.8, 3.2; L11: RDG 1.7, 1.8, 3.2;	L1: 2.1, 2.3, 2.9, 4.2; L2: 1.2, 2.1, 2.3, 4.2, 6.1, 6.2; L3: 2.3, 3.1, 4.1, 4.2; L4: 2.1, 2.3, 4.2; L5: 1.4, 2.1, 2.3, 4.2, 6.1, 6.2; L6: 2.1, 2.3, 3.9; L7: 2.1, 2.3, 4.2, 5.8, 6.1, 6.2; L8: 2.1, 2.3, 4.1, 4.2, 6.1, 6.2; L9: 3.9; L10: 2.1, 2.3, 3.11; L11: 2.1, 2.3, 4.1, 4.2;

CASAS: Comprehensive Adult Student Assessment System
CCRS: College and Career Readiness Standards (R=Reading; W=Writing; SL=Speaking/Listening; L=Language)
ELPS: English Language Proficiency Standards

CASAS Competencies (correlated to CASAS Competencies: Essential Life and Work skills for Youth and Adults)	CCRS Correlations, Level B	ELPS Correlations, Level 3
L1: 0.1.2, 0.1.5, 0.2.1, 7.4.1; **L2:** 0.1.2, 0.1.4, 0.1.5, 0.2.1; **L3:** 0.1.2, 0.1.5, 0.1.6, 0.2.1; **L4:** 0.1.2, 0.1.5, 6.7.2; **L5:** 0.1.2, 0.1.4, 0.1.5, 0.1.6, 0.2.1; **L6:** 0.1.2, 0.1.5, 0.1.6, 0.2.1; **L7:** 0.1.2, 0.1.5, 1.2.8, 3.5.3; **L8:** 0.1.2, 0.1.4, 0.1.5, 0.1.6, 0.2.1, 2.7.1; **L9:** 2.7.1; **L10:** 0.1.2, 0.1.5, 0.1.6, 0.2.1; **L11:** 0.1.2, 0.1.4, 0.1.5, 0.1.6, 0.2.1;	**L1:** RI.2.5, RI.3.7, RI.3.4, L.3.5b, L.2.6/L.3.6; **L2:** SL.3.1a, SL.3.1b, SL.3.1c, SL.3.1d, SL.3.2, SL.3.3, SL.3.6; **L3:** L.2.1/L.3.1b, L.2.1/L.3.1g, L.2.1/L.3.1h; **L4:** RI/RL.2.1, RI.3.2, RI.2.5, RI.3.7; **L5:** SL.3.1a, SL.3.1b, SL.3.1c, SL.3.1d, SL.3.2; **L6:** L.2.1/L.3.1b; **L7:** RI/RL.2.1, RI.3.3, W.3.7, W.3.8; **L8:** SL.3.2; **L9:** L.2.1/L.3.1a, L.2.1/L.3.1c; **L10:** W.2.3, W.3.4, W.3.5, L.3.3a; **L11:** SL.3.1a, SL.3.1b, SL.3.1c, SL.3.1d, SL.3.4, SL.3.6, L.3.3a;	ELPS 1–3, 5, 7–10
L1: 0.1.2, 0.1.5, 0.2.1, 7.1.1, 7.4.1; **L2:** 0.1.2, 0.1.4, 0.1.5, 0.2.1, 4.1.8, 7.1.1, 7.1.2; **L3:** 0.1.2, 0.1.5, 7.1.1; **L4:** 0.1.2, 0.1.5; **L5:** 0.1.2, 0.1.4, 0.1.5, 0.1.6, 0.2.1, 4.1.3; **L6:** 0.1.2, 0.1.5, 0.1.6, 0.2.1, 4.1.3, 7.1.1, 7.1.2; **L7:** 0.1.2, 0.1.5, 4.5.6, 7.1.1, 7.1.2, 7.1.3, 7.1.4, 7.4.4, 7.7.3; **L8:** 0.1.2, 0.1.4, 0.1.5, 0.1.6, 7.1.1, 7.1.2, 7.1.3; **L9:** 0.1.2, 0.1.5, 2.5.8, 8.3.2; **L10:** 0.1.2, 0.1.5, 0.1.6, 0.2.1, 2.6.3; **L11:** 0.1.2, 0.1.4, 0.1.5, 0.1.6, 0.2.1, 7.1.1, 7.1.3, 7.5.5;	**L1:** RI.3.4, L.2.2/L3.2k, L.2.4e, L.3.5b, L.2.6/L.3.6; **L2:** SL.3.2, SL.3.1a, SL.3.1b, SL.3.1c, SL.3.1d, SL.3.6, L.2.2/L3.2f; **L3:** L.2.1/L.3.1b, L.2.1/L.3.1h, SL.3.2; **L4:** RI/RL.2.1b, RI.3.2, RI.3.4; **L5:** SL.3.1a, SL.3.1b, SL.3.1c, SL.3.1d, SL.3.2, SL.3.3, SL.3.6; **L6:** L.2.1/L.3.1c; **L7:** RI/RL.2.1, W.3.7, W.3.8; **L8:** W.3.2a, W.3.2b, W.3.2c, W.3.4, W.3.5, SL.3.2, L.2.1/L.3.1l, L.2.1/L.3.1m, L.3.3a; **L9:** SL.3.1a, SL.3.1b, SL.3.1c, SL.3.1d; **L10:** SL.3.3; **L11:** RI/RL.2.1, SL.3.4, L.3.3a;	ELPS 1–3, 5, 7–10
L1: 0.1.2, 0.1.5, 2.8.6, 2.8.8, 7.4.1; **L2:** 0.1.2, 0.1.5, 2.8.6, 2.8.8; **L3:** 0.1.2, 0.1.3, 0.1.5, 2.8.8; **L4:** 0.1.2, 0.1.5, 0.2.1, 7.4.1; **L5:** 0.1.2, 0.1.5, 5.1.6; **L6:** 0.1.2, 0.1.4, 0.1.5, 4.6.5, 7.5.6; **L7:** 0.1.2, 0.1.3, 0.1.5, 2.8.8; **L8:** 0.1.2, 0.1.4, 0.1.5, 2.8.6, 2.8.8, 7.5.6; **L9:** 0.1.2, 0.1.5, 2.8.6, 2.8.8, 7.5.6; **L10:** 0.1.2, 0.1.5, 0.1.6, 2.8.8; **L11:** 0.1.2, 0.1.4, 0.1.5, 0.2.1, 4.8.3, 7.5.6;	**L1:** RI.3.4, L.2.1/L.3.1l, L.2.1/L.3.1m, L.3.5b, L.2.6/L.3.6; **L2:** SL.3.1a, SL.3.1b, SL.3.1c, SL.3.1d, SL.3.2, L.2.1/L.3.1b; **L3:** L.2.2/L3.2f, SL.3.1a, SL.3.1b, SL.3.1c, SL.3.1d, L.2.1/L.3.1l, L.2.1/L.3.1m; **L4:** RI.3.2, RI/RL.2.1, RI.3.4; **L5:** W.3.1a, W.3.1b, W.3.1c, W.3.1d, W.3.4, W.3.5, L.3.3a; **L6:** SL.3.2; **L7:** L.2.1/L.3.1b, L.2.1/L.3.1m, SL.3.1a, SL.3.1b, SL.3.1c, SL.3.1d; **L8:** RI/RL.2.1, RI.2.5; **L9:** SL.3.2, L.2.1/L.3.1b, L.2.1/L.3.1e; **L10:** L.2.1/L.3.1e, SL.3.6, L.2.6/L.3.6; **L11:** RI/RL.2.1, SL.3.1a, SL.3.1b, SL.3.1c, SL.3.1d, SL.3.4, L.3.3a, L.2.6/L.3.6;	ELPS 1–4, 7–10
L1: 0.1.2, 0.1.5, 0.2.1, 4.8.3, 7.4.1; **L2:** 0.1.2, 0.1.5,0.2.1, 4.1.5; **L3:** 0.1.2, 0.1.5, 0.2.1, 4.1.5; **L4:** 0.1.2, 0.1.5, 0.2.1, 4.1.2, 4.1.3, 4.5.6, 7.4.4, 7.7.3; **L5:** 0.1.2, 0.1.5, 0.1.6, 0.2.1, 4.1.5, 4.1.6, 4.1.7; **L6:** 0.1.2, 0.1.5, 0.1.6, 0.2.1, 4.1.5, 4.1.6, 4.1.7; **L7:** 0.1.2, 0.1.5, 4.1.5; **L8:** 0.1.2, 0.1.4, 0.1.5, 0.2.3, 4.1.2; **L9:** 0.1.2; **L10:** 0.1.2, 0.1.5, 0.1.6, 0.2.1; **L11:** 0.1.2, 0.1.5, 0.1.6, 4.8.3, 4.8.5;	**L1:** RI.3.4, L.3.5b, L.2.6/L.3.6, SL.3.1a, SL.3.1b, SL.3.1c, SL.3.1d; **L2:** SL.3.2b, SL.3.1a, SL.3.1b, SL.3.1c, SL.3.1d, SL.3.3; **L3:** L.2.1/L.3.1e; **L4:** RI/RL.2.1, W.3.7, W.3.8; **L5:** SL.3.2, SL.3.1a, SL.3.1b, SL.3.1c, SL.3.1d, SL.3.3, **L6:** L.2.1/L.3.1b; **L7:** RI.3.2, RI/RL.2.1; **L8:** W.3.4, W.3.5, L.3.3a; **L9:** SL.3.2; **L10:** L.2.1/L.3.1e, SL.3.1a, SL.3.1b, SL.3.1c, SL.3.1d; **L11:** RI/RL.2.1, SL.3.4, L.3.3a, L.2.6/L.3.6;	ELPS 1–3, 5, 7–10
L1: 0.1.2, 0.1.5, 7.4.1; **L2:** 0.1.2, 0.1.5, 2.2.7; **L3:** 0.1.2, 0.1.5, 2.2.6, 2.2.7; **L4:** 0.1.2, 0.1.5, 1.3.6, 2.2.4, 2.2.5, 4.5.6, 7.4.4, 7.7.3; **L5:** 0.1.2, 0.1.5, 0.1.6, 2.2.3, 7.3.1, 7.3.2, 7.3.4; **L6:** 0.1.2, 0.1.5, 0.1.6, 1.4.2, 7.5.6; **L7:** 0.1.2, 0.1.5, 2.2.7; **L8:** 0.1.2, 0.1.4, 0.1.5, 1.7.3, 2.2.5, 7.7.3,7.7.5, 7.7.6; **L9:** 0.1.2, 0.1.5, 2.2.7; **L10:** 0.1.2, 0.1.5, 0.1.7, 7.7.4; **L11:** 0.1.2, 0.1.4, 0.1.5, 4.8.3, 4.8.4, 7.3.1, 7.3.2;	**L1:** RI.3.4, L.3.5b, L.2.6/L.3.6, RI.3.7, SL.3.1a, SL.3.1b, SL.3.1c, SL.3.1d; **L2:** SL.3.2, SL.3.1a, SL.3.1b, SL.3.1c, SL.3.1d; **L4:** RI/RL.2.1, RI.2.5, RI.2.5, W.3.7; **L5:** SL.3.2, SL.3.3; **L6:** L.2.1/L.3.1b, L.2.2/L3.2g, SL.3.6, L.2.6/L.3.6; **L7:** RI.3.2, L.2.4a, L.3.5a, RI/RL.2.1; **L8:** W.3.2a, W.3.2b, W.3.2c, W.3.2d, W.3.4, W.3.5, L.3.3a; **L9:** SL.3.2, SL.3.3; **L11:** RI/RL.2.1, W.3.7, W.3.8, SL.3.4, L.3.3a, L.2.6/L.3.6;	ELPS 1–3, 5, 7–10
L1: 0.1.2, 0.1.5, 1.6.3, 7.4.1; **L2:** 0.1.2, 0.1.5, 1.6.3; **L3:** 0.1.2, 0.1.5, 1.6.3, 1.7.5; **L4:** 0.1.2, 0.1.5, 1.6.3, 1.7.1, 1.7.5; **L5:** 0.1.2, 0.1.5, 0.1.6, 0.2.1, 1.5.3, 1.6.3, 2.1.4; **L6:** 0.1.2, 0.1.5, 1.3.1; **L7:** 0.1.2, 0.1.5, 1.6.5; **L8:** 0.1.2, 0.1.5, 0.1.6, 0.2.1, 1.3.3; **L9:** 0.1.2, 0.1.5, 0.1.6, 0.2.1, 1.2.2, 1.3.1; **L10:** 0.1.2, 0.1.5, 0.1.6, 1.2.2, 1.3.1; **L11:** 0.1.2,0.1.5, 0.1.6, 0.2.1, 4.8.3, 4.8.4, 7.3.2;	**L1:** RI.3.4, L.3.5b, L.2.6/L.3.6, W.3.4, L.3.3a; **L2:** SL.3.2, SL.3.1a, SL.3.1b, SL.3.1c, SL.3.1d, SL.3.3; **L3:** SL.3.1a, SL.3.1b, SL.3.1c, SL.3.1d; **L4:** RI.3.2, RI.2.5, RI/RL.2.1, W.3.4, L.3.3, L.2.6/L.3.6; **L5:** SL.3.2; **L6:** L.2.1/L.3.1b; **L7:** RI/RL.2.1, W.3.7, W.3.8; **L8:** SL.3.2, SL.3.1a, SL.3.1b, SL.3.1c, SL.3.1d, SL.3.3; **L9:** L.2.4a, L.2.6/L.3.6; **L10:** W.3.2a, W.3.2b, W.3.2d, W.3.4, W.3.5, L.3.3a; **L11:** RI/RL.2.1a, SL.3.4, SL.3.6, L.2.6/L.3.6;	ELPS 1–3, 5, 7–10
L1: 0.1.2, 0.1.5, 2.2.3, 7.4.1; **L2:** 0.1.2, 0.1.5, 1.1.6, 1.9.6; **L3:** 0.1.2, 0.1.5, 1.9.7, 1.9.9; **L4:** 0.1.2, 0.1.5, 1.9.9, 4.5.6, 7.7.3, 7.4.4; **L5:** 0.1.2, 0.1.5, 0.1.6, 1.9.7; **L6:** 0.1.2, 0.1.5, 0.1.6, 1.9.7; **L7:** 0.1.2, 0.1.5, 1.9.7, 6.7.2; **L8:** 0.1.2, 0.1.5, 0.1.6, 1.9.7; **L9:** 0.1.2, 1.9.7; **L10:** 0.1.2, 0.1.5, 0.1.6, 1.9.5, 1.9.6; **L11:** 0.1.2, 0.1.4, 0.1.5, 0.1.6, 0.2.1, 4.8.1, 4.8.5, 7.3.2;	**L1:** RI.3.4, L.2.6/L.3.6, SL.3.1a, SL.3.1b, SL.3.1c, SL.3.1d, L.3.5b; **L2:** SL.3.2, SL.3.1a, SL.3.1b, SL.3.1c, SL.3.1d, SL.3.3; **L3:** W.3.4, L.3.3a; **L4:** RI.3.7, W.3.7, W.3.8; **L5:** SL.3.2, SL.3.3, SL.3.1a, SL.3.1b, SL.3.1c, SL.3.1d; **L6:** L.2.1/L.3.1m, RI/RL.2.1, W.3.4, L.3.3a; **L7:** RI.3.2, RI.2.5, W.3.4, L.3.3a, L.2.6/L.3.6; **L8:** W.3.1a, W.3.1b, W.3.1d, W.3.5; **L9:** SL.3.1a, SL.3.1b, SL.3.1c, SL.3.1d, SL.3.2; **L10:** L.2.1/L.3.1l, L.2.1/L.3.1m, L.2.6/L.3.6; **L11:** RI/RL.2.1, SL.3.1a, SL.3.1b, SL.3.1c, SL.3.1d, SL.3.4, SL.3.6, L.3.3a, L.2.6/L.3.6;	ELPS 1–5, 7–10
L1: 0.1.2, 0.1.5, 3.5.2, 7.4.1; **L2:** 0.1.2, 0.1.4, 0.1.5, 0.2.1, 0.2.4, 3.5.2, 3.5.3; **L3:** 0.1.2, 0.1.5, 0.2.1; **L4:** 0.1.2, 0.1.5, 3.5.1, 3.5.2, 4.5.6, 7.4.4, 7.7.3; **L5:** 0.1.2, 0.1.5, 0.1.6, 0.2.1, 3.5.2, 3.5.9; **L6:** 0.1.2, 0.1.5, 3.5.2, 3.5.9; **L7:** 0.1.2, 0.1.5, 0.2.1, 7.6.3; **L8:** 0.1.2, 0.1.4, 0.1.5, 0.1.6, 0.2.1, 3.5.4; **L9:** 0.1.2, 3.5.4; **L10:** 0.1.2, 0.1.5, 3.5.1, 3.5.2, 7.6.3; **L11:** 0.1.2, 0.1.4, 0.1.5, 0.1.6, 0.2.1, 4.8.4, 4.8.5, 7.3.1, 7.3.2;	**L1:** RI.3.4, L.3.5b, L.2.6/L.3.6; **L2:** SL.3.1a, SL.3.1b, SL.3.1c, SL.3.1d, SL.3.2, SL.3.3, SL.3.6; **L3:** L.2.1/L.3.1j, L.2.2/L3.2h, L.2.2/L3.2i, L.2.2/L3.2j, W.3.4, L.3.3, L.2.6/L.3.6; **L4:** RI.2.5, W.3.7, W.3.8, SL.3.2; **L5:** SL.3.2, SL.3.3, SL.3.6, L.2.6/L.3.6; **L6:** L.2.1/L.3.1b, W.3.4, SL.3.1a, SL.3.1b, SL.3.1c, SL.3.1d, L.3.3a, L.2.6/L.3.6; **L7:** RI.3.2, RI.2.8, RI/RL.2.1, RI.3.4, W.3.4, L.3.3a; **L8:** SL.3.2a, SL.3.1a, SL.3.1b, SL.3.1c, SL.3.1d, SL.3.6, L.2.6/L.3.6; **L9:** L.2.1/L.3.1i; **L10:** W.3.1a, W.3.1b, W.3.1d, W.3.4, W.3.5, W.3.7, L.3.3a; **L11:** RI/RL.2.1a, W.3.8, SL.3.4, SL.3.6, L.3.3, L.2.6/L.3.6;	ELPS 1–5, 7–10
L1: 0.1.2, 0.1.5, 4.1.9, 7.4.1; **L2:** 0.1.2, 0.1.5, 0.1.6; **L3:** 0.1.2, 0.1.5; **L4:** 0.1.2, 0.1.5, 4.1.6; **L5:** 0.1.2, 0.1.5, 4.1.3; **L6:** 0.1.2, 0.1.4, 0.1.5, 4.4.4, 4.4.6, 4.6.1, 4.6.4, 4.8.1, 4.8.7; **L7:** 0.1.2, 7.3.1, 7.3.2, 7.3.4; **L8:** 0.1.2, 0.1.5, 4.3.1, 4.3.2, 4.5.6, 7.4.4, 7.7.3; **L9:** 0.1.2, 0.1.5, 4.6.1, 4.8.3; **L10:** 0.1.2, 0.1.5, 0.1.7, 4.6.1; **L11:** 0.1.2, 0.1.5, 0.1.6, 4.6.1, 7.3.1, 7.3.2;	**L1:** RI.3.4, L.3.5b, L.2.6/L.3.6, W.3.4, SL.3.1, L.3.3a; **L2:** SL.3.2, SL.3.3; **L3:** L.2.1/L.3.1b, L.2.1/L.3.1c, W.3.4, SL.3.1a, SL.3.1b, SL.3.1c, SL.3.1d, L.3.3a; **L4:** RI.3.2, RI/RL.2.1, W.3.4, L.2.1/L.3.1l, L.2.1/L.3.1m, L.3.3a; **L5:** W.3.2a, W.3.2b, W.3.4, W.3.5, L.3.3a; **L6:** SL.3.1a, SL.3.1b, SL.3.1c, SL.3.1d, SL.3.6; **L7:** L.2.1/L.3.1b, L.2.1/L.3.1g, L.2.1/L.3.1i, L.2.1/L.3.1l, L.2.1/L.3.1m; **L8:** RI/RL.2.1, RI.3.2, RI.3.4, RI.2.5, W.3.7, W.3.8; **L9:** SL.3.2, L.2.6/L.3.6; **L10:** L.2.1/L.3.1m, L.2.2/L3.2g, W.3.4, L.3.3a, L.2.6/L.3.6; **L11:** W.3.4, SL.3.4, L.3.3a, L.2.6/L.3.6;	ELPS 1–3, 5, 7–10
L1: 0.1.2, 0.1.5, 3.1.2, 3.1.3, 3.6.2, 7.4.1; **L2:** 0.1.2, 0.1.5, 3.1.2, 3.1.3; **L3:** 0.1.2, 0.1.5; **L4:** 0.1.2. 0.1.5. 3.2.1. 3.6.9. 4.5.6. 7.4.4. 7.7.3; **L5:** 0.1.2, 0.1.4, 0.1.5, 0.1.6, 3.6.3, 3.6.4; **L6:** 0.1.2, 0.1.5, 0.1.6, 3.6.4; **L7:** 0.1.2, 0.1.5, 0.2.1, 3.4.6, 3.6.5, 3.6.8; **L8:** 0.1.2, 0.1.5, 0.1.6, 3.5.9; **L9:** 0.1.2, 0.1.5, 3.6.4, 3.6.8; **L10:** 0.1.2, 0.1.5, 3.6.3, 3.6.4, 3.6.9; **L11:** 0.1.2, 0.1.5, 0.1.6, 7.1.2, 7.3.1, 7.3.2;	**L1:** RI.3.4, W.3.4, L.3.5b, L.2.6/L.3.6; **L2:** SL.3.2, SL.3.1a, SL.3.1b, SL.3.1c, SL.3.1d, L.2.6/L.3.6; **L3:** L.2.1/L.3.1b, W.3.4, SL.3.1a, SL.3.1b, SL.3.1c, SL.3.1d, L.2.6/L.3.6; **L4:** RI/RL.2.1, W.3.7, W.3.8; **L5:** SL.3.2, L.2.6/L.3.6; **L6:** L.2.1/L.3.1b, W.3.4, SL.3.1a, SL.3.1b, SL.3.1c, SL.3.1d; **L7:** RI.3.2, RI.2.5, RI/RL.2.1, W.3.4; **L8:** W.3.1a, W.3.1b, W.3.1d, W.3.4, W.3.5, L.3.3; **L9:** SL.3.2; **L10:** L.2.1/L.3.1m, W.3.4, L.3.3a; **L11:** RI/RL.2.1, W.3.4, SL.3.4, SL.3.6	ELPS 1–5, 7–10
L1: 0.1.2, 0.1.5, 1.8.1, 7.4.1; **L2:** 0.1.2, 0.1.4, 0.1.5, 1.8.1, 1.8.3; **L3:** 0.1.2, 0.1.5, 1.6.7; **L4:** 0.1.2, 0.1.5, 1.8.6; **L5:** 0.1.2, 0.1.5, 0.1.6, 3.5.9; **L6:** 0.1.2, 0.1.5, 1.5.1; **L7:** 0.1.2, 0.1.3, 0.1.5; **L8:** 0.1.2, 0.1.5, 0.1.6, 1.5.3, 6.7.2; **L9:** 0.1.2, 0.1.4, 0.1.5, 1.4.2; **L10:** 0.1.2, 0.1.5, 0.1.6, 1.4.1; **L11:** 0.1.2, 0.1.5, 0.1.6, 7.2.2, 7.2.5, 7.2.6, 7.2.7, 7.3.1, 7.3.2, 7.3.3;	**L1:** RI.3.4, W.3.4, L.2.4a, L.3.5b; **L2:** SL.3.1a, SL.3.1b, SL.3.1c, SL.3.1d, SL.3.2, SL.3.3; **L3:** L.2.1/L.3.1b, W.3.4, SL.3.1a, SL.3.1b, SL.3.1c, SL.3.1d, L.2.6/L.3.6; **L4:** RI.3.2, RI.2.6, RI/RL.2.1, RI.2.6, W.3.4; **L5:** W.3.2a, W.3.2b, W.3.2c, W.3.2d, W.3.4, W.3.5, L.3.3a; **L6:** SL.3.2; **L7:** L.2.1/L.3.1b, L.2.6/L.3.6, **L8:** RI/RL.2.1, RI.2.5, W.3.7, W.3.8, SL.3.1a, SL.3.1b, SL.3.1c, SL.3.1d; **L9:** RI.3.4, SL.3.2, L.2.6/L.3.6, SL.3.1a, SL.3.1b, SL.3.1c, SL.3.1d; **L11:** W.3.4;	ELPS 1–3, 5–10
L1: 0.1.2, 0.1.5, 5.2.6, 7.4.1; **L2:** 0.1.2, 0.1.4, 0.1.5, 5.2.6; **L3:** 0.1.2, 0.1.5, 5.2.6; **L4:** 0.1.2, 0.1.5, 2.2.1, 2.2.3, 2.2.4, 2.2.5, 4.5.6, 7.4.4, 7.7.3; **L5:** 0.1.2, 0.1.4, 0.1.5, 0.1.6, 5.2.6; **L6:** 0.1.2, 0.1.5, 0.1.6, 2.7.1; **L7:** 0.1.2, 0.1.5; **L8:** 0.1.2, 0.1.5, 0.1.6, 5.2.6; **L9:** 0.1.2, 4.5.6, 5.2.1, 7.4.4, 7.7.3; **L10:** 0.1.2, 0.1.5, 0.1.6; **L11:** 0.1.2, 0.1.5, 0.1.6, 7.3.1, 7.3.2;	**L1:** RI.3.4, W.3.4, L.3.5b; **L2:** SL.3.2, SL.3.1a, SL.3.1b, SL.3.1c, SL.3.1d, SL.3.3, L.2.6/L.3.6; **L3:** L.2.1/L.3.1h, W.3.4, SL.3.1a, SL.3.1b, SL.3.1c, SL.3.1d, L.2.1/L.3.1h; **L4:** RI.2.5, RI/RL.2.1, W.3.7, W.3.8; **L5:** SL.3.2, SL.3.1a, SL.3.1b, SL.3.1c, SL.3.1d, SL.3.3; **L6:** L.2.1/L.3.1h, W.3.4; **L7:** RI/RL.2.1, RI.3.2, RI.3.4, W.3.4; **L8:** SL.3.2, SL.3.1a, SL.3.1b, SL.3.1c, SL.3.1d; **L9:** W.3.4, W.3.7, W.3.8, L.2.1/L.3.1e; **L10:** W.3.2a, W.3.2b, W.3.2d, W.3.4, W.3.5; **L11:** RI/RL.2.1, W.3.4, SL.3.4, SL.3.6, L.3.3a, L.2.6/L.3.6;	ELPS 1–3, 5, 7–10

All units of *Future* meet most of the **EFF Content Standards**. For details, as well as for correlations to other state standards, go to www.pearsoneltusa.com/future 2e.

AUTHOR, SERIES CONSULTANT, AND LEARNING EXPERT

Sarah Lynn is an ESOL teacher trainer, author, and curriculum design specialist. She has taught adult learners in the U.S. and abroad for decades, most recently at Harvard University's Center for Workforce Development. As a teacher-trainer and frequent conference presenter throughout the United States and Latin America, Ms. Lynn has led sessions and workshops on topics such as: fostering student agency and resilience, brain-based teaching techniques, literacy and learning, and teaching in a multilevel classroom. Collaborating with program leaders, teachers, and students, she has developed numerous curricula for college and career readiness, reading and writing skill development, and contextualized content for adult English language learners. Ms. Lynn has co-authored several Pearson ELT publications, including *Business Across Cultures, Future, Future U.S. Citizens,* and *Project Success.* She holds a master's degree in TESOL from Teachers College, Columbia University.

SERIES CONSULTANTS

Ronna Magy has worked as an ESOL classroom teacher, author, teacher-trainer, and curriculum development specialist. She served as the ESL Teacher Adviser in charge of professional development for the Division of Adult and Career Education of the Los Angeles Unified School District. She is a frequent conference presenter on the College and Career Readiness Standards (CCRS), the English Language Proficiency Standards (ELPS), and on the language, literacy, and soft skills needed for academic and workplace success. Ms. Magy has authored/co-authored and trained teachers on modules for CALPRO, the California Adult Literacy Professional Development Project, including modules on integrating and contextualizing workforce skills in the ESOL classroom and evidence-based writing instruction. She is the author of adult ESL publications on English for the workplace, reading and writing, citizenship, and life skills and test preparation. Ms. Magy holds a master's degree in social welfare from the University of California at Berkeley.

Federico Salas-Isnardi has worked in adult education as a teacher, administrator, professional developer, materials writer, and consultant. He contributed to a number of state projects in Texas including the adoption of adult education content standards and the design of statewide professional development and accountability systems.

Over nearly 30 years he has conducted professional development seminars for thousands of teachers, law enforcement officers, social workers, and business people in the United States and abroad. His areas of concentration have been educational leadership, communicative competence, literacy, intercultural communication, citizenship, and diversity education. He has taught customized workplace ESOL and Spanish programs as well as high-school equivalence classes, citizenship and civics, labor market information seminars, and middle-school mathematics. Mr. Salas-Isnardi has been a contributing writer or series consultant for a number of ESL publications, and he has co-authored curriculum for site-based workforce ESL and Spanish classes.

Mr. Salas-Isnardi is a certified diversity trainer. He has a Masters Degree in Applied Linguistics and doctoral level coursework in adult education.

AUTHOR

Irene Schoenberg has taught ESL for more than two decades at Hunter College's International English Language Institute and at Columbia University's American Language Program. Ms. Schoenberg holds a master's degree in TESOL from Teachers College, Columbia University. She has trained teachers at Hunter College, Columbia University, and the New School University, and she has given workshops and academic presentations at ESL programs and conferences throughout the world. Ms. Schoenberg is the author or co-author of numerous publications, including *True Colors; Speaking of Values 1; Topics from A to Z,* Books 1 and 2; and *Focus on Grammar: An Integrated Skills Approach* (levels 1 and 2).

ACKNOWLEDGMENTS

The Publisher would like to acknowledge the teachers, students, and survey and focus-group participants for their valuable input. Thank you to the following reviewers and consultants who made suggestions, contributed to this *Future* revision, and helped make *Future: English for Work, Life, and Academic Success* even better in this second edition. There are many more who also shared their comments and experiences using *Future* — a big thank you to all.

Fuad Al-Daraweesh The University of Toledo, Toledo, OH

Denise Alexander Bucks County Community College, Newtown, PA

Isabel Alonso Bergen Community College, Hackensack, NJ

Veronica Avitia LeBarron Park, El Paso, TX

Maria Bazan-Myrick Houston Community College, Houston, TX

Sara M. Bulnes Miami Dade College, Miami, FL

Alexander Chakshiri Santa Maria High School, Santa Maria, CA

Scott C. Cohen, M.A.Ed. Bergen Community College, Paramus, NJ

Judit Criado Fiuza Mercy Center, Bronx, NY

Megan Ernst Glendale Community College, Glendale, CA

Rebecca Feit-Klein Essex County College Adult Learning Center, West Caldwell, NJ

Caitlin Floyd Nationalities Service Center, Philadelphia, PA

Becky Gould International Community High School, Bronx, NY

Ingrid Greenberg San Diego Continuing Education, San Diego Community College District, San Diego, CA

Steve Gwynne San Diego Continuing Education, San Diego, CA

Robin Hatfield, M.Ed. Learning Institute of Texas, Houston, TX

Coral Horton Miami Dade College, Kendall Campus, Miami, FL

Roxana Hurtado Miami-Dade County Public Schools, Miami, FL

Lisa Johnson City College of San Francisco, San Francisco, CA

Kristine R. Kelly ATLAS @ Hamline University, St. Paul, MN

Jennifer King Austin Community College, Austin, TX

Lia Lerner, Ed.D. Burbank Adult School, Burbank, CA

Ting Li The University of Toledo, Ottawa Hills, OH

Nichole M. Lucas University of Dayton, Dayton, OH

Ruth Luman Modesto Junior College, Modesto, CA

Josephine Majul El Monte-Rosemead adult School, El Monte, CA

Dr. June Ohrnberger Suffolk County Community College, Selden, NY

Sue Park The Learning Institute of Texas, Houston, TX

Dr. Sergei Paromchik Adult Education Department, Hillsborough County Public Schools, Tampa, FL

Patricia Patton Uniontown ESL, Uniontown, PA

Matthew Piech Amarillo College, Amarillo, TX

Guillermo Rocha Essex County College, NJ

Audrene Rowe Essex County School, Newark, NJ

Naomi Sato Glendale Community College, Glendale, CA

Alejandra Solis Lone Star College, Houston, TX

Geneva Tesh Houston Community College, Houston, TX

Karyna Tytar Lake Washington Institute of Technology, Kirkland, WA

Miguel Veloso Miami Springs Adult, Miami, FL

Minah Woo Howard Community College, Columbia, MD

Pre-Unit

1 LEARN YOUR CLASSMATES' NAMES

A **WORK TOGETHER.** Tell your group your name and repeat the names of the students before you.

Diana: My name is Diana.

Luis: This is Diana. My name is Luis.

Olga: This is Diana. This is Luis. My name is Olga.

Tran: This is Diana. Excuse me. What's your name again, please?

Luis: Luis.

Tran: OK, thanks. This is Diana. This is Luis. This is Olga. My name is Tran.

Laila: This is Diana. This is Luis. This is Olga. This is Tran. My name is Laila.

B How many classmates' names do you remember?

2 FIND THINGS YOU HAVE IN COMMON

A Read the sentences. Check (✓) all the statements that are true for you.

- ☐ I have a small family.
- ☐ I have a large family.
- ☐ Most of my family lives in the U.S.
- ☐ Most of my family lives in my native country.
- ☐ I live with my family.
- ☐ I live with friends.

- ☐ I'm married.
- ☐ I'm single.
- ☐ I have children.
- ☐ I work in a restaurant.
- ☐ I work in a hospital.
- ☐ I am a student.

B Complete the statements about things you like.

My favorite food is _____.

My favorite kind of music is _____.

My favorite free-time activity is _____.

My favorite holiday is _____.

C Walk around the room. Ask your classmates questions. For example, *Do you have a large family?* Find classmates who have things in common with you. Take notes.

D **TALK ABOUT IT.** Share your results.

Getting Started

3 ASK FOR AND GIVE CLARIFICATION

A Complete the conversations. Use the questions and statement in the box.

~~Could you explain that?~~

Did you say a pen?

Do you mean first we should work alone?

I'm sorry. What page?

What's the word for this in English?

What I mean is that you shouldn't read out loud.

1.

OK, everyone. Ask your partner the questions on page 28.

I'm sorry. I don't understand. *Could you explain that?*

Sure. Turn to page 28. Work in pairs. Ask your partner the questions.

2.

Could I borrow a pen, please?

Yes, a pen. Thanks.

3.

Excuse me, Sue. _____

That? That's an outlet.

An outlet? Thanks.

4.

When you finish, please check your answers with a partner.

Sorry, _____ . . . and then work with a partner?

Yes, that's right.

5.

Class, please look at the article on page 74 and read it to yourselves.

Sorry, I don't understand.

_____ .

Read silently.

6.

OK, everyone. Open your books to page 85.

Page 85.

B ▶ SELF-ASSESS. Listen and check your answers.

C WORK TOGETHER. Choose one conversation from Exercise A. Create a new conversation with different information.

Getting Started

4 LEARN ABOUT *FUTURE*

A Turn to page iii. Answer the questions.

1. What information is on this page? _____

2. How many units are in this book? _____

3. Which two units are about health? _____

4. Which two units are about work? _____

B Sometimes you will need to go to the back of the book to do activities. Look at the chart. Find the pages in the book and complete the chart.

Page	Activity
245	My Soft Skills Log
247	

C Look in the back of the book. Find each section. Write the page number.

Grammar Reference _____   Map of the U.S. and Canada _____

Audio Script _____   Map of the World _____

Word List _____   Index _____

D Look inside the front cover. How will you get the audio?

_____

1 Living in a Neighborhood

PREVIEW

Where are you from? Where do you live now? What's your neighborhood like?

UNIT GOALS

- [ ] Identify different countries
- [ ] Make small talk
- [ ] Talk about places in the neighborhood
- [ ] Follow written instructions

- [ ] Talk about holidays and celebrations
- [ ] **Academic skill:** Understand the main idea
- [ ] **Writing skill:** Write a topic sentence
- [ ] **Workplace soft skill:** Be inclusive

5

Vocabulary

Countries

A **PREDICT.** Look at the map. How many countries can you name?

B ▶ **LISTEN AND POINT.** Then listen and repeat.

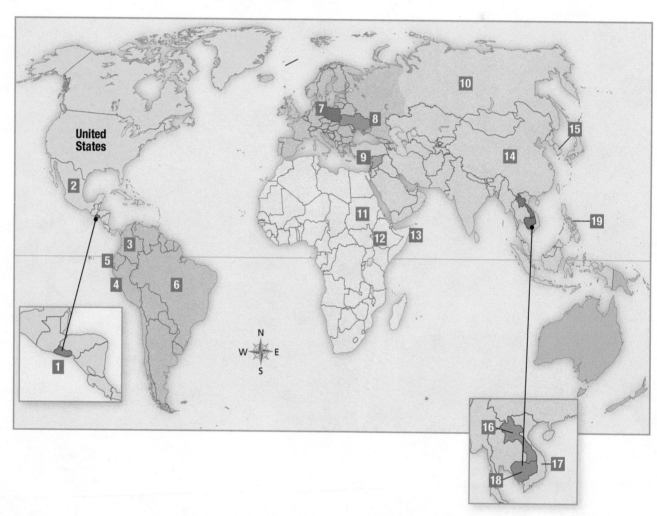

C **LOCATE.** Match the countries on the map with their names. Write the numbers.

Countries			
_____ Brazil	_____ El Salvador	_____ the Philippines	_____ Sudan
_____ Cambodia	_____ Ethiopia	_____ Poland	_____ Syria
_____ China	_____ Laos	_____ Russia	_____ Ukraine
_____ Colombia	_____ Mexico	_____ Somalia	_____ Vietnam
_____ Ecuador	_____ Peru	_____ South Korea	

Vocabulary

D **MATCH.** What is the most common language in each country? Write the correct letters.

___e___ **1.** Brazil   **a.** Polish

_____ **2.** China   **b.** Spanish

_____ **3.** Peru   **c.** Filipino

_____ **4.** the Philippines   **d.** Vietnamese

_____ **5.** Poland   **e.** Portuguese

_____ **6.** Vietnam   **f.** Mandarin

E **IDENTIFY.** Underline the countries. Circle the languages.

My name is Jamila, and my family is from Sudan. We came to the U.S. two years ago. Now we live in Kansas City. We like our neighbors in Kansas City. They are very friendly. We met many people at a community garden where we grow our own vegetables. We met people from Syria, Ethiopia, Vietnam, Mexico, and other countries. People speak different languages—like Arabic and Spanish—but everyone speaks at least a little English.

The Philippines

Las Filipinas

Show what you know!

1. **DISCUSS.** Where are you from? What languages do you speak? Do you like your community now? What do you like about it?

   A: Where are you from?
   B: I'm from Mexico City.
   A: What languages do you speak?
   B: I speak Spanish and some English.
   A: Do you like your community now?
   B: Yes, I really like my school and my job. I also have nice neighbors.

2. **WRITE.** Where is your partner from? What languages does he or she speak?

   My partner is from Mexico City. She speaks English and Spanish. She likes her school and her job. She also likes her neighbors.

I can talk about different countries and languages. ☐   I need more practice. ☐

For more practice, go to MyEnglishLab.

Make small talk

1 BEFORE YOU LISTEN

A **MATCH. Look at the pictures. Write the correct letters.**

_____ **1.** go to a park

_____ **2.** walk a dog

_____ **3.** take an exercise class

_____ **4.** watch a soccer game

B **MAKE CONNECTIONS. How do you meet people in your neighborhood?**

A: I meet new people when I walk my dog.
B: I talk to my neighbors when I go to the park with my children.

2 LISTEN

Edwin and Marco are watching a soccer game. They meet and introduce themselves.

A ▶ **LISTEN FOR MAIN IDEA. Circle the answer.**

Edwin and Marco are _____.
   a. teammates   **b.** old friends   **c.** new friends

B ▶ **LISTEN FOR DETAILS. Circle the answers.**

1. When does the Atlas soccer league meet?
   a. Saturdays
   b. Sundays
   c. Saturdays and Sundays

2. What happens when it rains?
   a. They play indoors.
   b. They still play.
   c. They don't play.

C ▶ **EXPAND. Listen to the rest of the conversation. Write _T_ (true) or _F_ (false).**

_____ **1.** Marco knows many players in Edwin's soccer league.

_____ **2.** Marco and Hector are both from Brazil but from different towns.

_____ **3.** Hector is surprised to see Marco.

Listening and Speaking

3 PRONUNCIATION

A ▷ PRACTICE. Listen. Then listen and repeat.

Po land   Bra **zil**   Cam **bo** di a   **Chi** na   U **ni** ted **States**

B ▷ APPLY. Listen. Mark (•) the stressed syllable.

1. La os

2. Ko re a

3. Mex i co

4. Russ ia

5. Vi et nam

6. Co lom bi a

> **Syllables**
>
> Words are made up of syllables. In English, one syllable in a word has the strongest stress. It is longer and louder than other syllables.

4 CONVERSATION

A ▷ LISTEN AND READ. Then practice the conversation with a partner.

A: Great game. Is this the Atlas soccer league? I've heard about them.

B: Yes. I love to come here and watch them.

A: Do they play every Saturday?

B: Yes, unless it rains. By the way, my name's Edwin.

A: Hi, I'm Marco. Nice to meet you.

B: Nice to meet you, too. Do you live around here?

A: Nearby. I live in Southside. I'm originally from Brazil.

B INTERVIEW. Get to know your partner. Introduce yourself. Ask questions.

Are you a new student in this school?
Do you live far from school? How do you get to school?
Why do you want to learn English?

I can make small talk. ■   I need more practice. ■

For more practice, go to MyEnglishLab.

Grammar

Simple present

Affirmative Statements		
I		
We	**play**	
You		
They		soccer.
He	**plays**	
She		

Negative Statements		
I		
We	**don't**	**play**
You		
They		soccer.
He	**doesn't**	**play**
She		

Grammar Watch
• Use the simple present for habits, routines, and facts.
• Use the simple present for feelings and possessions.
• For the third-person singular (*she, he, it*), add -*s* or -*es* to the verb.

Yes/No Questions		
Do	you	
		play soccer?
Does	she	

Short Answers	
Yes, I **do**.	No, I **don't**.
Yes, she **does**.	No, she **doesn't**.

Wh- Questions		
Who	**plays**	soccer on Saturdays?

Other *wh-* Questions			
How often			
Where	**do**	you	**play** soccer?
When			

A **INVESTIGATE.** Underline the simple present verbs.

My family comes from Sichuan province in China. Now we live in downtown Seattle. People from all parts of Asia live here. My family has an apartment near Hing Hay Park. I like the park a lot. It reminds me of parks in China. Hing Hay Park has benches and tables for Chinese chess. My grandfather plays there with other older men. My grandmother doesn't play chess, but she exercises with her friends almost every morning.

Grammar

Unit 1, Lesson 3 11

B PRACTICE. Complete the conversation. Use verbs from the word box. Use the simple present.

cook	do	eat	go	have	~~spend~~	want

A: How _____do_____ you _____spend_____ your spare time?

B: We _____ to the park almost every weekend.

A: Oh, yeah? What _____ you _____ there?

B: We _____ a barbecue and spend the day together.

A: That's nice. What kind of food _____ you _____?

B: We usually _____ beef or chicken, rice and beans, and tamales.

A: Delicious!

B: _____ you _____ to come with us this weekend?

A: Sure! That sounds great.

C APPLY. Write questions. Use the simple present.

1. What / country / you from? _What country are you from?_ _____

2. Where / you live / now? _____

3. you / like / your neighborhood? _____

4. What / you / like / about your neighborhood? _____

5. Who / you / live with? _____

6. Who / help you the most / in the U.S.? _____

Show what you know!

1. **INTERVIEW.** Ask a partner the questions from Exercise C. Take notes.

2. **WRITE.** Share some information you learned about your partner.

   Jun Park is from Seoul, Korea. Now Jun lives in Koreatown, Los Angeles.

I can use simple present verbs. ☐	I need more practice. ☐

For more practice, go to MyEnglishLab.

Reading

Read about where Americans live

1 BEFORE YOU READ

PREDICT. Where do you think most people in the U.S. live?
Do they live in the countryside or in a city?

2 READ

▶ Listen and read.

> **Academic Skill: Understand the main idea**
>
> The main idea is the most important idea in an article. The main idea is often found in the first paragraph.

Population Changes in the U.S.

Where do people live in the U.S.? The answer to this question is changing. In the past, most people lived in the countryside. Nowadays, not many Americans want to live in rural areas. So who will live in these areas?
5 Who will keep them alive? One idea is immigrants.

Hundreds of years ago, most Americans lived and worked on farms. In 1790, almost all Americans lived in rural areas. During the 1800s and 1900s, more people began to move to cities. They moved to find
10 jobs in factories and businesses. By 1920, more people lived in urban areas than in the countryside. Today, most Americans live in urban areas. In July 2016, less than 15 percent of the population lived in the countryside. The rural population of the U.S. is
15 falling.

This is a big problem for rural areas. What happens when many people leave an area? Stores and restaurants lose their customers. Schools and hospitals close. Residents have to travel many miles
20 every day. The area begins to die.

What is a possible solution to this problem? People from other countries, like refugees, can help. Refugees have to leave their own countries. They need to escape from war or poverty. Sometimes, they
25 come to the U.S. The government sends them to live in different places. Why not send them to rural areas?

For example, consider the small town of Clarkston, Georgia. Clarkston didn't have enough people. It asked the government to send 40,000 refugees. The
30 government agreed. Many refugees live in Clarkston now. They have brought new life to the town. People in places like Clarkston welcome immigrants. They know that immigrants are their hope for the future.

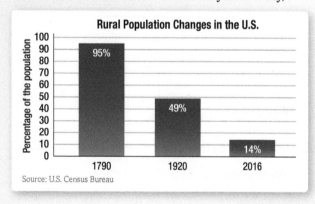

Rural Population Changes in the U.S.

Percentage of the population

95% — 1790
49% — 1920
14% — 2016

Source: U.S. Census Bureau

3 CLOSE READING

A IDENTIFY. What is the main idea of the article?

a. Hundreds of years ago, most people in the U.S. lived in the countryside.
b. The rural population of the U.S. is falling, and immigrants can solve this problem.
c. Clarkston, Georgia, asked the government to send refugees to their town.

Reading

B CITE EVIDENCE. Answer the questions. Where is the information? Write the line numbers.

Lines

1. Where did most U.S. residents live in 1790?

_____   _____

2. Why did many people move to urban areas?

_____   _____

3. What percentage of U.S. residents lived in rural areas in 2016?

_____   _____

4. Why is low population a problem for rural areas?

_____   _____

5. What solution does the article suggest for this problem?

_____   _____

C INTERPRET GRAPHICS. Complete the sentences about the bar graph.

1. According to the bar graph, _____.
   a. the population in urban areas is falling
   b. the population in the countryside is growing
   c. the number of people living in rural areas is falling

2. From 1790 to 1920, the population in rural areas in the U.S. _____.
   a. decreased by more than 50%
   b. decreased by more than 40%
   c. decreased by less than 40%

4 SUMMARIZE

What are the most important ideas in the article? Write three sentences in your notebook.

Show what you know!

1. **DISCUSS.** Look at the graph on page 12. What kinds of population changes are happening in the U.S.? Is the population in your area changing? If so, how is it changing?

2. **WRITE.** Describe how the population in your area is changing and how it affects your community.

   The population of my city is changing because more immigrants are moving here. That means there are many different kinds of restaurants, and . . .

I can understand the main idea while reading. ☐   I need more practice. ☐

To read more, go to MyEnglishLab.

Lesson 5

Talk about places in the neighborhood

1 BEFORE YOU LISTEN

MATCH. Look at the pictures. Write the correct letters.

_____ **1.** movie theater _____ **5.** supermarket

_____ **2.** café _____ **6.** hair salon

_____ **3.** post office _____ **7.** shopping mall

_____ **4.** pharmacy

2 LISTEN

Eden is moving into a new apartment. Her new neighbor, Sara, comes over to introduce herself.

A ▶ **LISTEN FOR MAIN IDEA.** Circle the answer.

Why does Sara go to Eden's house?
  a. She wants to ask about Eden's family.
  b. She wants to find out where Eden is from.
  c. She wants to introduce herself.

B ▶ **LISTEN FOR DETAILS.** Write *T* (true) or *F* (false).

_____ **1.** Sara doesn't like her neighborhood.

_____ **2.** The supermarket is crowded on weekends.

_____ **3.** The pharmacy is open 24 hours.

_____ **4.** The post office is closed on Saturdays.

_____ **5.** Sara likes to go to the movie theater.

_____ **6.** Eden needs a haircut.

Listening and Speaking

3 PRONUNCIATION

A ▶ **PRACTICE. Listen to the sentences. Then listen and repeat.**

When **do** they open?

Do you ("d'ya") have any questions?

Where **do you** ("d'ya") go shopping?

Do you

The word *do* usually has a weak pronunciation with a short, quiet vowel sound when the word *you* comes after it. *Do you* is often pronounced "d'ya."

B ▶ **APPLY. Listen to the sentences. Check (✓) the sentences that have a weak pronunciation of** *do* **(as in "d'ya").**

☐ **1.** Do you want to play basketball?

☐ **2.** Where do we go for class?

☐ **3.** Do they work at the post office?

☐ **4.** Where do you want to go for dinner?

4 CONVERSATION

A ▶ **LISTEN AND READ. Then practice the conversation with a partner.**

A: Where do you go shopping?

B: Sometimes I go to the supermarket, but I usually go to the discount store down the street.

A: What do they sell there?

B: Almost everything! They have food, clothes, and stuff for the house.

A: What do you usually do on the weekend?

B: I usually go to the park with my family. Sometimes I go to the mall.

A: Do you go to the movie theater often?

B: No, I rarely watch movies.

B **ROLE-PLAY. You move to a new home. Talk to your neighbor and learn more about your new neighborhood. Then switch roles.**

A: You live in the neighborhood. Introduce yourself and ask your new neighbor if he or she has questions about the neighborhood.

B: You are new to the neighborhood. Ask about different places. Find out the location of the closest supermarket, post office, café, and pharmacy.

I can talk about places in the neighborhood. ■   I need more practice. ■

For more practice, go to MyEnglishLab.

Adverbs of frequency

Adverb	Subject	Adverb	Verb	
	We	**always**	shop	at the supermarket.
	She	**rarely**	watches	movies.
Sometimes Usually	they			
			play	in the park.
	They	**sometimes**		

Subject	*be*	Adverb	
I	am	**usually**	home on the weekend.
The café	is	**never**	open on Sunday.

Grammar Watch

- Adverbs of frequency appear before the verb.
- Adverbs of frequency appear after the verb *be* (*am, is, are, was,* and *were*).
- *Sometimes* and *usually* can also start a sentence.

Adverbs of Frequency

always	100%
usually	
often	
sometimes	
rarely	
never	0%

A INVESTIGATE. Underline the adverbs of frequency. Circle the verb that the adverb describes.

Simon loves his neighborhood. He lives close to his job. He <u>usually</u> (walks) to work. He is never late for work. He likes all of the restaurants near his house. He often goes to the café and talks with his friends after work. Sometimes Simon and his friends go to the movies, but they rarely agree. They usually spend a long time deciding what to watch.

B PRACTICE. Unscramble the sentences.

1. never / Thomas / popcorn / gets / at the movies
   <u>Thomas never gets popcorn at the movies.</u>

2. often / we / go / to the shopping mall
   _____

3. rarely / I / my friends / visit / during the week
   _____

4. gets home / sometimes / Selim / after midnight
   _____

5. is / usually / Sam / at the library
   _____

6. never / I / am / late / for work
   _____

Grammar

C **APPLY. Add adverbs of frequency to the sentences. Draw arrows.**

1. Lisa watches movies at the theater. (often)

2. I buy shampoo at the hair salon. (sometimes)

3. We go to the park after dinner. (always)

4. They shop for clothes at the mall. (usually)

5. The post office is closed on weekends. (always)

6. Dan is at the café with his friends. (never)

D **IDENTIFY. Read the paragraph. Find and correct the mistakes.**

I'm from El Salvador. People drink usually coffee and eat tortillas for breakfast. Often we eat tortillas for lunch, too. Lunch always is the biggest meal. For dinner, we have often a lighter meal. Now I live in the U.S. I eat sometimes the same foods I ate in El Salvador, but I have usually a big dinner and a small lunch.

Show what you know!

1. **SURVEY. Ask your classmates about places in the neighborhood. Begin with *How often*.**

   How often do you go to the pharmacy?

2. **WRITE. Report the results of your survey. Use adverbs of frequency.**

   Nadia never goes to the pharmacy. Chen and Ali often go to the mall.

I can use adverbs of frequency. ☐   I need more practice. ☐

For more practice, go to MyEnglishLab.

Workplace, Life, and Community Skills

Follow written instructions

1 FOLLOW A RECIPE

A **MAKE CONNECTIONS.** Do you own or work in a food truck? Do you know someone who does? What kind of food do they serve?

B **READ.** Look at the instructions for making tacos.

How to Make a Taco:
1. Take a warm taco shell from the oven.
2. Place two tablespoons of chicken, beef, or shrimp in the taco.
3. Add two or three pieces of lettuce.
4. Place one tablespoon of salsa on top of the lettuce.
5. Add a topping (peppers, onions, black beans, avocado).
6. Sprinkle cheese over the ingredients.
7. Wrap the taco in foil and place it in the oven for 2 minutes.

C **APPLY.** Complete the steps for how to make a taco.

1. Place _____ of chicken, beef, or shrimp in the warm taco.
   a. one tablespoon **b.** two pieces **c.** two tablespoons

2. Next, add _____ and salsa.
   a. peppers **b.** lettuce **c.** onions

3. Add the _____ last.
   a. cheese **b.** lettuce **c.** salsa

4. Put the taco in the oven for _____ minutes.
   a. two **b.** one **c.** three

D GO ONLINE. Look up other recipes you can use when making tacos.

Workplace, Life, and Community Skills

2 HANDLE FOOD SAFELY

A READ. Look at the food safety instructions.

Food Safety Tips

- Always clean your hands before and after touching food.
- Wash fresh produce, such as lettuce, thoroughly.
- Wash all surfaces, cutting boards, and utensils carefully after using them.
- Keep raw meat and seafood separate from other foods.
- Use separate cutting boards for meat and poultry.
- Cook foods to the correct temperature.
- Use a meat thermometer to make sure all meat is cooked thoroughly.
- Never thaw meat on a counter. Keep it in the refrigerator.
- Put away unused food as soon as possible.

B PUT IN ORDER. Complete the sentences. Write the correct letters.

1. When cutting raw meat, _____
2. After touching any food, _____
3. When you are cooking poultry, _____
4. If meat or chicken touches a surface, _____
5. Before using fresh lettuce, _____

a. clean the surface immediately.
b. wash it thoroughly.
c. use a meat thermometer.
d. you must wash your hands.
e. use a separate cutting board.

C DISCUSS. What other food safety tips do you know?

I can follow written instructions. ■   I need more practice. ■

For more practice, go to MyEnglishLab.

8 Listening and Speaking

Talk about holidays and celebrations

1 BEFORE YOU LISTEN

A **IDENTIFY.** The West Indies is made up of many islands and countries. Look at the map. Name two.

B **MAKE CONNECTIONS.** Every year, there are many parades that celebrate the cultures from these islands. Do you like parades? Why or why not?

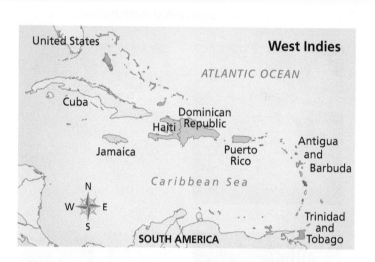

2 LISTEN

This is a radio announcement about the West Indian–American Day parade.

A ▶ **LISTEN FOR MAIN IDEA.** Circle the answer.

Where is the parade?
   a. the West Indies
   b. Brooklyn
   c. Labor Day

B ▶ **LISTEN FOR DETAILS.** Circle the correct answers. Some questions have more than one correct answer.

1. What can you see at the parade?
   a. costumes   **b.** musicians
   c. dancers   **d.** actors

2. What kind of music can you hear?
   a. reggae   **b.** rap
   c. jazz   **d.** calypso

3. What musical instruments can you hear?
   a. pianos   **b.** steel drums
   c. guitars   **d.** violins

4. What can you taste?
   a. fried chicken   **b.** potatoes
   c. rice and peas   **d.** eggs

5. What is free at the parade?
   a. food   **b.** tickets
   c. parking   **d.** music

Listening and Speaking

3 CONVERSATION

A ▶ **LISTEN AND READ.** Then practice the conversation with a partner.

A: There are a lot of choices at this food truck. What do you recommend?

B: Well, most people like the beef noodles.

A: I don't eat much meat. Are there any vegetarian dishes?

B: Yes, there are several vegetarian dishes. The vegetable fried rice is popular. There are also some vegetable dumplings, but they have a little fish sauce. There are a few sandwiches without meat.

B: Thanks! I'll have the fried rice. This is a nice food truck. Are you here often?

A: No, we're here only for the festival. We're usually at Smith Park on weekends.

B: That's close to my house. I'll go there next weekend and try something else.

B MAKE CONNECTIONS. Talk about a celebration you enjoy.

A: My favorite holiday is Chuseok, the Korean Harvest Moon festival.
B: What do you do on that day?

I can talk about holidays and celebrations. ■   I need more practice. ■

For more practice, go to MyEnglishLab.

	Quantifier	Count Noun	
There are	**a few** **some** **several** **a lot of** **many**	vegetables	in this dish.
There aren't	**many** **any**		

	Quantifier	Non-count Noun	
There's	**a little** **some** **a lot of**	meat	in this soup.
There isn't	**much** **any**		

Grammar Watch

- Quantifiers tell us *how much* or *how many* we have of something.
- Count nouns are things we can count separately (*an orange, two oranges*).
- Non-count nouns are things we can't count separately (*rice, water, information*).
- See page 259 for a list of common non-count nouns.

A INVESTIGATE. Circle the quantifiers. Underline the nouns they describe.

1. There are several parades in New York City each month.
2. Many children dress in costumes on Mexican Independence Day.
3. People carry a lot of flags at the Philippines Independence Day parade.
4. You can see several famous people at the Puerto Rican Day parade.
5. You can see some traditional dances at the Cinco de Mayo parade.
6. People set off a lot of firecrackers on Chinese New Year.

B CHOOSE. Cross out the incorrect words.

A: How did you know about this parade?

B: There were **a few / a little** announcements on the radio. But I often look for events on the internet.

A: Oh, yeah? I've never found **much / many** information like that on the internet.

B: It's easy. You just search for "free events in New York City." You'll find **a lot of / a few** information. You can click on the links and find **many / much** free events. Last year, I went to **several / a little** festivals I found on the internet.

I can use quantifiers with count and non-count nouns. ■   I need more practice. ■

For more practice, go to MyEnglishLab.

Lesson 10 Writing

Write about a move

1 STUDY THE MODEL

ANALYZE. Read the model and Writing Skill. Then answer the questions.

My Move

I moved to the U.S. in 2014. I moved with my parents and sisters. We moved from Oaxaca, Mexico, to Hammonton, New Jersey. We moved to Hammonton because many families from Oaxaca live there. My cousin moved there in 2012. He helped us a lot when we first arrived. Hammonton is in a rural area, so the cost of living is lower than in a big city. We are happy in Hammonton!

Writing Skill: Write a topic sentence

The topic sentence gives the main idea of a paragraph. It describes what the paragraph will be about.

1. What is the topic sentence in the paragraph?
2. What is the paragraph about?

2 PLAN YOUR WRITING

A BRAINSTORM. Ask and answer the questions.

Have you ever moved to a new place? Why did you move?

B OUTLINE. Complete each sentence.

Topic Sentence: _____

I moved with _____

I moved from _____

I moved to _____

I moved because _____

3 WRITE

EXPLAIN. Write about your move. Use the model, the Writing Skill, and your ideas from Exercise 2 to help you.

4 CHECK YOUR WRITING

COLLABORATE. Read the checklist. Read your writing together. Revise your writing.

WRITING CHECKLIST

☐ Does the paragraph have a topic sentence?

☐ Does the topic sentence give the main idea of the paragraph?

☐ Does the paragraph say who moved and where?

☐ Does the paragraph say why the writer moved?

I can write a topic sentence. ■

I need more practice. ■

For more practice, go to MyEnglishLab.

11 Lesson

Be inclusive

1 MEET ALEC

Read about one of his workplace skills.

> I try to make all of my co-workers feel included. For example, when I see co-workers sitting alone, I ask them to join the group.

2 ALEC'S PROBLEM

A READ. Write *T* (true) or *F* (false).

Alec is a laboratory assistant. He is very friendly and gets along well with everyone in the office. At lunch time, co-workers at his company usually eat together in the cafeteria.

Tony works on the same team as Alec. Tony is very shy and usually keeps to himself. He doesn't talk to anyone and eats lunch by himself. Some of his co-workers think Tony seems unfriendly. Alec wants Tony to feel included at work.

_____ **1.** Alec usually eats lunch by himself.

_____ **2.** Alec doesn't know Tony.

_____ **3.** Alec wants Tony to sit with him at lunch.

B ANALYZE. What is Alec's problem? Write your response in your notebook.

3 ALEC'S SOLUTION

A COLLABORATE. Alec is inclusive. He tries to make people feel welcome and part of a group. What should he do? Explain your answer.

1. Alec tells his co-workers that they should be nice to Tony.
2. Alec decides to eat lunch with Tony.
3. Alec invites Tony to join the group at lunch.
4. Alec _____.

B ROLE-PLAY. Act out Alec's solution with your partner.

Show what you know!

1. **REFLECT.** How have you made someone feel included at work? Give an example.

2. **WRITE.** Now write your example in your Skills Log.

   I am inclusive. I try hard to make everyone feel welcome and part of a group. For example, I invite new co-workers to lunch so I get to know them better.

3. **PRESENT.** Give a short presentation to show how you are inclusive.

I can give an example of how I am inclusive at work. ☐

Unit Review: Go back to page 5. Which unit goals can you check off?

2 Setting Goals

PREVIEW

What do you dream about for your future?
What are your plans for yourself or your family?

UNIT GOALS

- [ ] Identify goals for the future
- [ ] Identify steps to a better job
- [ ] Look for a new job
- [ ] Set goals
- [ ] Talk about obstacles and supports

- [ ] Identify community services
- [ ] **Academic skill:** Predict
- [ ] **Writing skill:** Write supporting sentences
- [ ] **Workplace soft skill:** Take responsibility for professional growth

25

Vocabulary

Goals

A **PREDICT.** Look at the pictures. What do you see?

B ▶ **LISTEN AND POINT.** Then listen and repeat.

Vocabulary

C **IDENTIFY. Read the paragraph. Underline the new vocabulary.**

My dream is to be an electrician. When I lived in Sudan, I got a high school diploma, but I couldn't go to college because of the war. Now I want to go back to school and get a college degree. First, I need to enroll in a college. Then I'll look at the schedule and register for classes. I'm going to sign up for weekend classes and apply for financial aid. I hope the school will give me some money for tuition. To become an electrician, I will have to work with a licensed electrician for two years and pass a test. After that, I can get a certificate and work for myself.

Study Tip

Build Vocabulary

Write the verbs *get* and *apply* on the front of two cards. On the back of each card, write two or three phrases that use the verb. Use a dictionary for help.

apply to college
apply for financial aid
apply for a job

Show what you know!

1. **DISCUSS. What are your goals for the future?**

   A: What's your goal?
   B: Well, I got my high school diploma. My goal is to get a college degree in nursing. What's your goal?
   A: My goal is to become a hotel manager.

2. **WRITE. List two goals you want to complete.**

   1. My goal is to _____

   2. _____

I can identify goals for the future. ■   I need more practice. ■

For more practice, go to MyEnglishLab.

Lesson 2

Identify steps to a better job

1 BEFORE YOU LISTEN

A **MATCH.** What training do these jobs require? Look at the pictures. Write the correct letters.

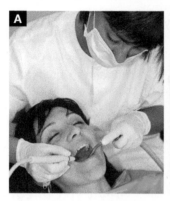

_____ **1.** auto body repairer, automotive service excellence (ASE) certificate

_____ **2.** dental assistant, state license

_____ **3.** registered nurse, associate's degree

2 LISTEN

Carmen tells Max about her plan to go back to school.

A ▶ **LISTEN FOR MAIN IDEA.** What are Carmen's plans?

She is going to _____ this fall.
  a. get a new job
  b. go back to school

B ▶ **LISTEN FOR DETAILS.** Circle the answers.

1. When will Carmen take courses?
  a. on weekends   **b.** at night

2. What will she study?
  a. nursing   **b.** medical billing

3. What will she do after her basic classes?
  a. apply to a clinical   **b.** get a job at a clinic
  program

C ▶ **LISTEN FOR DETAILS.** Listen again. Then answer the questions.

1. How long will it take Carmen to get her degree if she works hard?
2. What does Max give Carmen? Why?

Listening and Speaking

3 PRONUNCIATION

A ▶ **PRACTICE. Listen. Then listen and repeat.**

I'll start in the fall.
He'll work part-time.
When will you finish?

We'll help.
You'll study tonight.
What will you study?

> **Contraction of *will***
>
> *Will* is often contracted with nouns (*he'll, she'll*) and *wh-* questions (*what'll, when'll, where'll, how'll*).

B ▶ **APPLY. Listen to the sentences. Circle the words you hear.**

1. **I / I'll** work at night.

2. **I / I'll** take classes during the day.

3. **We / We'll** both go to City College.

4. **You / You'll** need to get a license.

4 CONVERSATION

A ▶ **LISTEN AND READ. Then practice the conversation with a partner.**

A: I'm going to take night classes this fall.

B: Yeah? Where?

A: At Los Angeles City College.

B: That's great. What will you study?

A: Well, I want to be a nurse.

B: What kind of training does that require?

A: I'll need to get an associate's degree.

B **ROLE-PLAY. Make a similar conversation. Then change roles.**

A: Talk about going back to school.

B: Ask about the certificate, license, or degree.

Welder
get a certificate

Real estate agent
get a license

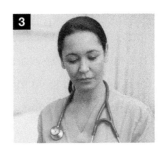

Medical assistant
get an associate's degree

I can identify steps to a better job. ■

I need more practice. ■

For more practice, go to MyEnglishLab.

Grammar

The future with *will* and *might*

Subject	*will* *might*		Verb	
She	**will** **might**	(not)	**go**	to school next fall.
We	**will** **might**	(not)	**work**	this weekend.

Yes/No questions			
Will	you she	**change**	jobs?

Short answers
Yes, I **will**. / Probably. / No, I **won't**.
Yes, she **will**. / Probably. / No, she **won't**.

Wh- questions				
When Where Why	**will**	you	**take**	classes?

Grammar Watch

- Use *will* to talk about the future.
- Use *might* to talk about a future possibility.
- Use *will* to ask questions about the future. Do not use *might*.
- *will* + *not* = *won't* I *will* = I'll He *will* = He'll
- See page 260 for more contractions.

A INVESTIGATE. Read about Cam. Underline *will / won't / might* and the verb that follows.

Cam

    I want to go to City College this fall. I want to get an associate's degree in computer programming. To get the degree, I'll need to take basic classes like English and math first. Then I will need to take classes in computer science and coding. It won't take long to finish the degree. It might take two or three years if I work part-time. After I get my degree, I'll work for a while and save money. Later, if I get financial aid, I might go to a four-year college and get a bachelor's degree. I will make more money with a bachelor's degree.

B COMPLETE. Use *will, might,* or *won't.*

1. Cam _____ go to college this fall.
2. Cam _____ get a degree next year.
3. Cam _____ get financial aid.

Grammar

C **PRACTICE.** Read the conversation between a husband and wife. Cross out the incorrect verbs.

A: My English class **will / ~~might~~** start on Monday at 5:30.

B: Oh, no! I forgot about your English class. I can't take you this Monday because I have to work. How **will / might** you get to school?

A: I'm not sure. I**'ll / might** take the bus, or I **won't / might** share a ride with a friend.

B: OK. I don't work the following Monday, so I**'ll / might** definitely drive you then.

A: Thanks, but next Monday is a holiday, and the school **will / might not** be closed. I **might / won't** need a ride that day.

D **INFER.** Read the situations. What do you think the people *might* or *might not* do?

1. Jun doesn't have enough money to pay the school tuition.

   He might apply for financial aid. He might not take classes this year.

2. Mona can't study full-time because she takes care of her kids during the day.

   _____

3. Pedro can't finish his degree because he works every day. His employer told him about some online classes.

   _____

4. Kate really wants to go to a community college, but she doesn't have a car.

   _____

5. Sam is in his first year of college. He's not getting good grades.

   _____

Show what you know!

1. **DISCUSS.** Talk about how you can improve your English this year.

   A: *I will need to study hard.*
   B: *I might work with an English tutor.*

2. **WRITE.** List three ways you can improve your English.

   1. *I will* _____

   2. *I won't* _____

   3. *I might* _____

I can use *will* and *might* to talk about the future. ■   I need more practice. ■

For more practice, go to MyEnglishLab.

Read about immigrant entrepreneurs

1 BEFORE YOU READ

PREDICT. Look at the picture and the title of the article.
What do you think the article is about?

2 READ

▶ Listen and read.

Immigrant Dreams: Small Businesses

People from all around the world move to the U.S.
every year. Many of these immigrants have an
important dream. Their dream is to start their own
business. They want to become entrepreneurs. Many
5 of them achieve this goal.

Ignacio and Eva Moreno are immigrant entrepreneurs.
They were both born in Mexico. Ignacio's parents had
a bakery. They taught him to bake. He was very good
at it. Then Ignacio met Eva. They moved to the U.S.
10 They settled in Little Rock, Arkansas. There, they
decided to open their own bakery.

Ignacio and Eva worked hard to reach their goal. First,
they got jobs in other people's bakeries. That way,
they learned about bakeries in the U.S. They saved
15 money. Then they found an old building. They fixed it
up. They bought ovens and other bakery equipment.

Fifteen years went by. Finally, the Morenos opened
their own bakery. Their goal became a reality. They
named their bakery La Flor del Trigo. They baked
20 special Mexican breads. People in Little Rock loved the
breads. La Flor del Trigo became very popular. Now,
Ignacio and Eva work 12-hour days, but they are happy.

The Morenos are not alone. Many immigrants are
successful entrepreneurs. The Small Business
25 Administration compared immigrants with
native-born Americans. What did they find?
Immigrants are more likely to own their own
businesses. In fact, 10.5 percent of U.S. immigrants
are entrepreneurs. Only 9.3 percent of people born
30 in the U.S. are entrepreneurs. Small businesses
create many new jobs. They are important in the
U.S. economy. The U.S. needs immigrant
entrepreneurs like the Morenos.

3 CLOSE READING

A **IDENTIFY.** What is the main idea of the article?

a. Many immigrants in the U.S. are successful entrepreneurs.
b. Ignacio and Eva Moreno own a bakery in Little Rock, Arkansas.
c. Only 9.3 percent of people born in the U.S. are entrepreneurs.

Reading

B CITE EVIDENCE. Answer the questions. Where is the information? Write the line numbers.

Lines

1. What did Ignacio Moreno do when he was a child?

_____   _____

2. What did the Morenos decide to do after they moved to Little Rock?

_____   _____

3. How did the Morenos reach their goal?

_____   _____

4. What do the Morenos do now?

_____   _____

5. What percentage of U.S. immigrants own their own businesses?

_____   _____

6. Why are immigrant entrepreneurs important in the U.S. economy?

_____   _____

C INTERPRET VOCABULARY. Complete the sentences.

1. The word *entrepreneurs* in line 4 means _____.
   a. people from another country
   b. people who own businesses

2. The word *achieve* in line 5 means _____.
   a. reach
   b. plan

3. The word *equipment* in line 16 means _____.
   a. tools or machines you need to do something
   b. food you can eat or cook with

4. The word *reality* in line 18 means _____.
   a. a dream or goal
   b. a real or true situation

5. The words *native-born* in line 26 means _____.
   a. born in this country
   b. born in another country

4 SUMMARIZE

What are the most important ideas in the article? Write three sentences in your notebook.

Show what you know!

1. **DISCUSS.** How did the Morenos achieve their goal? Talk about other entrepreneurs you know about. What did they have to do to achieve their goals?

2. **WRITE.** Describe one immigrant entrepreneur and the challenges he or she faced when starting a new business.

   My friend Lisa Chang is an immigrant from China. She owns a restaurant. She opened the restaurant after she moved to Los Angeles. She . . .

I can make predictions while reading. ■   I need more practice. ■

To read more, go to MyEnglishLab.

1 BEFORE YOU LISTEN

A **EXPLAIN.** How do social media sites and job fairs help people find jobs?

careerlinks.com

Main Street Clinic: Looking for experienced registered nurses. Must have excellent communication skills.
Nursing Home: Nurses needed immediately. Nights and weekends required.
Community Hospital: Emergency room nurses needed. Bilingual applicants preferred.

Social media site

Job fair

B **MAKE CONNECTIONS.** What are other ways to look for a job? How do you look for a job?

2 LISTEN

Min and Sheng are talking about finding a new job.

Sheng

Min

A ▶ **LISTEN FOR MAIN IDEA.** Circle the answer.

What is Min going to do?
a. work more hours
b. look for a new job
c. go back to school

B ▶ **LISTEN FOR DETAILS.** Circle the answers.

1. Why is Min going to look for a new job?
   a. She comes to work late.
   b. She doesn't like her manager.
   c. She doesn't like the restaurant.

2. Where is Sheng going to go this weekend?
   a. to a job fair
   b. to a restaurant
   c. to school

3. What is Sheng going to get next month?
   a. a certificate
   b. an associate's degree
   c. a license

C ▶ **EXPAND.** Listen to the rest of the conversation. Answer the questions.

Sheng finds a job listing for Min. Is Min going to apply for that job? Why or why not?

Listening and Speaking

3 PRONUNCIATION

A ▶ **PRACTICE. Listen. Then listen and repeat.**

What are you going to do?
I'm going to look for a job.

Are you going to the store right now?
No, I'm going to English class.

B ▶ **APPLY. Listen to the sentences. Check (✓) the sentences where *going to* is pronounced "gonna."**

☐ **1.** I'm going to the movies tonight.

☐ **2.** Is he going to do his homework?

☐ **3.** Are you going to be at the meeting today?

☐ **4.** They are going to New York next week.

4 CONVERSATION

A ▶ **LISTEN AND READ. Then practice the conversation with a partner.**

A: Why are you looking for a new job?

B: I'm going to graduate with an associate's degree in nursing next month. I'm looking for a job as a nurse.

A: Congratulations! Do you use careerlinks.com? It's a social media site with lots of job listings.

B **ROLE-PLAY. Make a similar conversation. Then change roles.**

A: You're looking for a new job. Explain how.

B: Suggest some other ways your partner can look for a new job.

- Look online.
- Go to a job fair.
- Look for Help Wanted signs.

I can talk about how to look for a new job. ■   I need more practice. ■

For more practice, go to MyEnglishLab.

Grammar

The future with *going to*

Subject	*be*		*going to*	Verb	
I	am				
She	is				
You		(not)	going to	look	for a new job.
We	are				
They					

Yes/No questions

Are	you	going to	**look** for a new job?	
Is	he			

Short answers

Yes, I am.	No, I'm not.
Yes, he is.	No, he's not.

Wh- questions

When	**are**	you	going to	look	for a new job?
Where	**is**	he			

Grammar Watch

- Use *going to* to talk about plans for the future.
- *I + am = I'm
  she + is = she's
  you + are = you're
  we + are = we're
  they + are = they're*

A **INVESTIGATE. Read the conversation between Omar and an employment counselor. Underline *going to* and the verb that follows.**

A: Thanks for meeting with me today. I'm <u>going to graduate</u> soon, and I want to find a job in my field.

B: That's a smart decision. What degree are you going to receive?

A: I'm going to get an associate's degree in accounting.

B: That's great. There are a lot of opportunities for accountants. When are you going to graduate?

A: In about three months.

B: OK, here's what we're going to do. First, I want you to attend a job fair. There's going to be one at the community college this weekend. I'm also going to set up a profile for you on our job site.

A: Thanks! This is very helpful.

B: No problem. Let's meet again after the job fair. I'm not going to be here next week. Do you want to meet again in two weeks?

A: Sounds good.

B **PRACTICE. Complete the sentences. Use the correct form of *be* + *going to*.**

1. He _____ graduate soon.

2. They _____ meet again in two weeks.

Grammar

C **COMPLETE. Use the correct form of *be + going to*. Use the negative form when necessary.**

1. Ana and Lisa _____*are going to*_____ take classes at the community center.

2. Pablo works at night. He _____ apply for a job with daytime hours.

3. I saw a Help Wanted sign at the mall. I _____ apply for the job today.

4. My sister _____ look for a part-time job. She _____ work full-time because she is still in school.

5. _____ you _____ look for a job on a social media site?

D **APPLY. Use the correct form of *be + going to* and the verb in parentheses.**

A: Ricardo and I _____*are going to visit*_____ a temp agency tomorrow.

(visit)

B: What's a temp agency?

A: It's a place where people help you find jobs for short periods of time. I _____

(ask)
them about an office job. Do you want to come?

B: Yes. That sounds great! I really need a job. My job _____ next month. Do I

(end)
need to bring anything?

A: I _____ my diploma from Russia. It's translated into English. Ricardo

(bring)
_____ a letter from his old employer.

(take)

B: That's a good idea. My manager really likes me, so I _____ her for a letter.

(ask)
Maybe that will help.

Show what you know!

1. **DISCUSS. Talk about the job you want to have five years from now. What are you going to do to get that job?**

   A: I'm going to be a medical assistant in five years.
   B: Are you going to go to school to get that job?
   A: Yes. I'm going to get a certificate from the community college.

2. **WRITE. Plan for your future job. List the steps you need to take to get that job. Use *going to*.**

   1. I am going to _____

   2. _____

I can use *going to* to talk about the future. ■   I need more practice. ■

For more practice, go to MyEnglishLab.

7 Workplace, Life, and Community Skills

Lesson **7**

Set goals and talk about obstacles and supports

1 SET GOALS

A **READ.** Think about time frames for goals.

When you set a goal, you need to decide on a realistic time frame to reach your goal. For example, if you want to get a certificate and are studying part-time, you probably won't be able to finish in a year. In this case, not having enough time is an *obstacle* to reaching your goal. So a realistic time frame might be two or three years. It also helps to have *support* to reach your goal. This can include advice or encouragement from a friend.

B **DISCUSS.** What makes a time frame realistic? How can you set a realistic time frame for your goals?

C **MAKE CONNECTIONS.** Complete the chart. Write one or two goals in each category. When do you want to reach them?

School	By when?	Job	By when?

Community	By when?	Family or personal	By when?

D **COLLABORATE.** Look at your partner's goals. Are the time frames realistic?

Workplace, Life, and Community Skills

2 TALK ABOUT OBSTACLES AND SUPPORTS

A COLLABORATE. Read about Amina. Answer the questions.

I grew up in Damascus, Syria. My father was a professor at Damascus University. When I turned 18, our family moved to the U.S. I didn't finish my education in Syria. I got my high school diploma (GED) when we got to Chicago. I work at a nursing home as an aide. My dream is to be a registered nurse. First, I need to improve my English skills. I'm in an English language program at the community college. Then I'll continue studying for an associate's degree in nursing. To reach my goal, I need financial aid and help from my family. Right now, my husband works, and my family helps take care of my daughter. They want me to become a nurse, and they think I can succeed.

1. What is Amina's goal?
2. What are some obstacles to Amina's goal?
3. What are Amina's supports?

B APPLY. Think about your most important goal. Is it difficult? Complete the chart.

Goal	What are some obstacles?	What are your supports?

C COLLABORATE. Look at your partner's chart. Can you think of obstacles or supports that he or she did not include? Discuss.

D GO ONLINE. Identify a certificate, license, or associate's degree. Find out how long it takes to get.

I can set goals and talk about obstacles and supports. ☐   I need more practice. ☐

For more practice, go to MyEnglishLab.

Write about your goal

1 STUDY THE MODEL

ANALYZE. Read the model and Writing Skill. Then answer the questions.

My Goal

My goal is to become a licensed real estate agent. First, I'm going to work and study English. Then I will take classes and learn about buying and selling homes. Next, I will work full-time in a real estate office to learn more about the job. Finally, I will pass the real estate license exam. It will be hard, but I know I can become a licensed real estate agent.

Writing Skill: Write supporting sentences

Remember that the topic sentence gives the main idea of the paragraph. Supporting sentences give more information to support the topic sentence. When supporting sentences are steps, they begin with words such as *first, second, then, next, last,* or *finally*.

1. What is the topic sentence in the paragraph?
2. What are the four steps the writer will take to reach her goal?

2 PLAN YOUR WRITING

A BRAINSTORM. Ask and answer the questions.

What is one of your goals? What steps will you take to reach your goal?

B OUTLINE. Complete with your ideas.

Topic Sentence: _____

Supporting Sentences:

    Step 1: _____

    Step 2: _____

    Step 3: _____

    Step 4: _____

3 WRITE

STATE. Write about your goal and the steps you will take to reach your goal. Use the model, the Writing Skill, and your ideas from Exercise 2 to help you.

4 CHECK YOUR WRITING

COLLABORATE. Read the checklist. Read your writing together. Revise your writing.

WRITING CHECKLIST

☐ Does the paragraph have a topic sentence?

☐ Does the topic sentence explain the goal?

☐ Does the paragraph have supporting sentences?

☐ Do the steps begin with *first, next, then, last,* or *finally*?

I can write supporting sentences. ■   I need more practice. ■

For more practice, go to MyEnglishLab.

Lesson 9

Identify community services

1 BEFORE YOU LISTEN

MAKE CONNECTIONS. Is there a community center in your neighborhood? What kinds of services and activities does it provide? Can it help you reach your goals?

2 LISTEN

This is a radio announcement about community events.

A ▶ **LISTEN FOR MAIN IDEA. Which services are mentioned in the announcement? Check (✓) the services you hear.**

☐ healthcare service

☐ food and clothing for families in need

☐ classes for adults

☐ babysitting services

☐ neighborhood improvement

B ▶ **LISTEN FOR DETAILS. Match the dates with the events.**

_____ **1.** Sept.–Oct.   **a.** English placement test

_____ **2.** Oct. 20   **b.** mural painting

_____ **3.** Sept. 8, 9   **c.** food and clothing distribution

_____ **4.** Oct. 1   **d.** food and clothing drive

_____ **5.** Sept. 10   **e.** English and computer classes

C **EXPAND. Write a list of community services available in your neighborhood that can help you reach your goals. Then share your list with the class.**

- _____   - _____
- _____   - _____
- _____   - _____

I can identify community services. ☐   I need more practice. ☐

For more practice, go to MyEnglishLab.

The future with present continuous

Subject	*be*		Verb	
I	**am**			
She	**is**			
You		(not)	**working**	tomorrow.
We	**are**			
They				

Grammar Watch

- Use the present continuous to talk about definite plans in the future.
- We usually use a time expression like *tomorrow* or *next week* to show the action is in the future.

Yes/No questions				
Are	you	**cleaning**	the office next week?	
Is	he			

Wh- questions				
Where	**are**	we	**meeting**	this afternoon?
What	**is**	he	**watching**	tonight?

A **INVESTIGATE.** Read the conversation between two people making plans for the future. Underline examples of the present continuous.

A: Hi. I work at the community center. We<u>'re having</u> a meeting next Saturday night. We're talking about how volunteers can help clean up our neighborhood parks.

B: Sorry, I'd like to come, but I'm working that night.

A: Oh, sure, I understand. But please tell your friends and neighbors. We're meeting at 7:00 p.m. We're having a potluck dinner and giving out prizes.

B **APPLY.** Complete the sentences with the present continuous. Use the words in parentheses.

1. The community center _____ next week.
   (meet)

2. They _____ pizza and fun activities for the children.
   (provide)

3. We _____ our children to the center tomorrow.
   (bring)

4. _____ to the meeting tomorrow night?
   (you, go)

Grammar

C **COMPLETE. Use the present continuous and the words in parentheses.**

1. **A:** <u>Are you coming</u> to the meeting tomorrow night?

        (you, come)

   B: No, I can't. _____ for my granddaughter.

               (I, babysit)

2. **A:** _____ English classes next semester?

   (your sister, take)

   B: She's still not sure. They don't have enough space right now, so they put her on

   a waiting list. _____ her back next week to let her know.

              (They, call)

3. **A:** _____ your children to the community center tomorrow?

   (you, bring)

   B: Yes, I am. _____ special activities for the kids.

          (They, have)

D **COLLABORATE. Mei Lu is a stay-at-home mother. Look at her calendar.
Ask your partner *yes / no* and *wh-* questions about her plans for next week.**

Monday	Tuesday	Wednesday	Thursday	Friday
4	**5**	**6**	**7**	**8**
Babysit for Feng 3:30 English class 7:00	Go shopping! Chinese community center – Legal Aid 5:00	Library – kids' story time 9:00 English class 7:00	Chinese community center – moms' group 6:00	take Jin to clinic 9:00

A: When is Mei Lu babysitting?
B: She is babysitting on Monday afternoon at 3:30.
A: What is she doing on Wednesday?

Show what you know!

1. **DISCUSS. What events are happening in your community this month? Are you going to the events?**

   A: The immigration center is having a citizenship meeting next Monday.
   B: Are you going to the meeting?
   A: No, I'm not. I'm working that day.

2. **WRITE. Describe a few events that are happening in your community this month. Use the present continuous.**

   My apartment building is having a picnic next weekend.

I can use the present continuous to talk about the future. ☐   I need more practice. ☐

For more practice, go to MyEnglishLab.

Soft Skills at Work

Take responsibility for professional growth

1 MEET EVAN

Read about one of his workplace skills.

> I take responsibility for my professional growth. I love my career. For example, I am always looking for opportunities to learn new skills and get better at what I do.

2 EVAN'S PROBLEM

A READ. Write *T* (true) or *F* (false).

    Evan is an electrician. He works at Energy Electric. His customers and his supervisor agree that Evan is very good at his job. When he has time, Evan takes classes to learn new skills and stay up to date.

    Energy Electric wants to hire a new project manager. Evan is interested in the job, but he's not sure he has the necessary skills. He has never been a manager, but he has a lot of great experience.

_____ **1.** Evan is very good at what he does.
_____ **2.** His supervisor makes him take extra courses.
_____ **3.** Evan isn't sure if he has the skills for the new job.

B ANALYZE. What is Evan's problem? Write your response in your notebook.

3 EVAN'S SOLUTION

A COLLABORATE. Evan takes responsibility for his professional growth. What should he do? Explain your answer.

1. Evan waits to see if his supervisor offers him the job.
2. Evan applies for the job. He knows he has a lot of experience.
3. Evan asks his supervisor if he has the necessary skills for the job.
4. Evan _____.

B ROLE-PLAY. Act out Evan's solution with your partner.

Show what you know!

1. **REFLECT.** Share an example of a decision you made that helped you grow professionally.

2. **WRITE.** Now write your example in your Skills Log.

I take responsibility for my professional growth. For example, I take classes to learn new skills.

3. **PRESENT.** Give a short presentation to show how you take responsibility for your professional growth.

I can show how I take responsibility for my professional growth. ☐

Unit Review: Go back to page 25. Which unit goals can you check off?

3 Going to School

PREVIEW

In the U.S., there are elementary schools, middle schools, and high schools. Is this the same as or different from other countries?

UNIT GOALS

- [ ] Identify and talk about school activities
- [ ] Help children with school
- [ ] Ask for time off work
- [ ] Communicate with your child's teacher
- [ ] Deal with bullies

- [ ] **Academic skill:** Use what you know
- [ ] **Writing skill:** Support an opinion with reasons
- [ ] **Workplace soft skill:** Separate work life and family life

Vocabulary

School activities

A IDENTIFY. Look at the pictures. What do you see?

B ▶ **LISTEN AND POINT.** Then listen and repeat.

Vocabulary

School Activities

1. do research
2. figure out an answer
3. go online
4. go over homework
5. go to a parent-teacher conference
6. hand in homework
7. help someone out
8. look up a word in a dictionary
9. make up a test

C **INTERPRET.** Read the email. Why is Jen's mother worried about her? What does *drop out* mean?

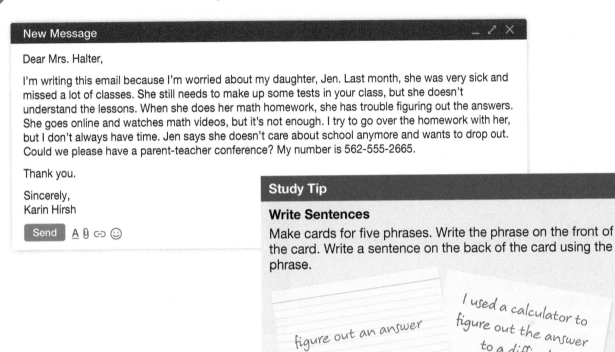

New Message _ ⤢ ✕

Dear Mrs. Halter,

I'm writing this email because I'm worried about my daughter, Jen. Last month, she was very sick and missed a lot of classes. She still needs to make up some tests in your class, but she doesn't understand the lessons. When she does her math homework, she has trouble figuring out the answers. She goes online and watches math videos, but it's not enough. I try to go over the homework with her, but I don't always have time. Jen says she doesn't care about school anymore and wants to drop out. Could we please have a parent-teacher conference? My number is 562-555-2665.

Thank you.

Sincerely,
Karin Hirsh

Send   A ⌨ ⊖ ☺

Study Tip

Write Sentences
Make cards for five phrases. Write the phrase on the front of the card. Write a sentence on the back of the card using the phrase.

figure out an answer

I used a calculator to figure out the answer to a difficult math problem.

Show what you know!

1. **PROBLEM SOLVE.** Why do children sometimes fall behind in school? What can parents do to help children keep up with school work?

   A: Some children don't finish their homework because they get distracted by TV or video games.
   B: Parents can limit screen time on school nights.

2. **WRITE.** Explain other ways parents can help their children succeed in school.

   Parents can . . .

I can identify and talk about school activities. ☐   I need more practice. ☐

For more practice, go to MyEnglishLab.

Lesson 2

Help children with school

1 BEFORE YOU LISTEN

EXPLAIN. What things can parents do to help their children continue their education?

2 LISTEN

A mother is talking to a school counselor about her daughter, Elena. School counselors help students with many kinds of problems—problems at school and personal problems.

A ▶ **LISTEN FOR MAIN IDEA.** Circle the answer.

Why is Ms. Cruz talking to the school counselor?
- **a.** She wants to plan for her daughter's future.
- **b.** Her daughter is depressed.
- **c.** Her daughter is having a problem with a teacher.

Counselor

Elena

Ms. Cruz

B ▶ **LISTEN FOR DETAILS.** Circle the answers.

1. Elena's grades are especially good in _____.
   - **a.** computers and math
   - **b.** math and social studies
   - **c.** math and science

2. Elena's mother wants her to _____.
   - **a.** attend a community college
   - **b.** attend a four-year college
   - **c.** become a doctor

C ▶ **EXPAND.** Listen to the second part of the conversation. How many years of each subject does Elena need to take?

_____4 years_____	English
_____	social studies
_____	math
_____	science
_____	foreign language

Listening and Speaking

3 PRONUNCIATION

A ▶ PRACTICE. Listen. Then listen and repeat.

hand it **in**   He hands it in on time.

fall be**hind**   You don't want to fall behind.

keep up with   Try to keep up with the work.

B ▶ APPLY. Listen. Mark (•) the stressed syllables in the phrasal verbs.

1. We have homework every day. Our teacher **goes over** it in the morning.
2. Paul missed a test. He'll **make it up** tomorrow.
3. My son's graduation is next week. I **look forward** to it.
4. Dina can't carry all those books. Can you please **help her out**?

4 CONVERSATION

A ▶ LISTEN AND READ. Then practice the conversation with a partner.

A: What would you like to see Elena do in the future?

B: We really want her to go to a four-year college.

A: Oh, that's great. Well, in that case, we have to make sure she takes the right courses. Elena should take certain classes to prepare for a four-year college.

B: OK. What classes should she take?

A: Well, she has to take four years of English. She needs three years of social studies, math, and science. She also has to take two years of a foreign language and a semester of computer science.

B PROBLEM SOLVE. What should teachers and counselors do to help children continue their education?

I can talk about ways to help children with school. ■   I need more practice. ■

For more practice, go to MyEnglishLab.

Questions with *should*			Answers
Should	he I	talk to a counselor today?	Yes. He **should** talk to a counselor. Yes, he **should**. No, you **shouldn't** talk to a counselor. No, you **shouldn't**.

Questions with *have to*			Answers
Does Do	he I	**have to** take English?	Yes. He **has to** take English. Yes, he **does**. No, you **don't have to** take English. No, you **don't**.

Grammar Watch

- Use *should* to give advice.
- Use *have to* when it is necessary to do something.
- *Don't / Doesn't have to* means there is a choice.
- *should not* = *shouldn't*

A INVESTIGATE. Read the advice from a high school counselor. Underline *should* or *have to* and the verb that follows.

You <u>have to take</u> four years of English, math, science, and social studies. You should choose electives in different subjects like computer science and art. You have to take the SAT during your senior year of high school. You don't have to take the PSAT, but it will help you prepare for the SAT. You should do some research on different colleges and majors now. You shouldn't wait until your senior year.

B SELECT. Read the advice. Check (✓) the statements with the same meaning.

1. It is a good idea to show your college essay to a few people before you hand it in.

    ☐ **a.** You have to show it to a few people.
    ☐ **b.** You should show it to a few people.

2. The application is due on December 31.

    ☐ **a.** You have to send it in before December 31.
    ☐ **b.** You should send it in before December 31.

3. Recommendations from teachers are a required part of a college application.

    ☐ **a.** You have to ask a teacher for a letter of recommendation.
    ☐ **b.** You should ask a teacher for a letter of recommendation.

Grammar

C **COMPLETE.** Use the affirmative or negative form of *should* or *have to.*

1. You can register for the exam online. You _____don't have to_____ register in person.

2. The test begins at 8:00. You _____ be in room 201 by 8:00. No one can enter the room after 8:00.

3. You _____ go to bed late the night before the test. You _____ get a good night's sleep.

4. Bring two number 2 pencils. You _____ use a number 2 pencil for the test.

5. You _____ work quickly. You only have two hours to complete the questions.

6. You _____ answer all questions. You _____ leave any blanks.

D **CHOOSE.** Cross out the incorrect words.

1. **A:** Does my daughter need algebra to graduate from high school?

   B: Yes, she ~~should~~ / **has to** take algebra. She can't graduate without it.

2. **A:** Does my son **should / have to** take four years of a foreign language?

   B: No. Students only need two years of a foreign language. They **have to / don't have to** take four years.

3. **A:** My son needs help with science. What can he do?

   B: He **should / has to** ask classmates who are good in science for help.

4. **A:** We want our daughter to go to college next year. How can we learn about financial aid?

   B: You **should / have to** look online. That's a good place to start. There's a lot of great information on our website.

Show what you know!

1. **COLLABORATE.** What do students have to do to prepare for college? What are some things parents should do to help their children prepare for college?

   Students have to take certain classes to prepare for college. Parents should take their children to visit colleges.

2. **WRITE.** Should children continue their education after they finish high school? Write three or four sentences explaining your answer. Use *should* and *have to.*

   I think all children should . . .

I can use *should* and *have to* in questions and statements. ■   I need more practice. ■

For more practice, go to MyEnglishLab.

Read about effective study habits

1 BEFORE YOU READ

RECALL. What do you do when you have to remember something you have learned? How do you study for a big test?

2 READ

▶ **Listen and read.**

> **Academic Skill: Use what you know**
>
> While you read, think about the topic. What do you already know about it? This can help you guess the meaning of unfamiliar words and ideas.

Effective Study Habits

a flashcard

草莓 / *cǎo méi* / strawberry

Learning is an important skill. Remembering what you learn is even more important. In the past,
5 what did people do to memorize new facts? They read the facts over and over again. Before an important test,
10 students "crammed." They studied for many hours. They didn't take breaks. Today, many people understand that this method is not very effective. It's better to use several different methods to study. These methods include spaced repetition, making personal connections, and self-testing.

15 **Spaced Repetition**
When people space out their studying over time, they remember more. Students should take breaks between study sessions. They should spread out the sessions over a long period of time. They should also start studying
20 right after they learn a new fact. They shouldn't wait until right before a test. That way, they can remember more. This is true even when they study for fewer hours. This method is called "spaced repetition."

Making Personal Connections
25 Making personal connections is another effective way to study. People can remember new concepts when they connect those concepts to their own lives. Here's an example. In an English class, students learn how to ask, "Where is the post office?" Then they go out. They ask
30 people on the street where another place is. Students write down the directions. Then they walk to the place. They remember the phrase better because they use it in real life.

Self-Testing
35 Students should test themselves when they study. It's one of the best ways to study. When students test themselves, they find out what they know. They also find out what they don't know. They should do this right after they learn something new. Then they should keep
40 testing themselves until they really remember what they learned. There are different ways to test yourself. You can ask a classmate to test you. You can use flashcards. You can practice on the computer.

Spaced repetition, making personal connections, and
45 self-testing are all effective study methods. They will help you remember what you learn.

3 CLOSE READING

Ⓐ IDENTIFY. What is the main idea of the article?

a. Learning is an important skill, but remembering what you learn is even more important.
b. You can remember more when you make personal connections to what you learn.
c. Use several different study methods if you want to remember what you learn.

Reading

B **CITE EVIDENCE. Complete the sentences. Where is the information? Write the line numbers.**

Lines

1. In the past, people usually _____ before big tests.
   - **a.** crammed
   - **b.** studied for a short time
   - **c.** studied in different ways
   _____

2. Spaced repetition means studying _____.
   - **a.** for many hours without a break
   - **b.** right after learning something
   - **c.** with breaks over a long period of time
   _____

3. When you make personal connections to what you learn, you _____.
   - **a.** study what you learn for many hours
   - **b.** connect what you learn to your own life
   - **c.** write down directions and walk
   _____

4. When you use flashcards, you practice the study method of _____.
   - **a.** spaced repetition
   - **b.** making personal connections
   - **c.** self-testing
   _____

5. Students should test themselves _____.
   - **a.** in the same way every time
   - **b.** in different ways
   - **c.** only right before they have a big test
   _____

C **INTERPRET VOCABULARY. Answer the questions.**

1. What's another word for *memorize* in line 6? _____
   - **a.** study
   - **b.** remember
   - **c.** understand

2. What's another word for *method* in line 12? _____
   - **a.** idea
   - **b.** person
   - **c.** way

3. What's another way to say *effective* in line 12? _____
   - **a.** works well
   - **b.** doesn't work
   - **c.** is fun

4. What's another word for *concepts* in line 26? _____
   - **a.** ideas
   - **b.** places
   - **c.** connections

4 SUMMARIZE

What are the most important ideas in the article? Write three sentences in your notebook.

Show what you know!

1. **IDENTIFY.** According to the article, what are some good ways to remember what you learn? Do you know other good ways? What do you think is the best way for you?

2. **WRITE.** Describe three different study methods that help people remember what they learn.

   These three study methods help people remember what they learn. The first method is . . .

I can use what I know while reading. ☐   I need more practice. ☐

To read more, go to MyEnglishLab.

Give your opinion about a school issue

1 STUDY THE MODEL

ANALYZE. Read the model and Writing Skill. Then answer the questions.

The Arts in Schools

I think schools should offer classes in the arts (music, art, and theater). Why? First, the arts help children express their creativity. Second, the arts improve student grades and test scores. Finally, the arts help many students feel better about themselves. For these reasons, I believe students should learn music, art, and theater in school.

Writing Skill: Support an opinion with reasons

Writers sometimes give an opinion about a topic and try to persuade the reader to agree. To persuade—or convince—the reader, the opinion must be supported with reasons. The words *first, second,* and *finally* help organize these reasons.

1. What is the writer's opinion?
2. What three reasons does the writer give to support this opinion?

2 PLAN YOUR WRITING

A BRAINSTORM. Ask and answer the questions.

What is something your school or program should do?
What are the reasons you think your school should do this?

B OUTLINE. List reasons to support your opinion.

Opinion	
Reason 1	
Reason 2	
Reason 3	

3 WRITE

JUSTIFY. Give your opinion about a school issue. Use the model, the Writing Skill, and your ideas from Exercise 2 to help you.

WRITING CHECKLIST

☐ Does the paragraph have a topic sentence that gives an opinion?

☐ Does the paragraph include reasons that support this opinion?

☐ Does the paragraph include words such as *first, second,* and *finally*?

4 CHECK YOUR WRITING

COLLABORATE. Read the checklist. Read your writing together. Revise your writing.

I can support an opinion with reasons. ■   I need more practice. ■

For more practice, go to MyEnglishLab.

Lesson 6

Ask for time off work

1 BEFORE YOU LISTEN

IDENTIFY. Sometimes people need to take time off work for school or their children. What are some good reasons to take time off?

2 LISTEN

Pilar is calling her manager, Dave, to ask for time off work.

A ▶ **LISTEN FOR MAIN IDEA. Circle the answer.**

Pilar   Dave

Why is Pilar calling her manager?
   a. She needs to take her son to the doctor.
   b. She needs to go to her daughter's school play.
   c. She needs to go to a parent-teacher conference.

B ▶ **LISTEN FOR DETAILS. Circle the answers.**

1. Pilar wants to _____ tomorrow.
   a. take the day off
   b. work another shift
   c. come in late

2. Why is Nestor taking the day off work?
   a. He is sick.
   b. His son is sick.
   c. He has a parent-teacher conference.

3. Pilar has a parent-teacher conference _____.
   a. next Friday
   b. tomorrow
   c. at 2:00

C **EXPAND.** Talk about a time you had to ask for time off work. How did you ask your manager?

I can ask for time off work. ▪   I need more practice. ▪

For more practice, go to MyEnglishLab.

Grammar

Adjective or noun phrase + infinitive

It	is	Adjective or Noun Phrase		Infinitive	
		important **a good idea**	(for you)	**to ask**	for time off in advance.
		difficult **necessary**	(for me)	**to talk**	to my child's teacher.

A **INVESTIGATE.** Underline the adjective or noun phrase + infinitive.

It's <u>hard to say</u> much about my son's new school. He's only been there a week. I know that it's important to be in class every day. It's a good idea to tell his teacher if he will not be in class. Yesterday, my son was sick and missed a day of school. It is difficult for me to stay home with him when I have to work. It was necessary to take a day off work.

B **PRACTICE.** Unscramble the sentences.

1. _It's important for high school students to study for exams._
   (important / to study / for high school students / for exams / it's)

2. _____
   (it's / for me / difficult / time off work / to take)

3. _____
   (necessary / it's / for parents / to help / in school / their children)

4. _____
   (it's / to meet / with your children's teachers / a good idea)

5. _____
   (easy / to fall behind / it's / for kids / in their school work)

6. _____
   (for parents and teachers / to discuss problems / important / it's)

Grammar Watch

- A noun phrase is a noun plus other words that describe that noun and make it unique (*idea* → *a good idea*).
- An infinitive is the word *to* plus the base form of a verb.

Grammar

C **COMPLETE.** Write sentences with the words in parentheses. Use the infinitive form of the verb.

1. College is expensive, but students can sometimes get financial aid.

   It's _____*important to apply*_____ for financial aid early.

(important / apply)

2. Marta needs to take off work to attend her daughter's graduation.

   It's _____ her manager in advance.

(a good idea / ask)

3. Clara is nervous because she is giving a speech at her graduation. She's very shy.

   It's _____ in front of a large crowd.

(difficult / for her / speak)

4. Graduates have to wear special clothes.

   It's _____ a cap and gown at graduation.

(necessary / for students / wear)

Show what you know!

1. **DISCUSS.** Is it easy to graduate from high school? Is it important to attend your child's graduation ceremony?

   It is not easy to graduate from high school. Students need to work hard. It is important to support your child and attend his or her graduation.

2. **WRITE.** Take notes about why it is important to support children when they are in school. Use an adjective or a noun phrase + infinitive.

   I think it's important to support children because . . .

I can use adjectives or noun phrases + infinitives. ■   I need more practice. ■

For more practice, go to MyEnglishLab.

Workplace, Life, and Community Skills

Communicate with your child's teacher

1 READ A REPORT CARD

A **READ.** Learn about the grading system in the U.S.

In the U.S., most high school students receive letter or number grades on their tests, homework, and papers. They usually receive grades four times a year, called a quarter. At the end of the school year, they get a final grade for each class. Look at the chart. Which grades are good? Which are bad?

A+	A	B+	B	C+	C	D	F
95–100%	90–94%	85–89%	80–84%	75–79%	70–74%	65–69%	Below 65%

B **INTERPRET.** Look at the report card.

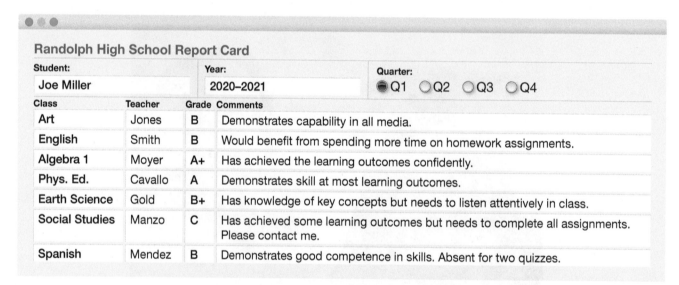

Randolph High School Report Card

Student: Joe Miller

Year: 2020–2021

Quarter: ● Q1 ○ Q2 ○ Q3 ○ Q4

Class	Teacher	Grade	Comments
Art	Jones	B	Demonstrates capability in all media.
English	Smith	B	Would benefit from spending more time on homework assignments.
Algebra 1	Moyer	A+	Has achieved the learning outcomes confidently.
Phys. Ed.	Cavallo	A	Demonstrates skill at most learning outcomes.
Earth Science	Gold	B+	Has knowledge of key concepts but needs to listen attentively in class.
Social Studies	Manzo	C	Has achieved some learning outcomes but needs to complete all assignments. Please contact me.
Spanish	Mendez	B	Demonstrates good competence in skills. Absent for two quizzes.

C **COLLABORATE.** Answer the questions about the report card.

1. In which classes does Joe need to work harder?
2. In which classes did Joe miss assignments, tests, or quizzes?
3. In which class does Joe need to listen to the teacher more?
4. Which teacher wants to speak to Joe's parents?

Workplace, Life, and Community Skills

2 LISTEN TO A VOICEMAIL

A DISCUSS. Why do parents sometimes call their child's school or teacher?

B ► LISTEN FOR DETAILS. Listen to a voicemail from a high school.
Circle the words you hear.

a. main office   **b.** weather   **c.** school closing

C ► LISTEN AND READ. Read the statements. Then listen again and write
the correct numbers.

1. You don't know where the school is. You need to press _____.

2. You need to call the main office. Press _____.

3. Your daughter got sick at school. The school nurse left a voicemail on your cell phone.

Press _____ to call her back.

4. A boy in school hit your son. Press _____ for the vice principal.

5. Your child is doing poorly in Mr. Manzo's class. You want to talk to Mr. Manzo. Press _____.

3 TALK TO A TEACHER

A ROLE-PLAY. Act out the following situation with your partner.

A: You are Joe's teacher. Explain that Joe doesn't hand in his homework. He comes to class late,
and his test scores are low. Give Joe's parent some advice.
B: You are Joe's parent. Ask how Joe can do better in class.

B GO ONLINE. Find a video that shows a meeting between a parent and a teacher. What do they
talk about?

I can communicate with my child's teacher. ■   I need more practice. ■

Listening and Speaking

Deal with bullies

1 BEFORE YOU LISTEN

DISCUSS. Sometimes children are mean and bully other children. Sometimes problems happen in class or on the playground. What should parents do if another child bullies their child?

playground

2 LISTEN

Rafael is in middle school. He is talking to his mother.

A ▶ **LISTEN FOR MAIN IDEA.** Circle the answer.

How does Rafael feel?
  a. upset
  b. bored
  c. confused

Rafael

B ▶ **LISTEN FOR DETAILS.** Answer the questions. Write *T* (true) or *F* (false).

_____ **1.** Rafael is not doing well in class.

_____ **2.** Two boys are bullying Rafael at school.

_____ **3.** The boys took Rafael's backpack.

_____ **4.** Rafael got in a fight far away from school.

_____ **5.** The boys made fun of Rafael's name.

C **EXPAND.** Discuss the questions.

1. Why doesn't Rafael want to talk to his mother about the problem?
2. How do you think Rafael's mother feels?
3. What do you think Rafael and his mother should do?

Listening and Speaking

3 PRONUNCIATION

A ▶ PRACTICE. Listen. Then listen and repeat.

When a past-tense verb ends in *t* or *d*, we add an extra syllable to pronounce the *-ed* ending. When the verb does not end in *t* or *d*, we do not add an extra syllable.

What happened?
He asked a question.
She agreed to help.

I needed to meet someone.
He wanted an answer.
We decided to stay.

B ▶ APPLY. Listen. Decide if the past tense of the verb has an extra syllable. Check (✓) the correct column.

		Extra Syllable	No Extra Syllable
1. happen	happened		
2. agree	agreed		
3. want	wanted		
4. need	needed		
5. ask	asked		
6. decide	decided		
7. like	liked		
8. call	called		
9. suspend	suspended		
10. bully	bullied		

4 CONVERSATION

A ▶ LISTEN AND READ. Then practice the conversation with a partner.

A: What happened yesterday? You left work early, and you seemed upset.
B: I needed to meet with my son's teacher. Someone hit him at school.
A: That's terrible! Who hit him?
B: Another boy in his class.
A: Why did he hit him?
B: He wanted to copy his homework, but my son said no.
A: What did you do?
B: Well, at first I wanted my son to be in a different class. I asked to move him. The school principal agreed, but my son was not happy about it. He likes his teacher and friends. We decided to keep him in the class. The teacher talked to the other boy's parents. We hope it won't happen again.
A: I hope so, too. It's hard to deal with bullies.

B MAKE CONNECTIONS. If a bully picks on your child, what would you say? How would you help solve the problem?

I can deal with bullies. ☐   I need more practice. ☐

For more practice, go to MyEnglishLab.

Grammar

Simple past

Affirmative		
She	**called**	the teacher.
He	**hit**	me.
They	**took**	his money.

Negative			
She		**call**	the principal.
I	**didn't**	**hit**	him.
We		**take**	his money.

Grammar Watch

- Regular past-tense verbs end in *-ed*.
- Irregular past-tense verbs don't end in *-ed*.
- The past of *be* is *was* and *were*.
- See page 260 for a list of irregular verbs.

Yes/No Questions			Short Answers	
Did	you	**tell** anyone?	Yes, I **did**.	No, I **didn't**.

Wh- Questions		Answers
What	**happened**?	Someone **hit** me.
Who	**hit** you?	Tom **hit** me.

Other wh- Questions		Answers
Who	**did** you **tell**?	I **told** the teacher.
What	**did** he **do**?	He **called** the principal.
When	**did** this **happen**?	It **happened** yesterday.
Where	**did** it **happen**?	It **happened** on the playground.

A **INVESTIGATE.** Underline all regular verbs in the simple past. Circle all irregular verbs.

Last year, my son (was) in third grade. One day, he came home late. He was very upset. Some students in his class made fun of his name. He has a beautiful Vietnamese name, but many Americans can't pronounce it. My son wanted to change his name. At first, I didn't want him to change his name. Finally, I said OK. He decided to call himself Henry. He loves his new name. I'm happy for him, but for me he will always be Hao.

Grammar

B **PRACTICE. Complete the conversation with the simple past and the words in parentheses.**

A: On Monday, Tom _____*hit*_____ me after school.
(hit)

B: _____ your mom _____ the vice principal's office?
(call)

A: Yes, but the vice principal _____ in the office, so my mom _____
(not / be)   (leave)

a message.

B: _____ Tom _____ into trouble?
(get)

A: Yes, he _____. The vice principal _____ him for three days.
(do)   (suspend)

C **COMPLETE. Write each question in the simple past. Use the words in parentheses.**

A: Some kids got into a big fight at school today.

B: Oh? _____*What happened?*_____
(What / happen)

A: Tom started a fight and hit someone.

B: _____
(Who / he / hit)

A: Angel.

B: _____ that?
(When / he / do)

A: It happened in the afternoon. Right after school let out.

B: _____ Angel?
(Why / Tom / hit)

A: They got in an argument at the end of the day. Then they went outside and started to fight.

B: _____
(Where / the fight / happen)

A: It happened on the playground next to the school.

Show what you know!

1. **DESCRIBE. Talk about a time you (or your child) had a problem with a bully or something else at school. What happened?**

2. **WRITE. Describe a time you had a problem or got into trouble at school. Use past-tense verbs.**

   When I was in school, I had to deal with a bully on the school bus. He made fun of everybody. Sometimes he hit other kids or took their backpacks. One day, he threw my bag out the bus window. The bus driver got very upset and called his parents. After that day, the bully didn't ride the bus. He had to walk or ride his bike to school.

I can use the past tense in questions and statements. ☐   I need more practice. ☐

For more practice, go to MyEnglishLab.

Lesson 11

Soft Skills at Work

Separate work life and family life

1 MEET PING

Read about one of her workplace skills.

> I do not bring personal problems to my workplace. I love my family, and I love my job. When I have problems at home, I solve them at home. I don't let those problems affect my work.

2 PING'S PROBLEM

A READ. Write *T* (true) or *F* (false).

Ping works at a small real estate office. Her son Jack is having problems at school. He is in fourth grade, and several other kids are making fun of him. Jack doesn't want to go to school. Ping often gets calls from the nurse that her son is not feeling well. She has to pick him up from school at least once a week. When this happens, she misses work.

Ping is worried. The situation is making her distracted at work. She cannot focus on her job. She is worried about missing more time at work because of the problem at home.

_____ **1.** Jack gets sick in school often.

_____ **2.** Kids are making fun of Jack at school.

_____ **3.** Jack's problems at school are affecting Ping's work.

B ANALYZE. What is Ping's problem? Write your response in your notebook.

3 PING'S SOLUTION

A COLLABORATE. Ping needs to separate work life and family life. What should she do? Explain your answer.

1. Ping tells Jack to stop going to the nurse when he's not really sick.
2. Ping doesn't take personal phone calls while she's at work.
3. Ping takes a personal day to meet with the other kids' parents to try and solve the problem.
4. Ping _____.

B ROLE-PLAY. Act out Ping's solution with your partner.

Show what you know!

1. **REFLECT.** Do you keep your family life separate from work? Give an example.

2. **WRITE.** Now write your example in your Skills Log.

   I separate work life and family life. For example, I try not to miss work when my kids are sick. I ask my mother to take care of them so I don't have to take a day off.

3. **PRESENT.** Give a short presentation to show how you separate work life and family life.

I can give an example of how I separate work life and family life. ■

Unit Review: Go back to page 45. Which unit goals can you check off?

4 Getting a Job

PREVIEW

Do you have a job now?
Are you looking for a job?
What experience and skills do you have?

UNIT GOALS

- ☐ Identify qualities of good employees
- ☐ Talk about work experience
- ☐ Read a job application
- ☐ Describe your work history

- ☐ Talk about the past and the present
- ☐ **Academic skill:** Make inferences
- ☐ **Writing skill:** Add specific details
- ☐ **Workplace soft skill:** Be positive

Qualities of good employees

A **LABEL.** Use the words in the box to complete the descriptions of the pictures. Use the word that has the same meaning as the first sentence.

B ▶ **LISTEN AND POINT.** Then listen and repeat.

Qualities of good employees		
cooperative	flexible	organized
dependable	hardworking	pleasant
efficient	motivated	punctual

Carmella comes to work every day and helps her patients. She is _____.

John is very fast. He is an _____ worker.

Alisa is neat and knows where everything is. She is always _____.

Bill always comes to work on time. He's very _____.

Carlo smiles a lot and is always friendly to customers. He is _____.

May and her co-workers work well together. They are _____.

These men want to do a good job and finish the project soon. They are _____.

Yusef works hard at the fabric store. He is very _____, so he might get a promotion.

Rana can do many different things at work. She is _____.

Vocabulary

C **PRACTICE.** Sometimes former employers write a letter of recommendation. This letter tells a new employer good things about the employee. Read the letter and the statements. Write *T* (true) or *F* (false).

To Whom It May Concern:

I would like to recommend Omar Ramos as a sales associate for your car dealership. Omar worked at my car dealership for five years. We'll miss him when he moves to Los Angeles.

Omar is a very good salesperson. He is always friendly and pleasant. He knows how to talk to customers and make them comfortable. Omar is sincere. Customers feel like they can buy a good car from him. He's also hardworking and almost never misses work. Please call me at 312-555-6571 if you have any questions.

Sincerely,
Sam Banks
Sam Banks
Manager

_____ **1.** Omar is leaving his current job.

_____ **2.** Customers feel that Omar is honest.

_____ **3.** Omar's manager thinks Omar needs to work harder.

_____ **4.** Omar's manager thinks Omar is a good salesperson.

Show what you know!

1. **COLLABORATE.** Look at the list of qualities. Which qualities do you have? Which qualities do you need to work on?

   A: Which qualities do you have?
   B: I like to work fast, so I'm really efficient. I'm also punctual and dependable. I arrive at work on time every day. How about you? Which qualities do you have?
   A: I'm very organized.

2. **WRITE.** Write a letter of recommendation you would like to receive from an employer.

   To Whom It May Concern:

   I am happy to write this reference for Yi Wang. Yi worked at my restaurant for over a year. She is hardworking and efficient. She is also punctual and dependable. Yi is very friendly and enjoys meeting new people. She has my highest recommendation.

   Sincerely,
   Kevin Clement

I can identify qualities of good employees. ■   I need more practice. ■

For more practice, go to MyEnglishLab.

Listening and Speaking

Talk about work experience

1 BEFORE YOU LISTEN

A **EXPLAIN.** Do you know any technicians? What do they fix?

B **MATCH.** Look at the pictures. Write the correct letters.

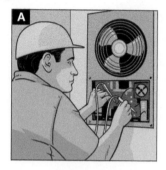   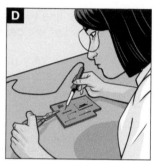

____ **1.** refrigeration

____ **2.** automotive

____ **3.** air conditioning

____ **4.** electronics

2 LISTEN

This is a radio commercial for a technical school.

A ▶ **LISTEN FOR MAIN IDEA.** Circle the answer.

Why does the commercial say it is a good idea to be a technician?
  a. There are always jobs.
  b. Technicians make good money.
  c. Technicians decide their own hours.

B ▶ **LISTEN FOR DETAILS.** Read the statements. Write *T* (true) or *F* (false).

_____ **1.** ACME has programs in refrigeration.

_____ **2.** ACME has classes at night but not on weekends.

_____ **3.** ACME has part-time and full-time programs.

_____ **4.** Financial aid is not available at ACME.

_____ **5.** ACME helps students find a job when they finish the program.

Listening and Speaking

3 PRONUNCIATION

A ▶ PRACTICE. Listen. Then listen and repeat.

/s/	/z/	/ɪz/
shirts	programs	classes

B ▶ APPLY. Listen. What ending sound do you hear? Write /s/, /z/, or /ɪz/.

1. technicians _____
2. things _____
3. nights _____
4. schools _____
5. services _____
6. laptops _____
7. employers _____
8. watches _____

Plural Pronunciation

- When a word ends in *t*, *p*, or *k*, the plural ending -*s* is pronounced /s/.
- When a word ends in *d*, *b*, *g*, *l*, *m*, *n*, or *r*, the plural ending -*s* is pronounced /z/.
- When a word ends in *sh*, *ch*, *s*, *z*, or *x*, the plural ending -*es* is a separate syllable and is pronounced /ɪz/.

4 CONVERSATION

A ▶ LISTEN AND READ. Then practice the conversation with a partner.

A: Can you tell me about your experience?

B: Sure. I started out five years ago. My uncle is a manager for an apartment building. I used to help him fix the heating and air conditioning equipment. So then last year, I got a certificate in HVAC from the ACME school.

A: And what kinds of equipment did they train you on?

B: We worked on all kinds of air conditioners, heaters, and ventilation systems.

A: What about walk-in refrigerators? Have you ever worked on those?

B: Yes, I've repaired walk-in refrigerators and freezers in a few restaurants.

HVAC = heating, ventilation, and air conditioning

B MAKE CONNECTIONS.

1. Think of a job. Write a list of questions you think an employer would ask at a job interview. Then write your answers.
2. Give your list of questions to a partner. Then role-play a job interview.

I can talk about work experience. ■   I need more practice. ■

For more practice, go to MyEnglishLab.

Grammar

Present perfect: Questions with *ever* and *never*

	Subject	*ever*	Verb	
Has	he she			
Have	you we they	**ever**	**worked**	at night?

Affirmative			Negative		
Yes,	he she	**has.**	No,	he she	**hasn't.** **has never worked** at night.
	I you they	**have.**		I you they	**haven't.** **have never worked** at night.

Grammar Watch

- Use the present perfect with *ever* to ask about any time before now.
- Use the simple past to talk about a specific time in the past.
- See page 261 for a list of irregular verbs.

A INVESTIGATE. Underline examples of the present perfect. Circle the simple past.

A: Have you ever driven a truck? There's a job here for a driver with Safe Way Moving Company in Los Altos.

B: No. I've driven a taxi, but I've never driven a truck.

A: Where did you drive a taxi?

B: In Los Angeles. My brother and I shared the cab. The money was OK until gas became so expensive.

B PRACTICE. Write the past participle form of the verbs in parentheses.

1. Have you ever _____worked_____ in an office?
   (work)

2. Have you ever _____ a taxi?
   (drive)

3. Have you ever _____ a commercial license?
   (get)

4. Have you ever _____ cars?
   (sell)

5. Have you ever _____ problems on the job?
   (solve)

Grammar

C COMPLETE. Use the present perfect or the simple past of the verbs in parentheses.

1. **A:** _____*Have*_____ you ever _____*had*_____ your own business?
   _(have)

   B: Yes, I _____. My husband and I _____ a small grocery store in
   _(own)

   Guatemala ten years ago.

2. **A:** _____ you ever _____ at a bank?
   _(work)

   B: No, I _____, but my wife _____ a bank teller from 1990 to 2005.
   _(be)

3. **A:** _____ you ever _____ phones for an office?
   _(answer)

   B: No, I _____. But I _____ documents and _____
   _(scan)   _(make)

   copies in an office last year.

D APPLY. Write questions in the present perfect with *ever.*

1. you / take care of patients   *Have you ever taken care of patients?* _____

2. she / work in a hospital   _____

3. he / teach at a school   _____

4. you / do office work   _____

5. they / repair a car   _____

6. he / fix computers   _____

7. you / own a business   _____

8. she / operate heavy machinery   _____

Show what you know!

1. **COLLABORATE.** Ask and answer the questions in Exercise D. If the answer is yes, explain.

   A: *Have you ever taken care of patients?*
   B: *Yes, I have. I was a nurse in the Philippines. Have you ever worked in a hospital?*
   A: *No, I haven't.*

2. **WRITE.** Describe your work experience. Use the present perfect.

   I work on a computer all day. I have never worked with customers.

I can use the present perfect. ■	I need more practice. ■

For more practice, go to MyEnglishLab.

Workplace, Life, and Community Skills

Lesson 4 — Read a job application

1 READ A JOB APPLICATION

A **READ.** Look at the job application. Talk about any words you don't understand.

Caruso's Application For Employment

We are an Equal Opportunity Employer and committed to excellence through diversity.
Please print or type. The application must be fully completed to be considered. Please complete each section, even if you attach a résumé.

Personal Information

Name	Address	City	State	ZIP
Chu, Li	342 Sycamore Street	Alhambra	CA	91803

Phone Number	Mobile Number	Email Address
(520) 555-9832		Li.Chu@email.com

Are you a U.S. citizen? ● Yes ○ No   Have you ever been fired from a job? ○ Yes ● No

Can you legally work in the U.S.? (If hired, verification within 3 days is required.) ● Yes ○ No

Position

Position	Available Start Date	Desired Pay
Inventory Supervisor	Immediately	$20.00/hr.

Employment desired ● Full Time ○ Part Time ○ Seasonal/Temporary

Education

School Name	Location	Years Attended	Degree Received	Major
East Los Angeles College	Los Angeles, CA	2011–2012	no	Business
Caballero High School	Los Angeles, CA	2006–2010	yes	n/a

B **INTERPRET.** Read the statements. Write *T* (true) or *F* (false).

_____ **1.** Li is looking for a part-time job.

_____ **2.** Li wants to be a store manager.

_____ **3.** If Li gets the job, he needs to prove that he can work in the U.S.

_____ **4.** Li was fired from his last job.

_____ **5.** Li graduated from high school.

C **READ.** Look at the next screen of the job application.

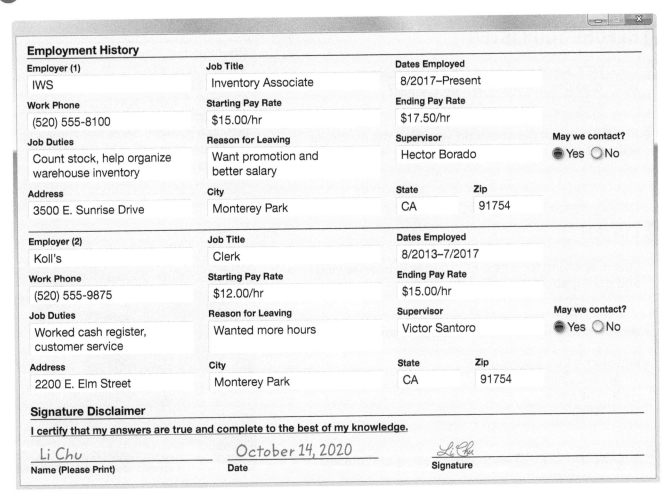

Employment History

Employer (1)	**Job Title**	**Dates Employed**
IWS	Inventory Associate	8/2017–Present
Work Phone	**Starting Pay Rate**	**Ending Pay Rate**
(520) 555-8100	$15.00/hr	$17.50/hr

Job Duties	**Reason for Leaving**	**Supervisor**	**May we contact?**
Count stock, help organize warehouse inventory	Want promotion and better salary	Hector Borado	◉ Yes ○ No

Address	**City**	**State**	**Zip**
3500 E. Sunrise Drive	Monterey Park	CA	91754

Employer (2)	**Job Title**	**Dates Employed**
Koll's	Clerk	8/2013–7/2017
Work Phone	**Starting Pay Rate**	**Ending Pay Rate**
(520) 555-9875	$12.00/hr	$15.00/hr

Job Duties	**Reason for Leaving**	**Supervisor**	**May we contact?**
Worked cash register, customer service	Wanted more hours	Victor Santoro	◉ Yes ○ No

Address	**City**	**State**	**Zip**
2200 E. Elm Street	Monterey Park	CA	91754

Signature Disclaimer

I certify that my answers are true and complete to the best of my knowledge.

Li Chu	October 14, 2020	Li Chu
Name (Please Print)	Date	Signature

D **CONNECT.** Answer the questions.

Where does Li work now? Where did he work before?
Why does he want to leave his job?
Is it OK for Caruso's to call Li's supervisor at Koll's?

E **ROLE-PLAY.** Practice a conversation between an applicant and the supervisor at Caruso's.

F GO ONLINE. Search for a company you want to work for. Do they have an online application?

I can read a job application. ■   I need more practice. ■

For more practice, go to MyEnglishLab.

Describe your work history

1 BEFORE YOU LISTEN

A **IDENTIFY.** Read the online job advertisement. What qualities are important for the job?

B **PREDICT.** What questions do you think the employer will ask?

> **Chef needed.** Small busy restaurant. Must be fast, efficient, dependable, and able to work under pressure. Minimum 5 years experience. Management experience necessary. Full-time position. Some night hours. Health benefits available. References necessary. Email JMorgan@PJs.com or call (520) 555-9786.

2 LISTEN

Luis is applying for a new job. James is interviewing Luis and asking about his work history.

A ▶ **LISTEN FOR MAIN IDEA.** Circle the answer.

What job is Luis applying for?
   a. assistant manager
   b. line cook
   c. chef

B ▶ **LISTEN FOR DETAILS.** Write *T* (true) or *F* (false).

_____ **1.** Luis worked at El Norte for five years.

_____ **2.** Luis was the assistant manager at El Norte.

_____ **3.** Luis owned a restaurant in Mexico City.

_____ **4.** Luis is unhappy at El Norte because it isn't a good restaurant.

C ▶ **EXPAND.** Listen to the second part of the conversation. Check (✓) the skills that are mentioned.

☐ managing employees
☐ planning menus
☐ preparing meals
☐ using kitchen equipment

Listening and Speaking

3 PRONUNCIATION

A ▶ PRACTICE. Listen. Then listen and repeat.

repu**ta**tion   situ**a**tion   tra**di**tion

Syllable Stress

When words end in -*sion* or -*tion*, we stress the syllable before the last syllable.

B ▶ APPLY. Listen. Mark (•) the stressed syllable.

1. permission   **2.** conversation   **3.** discussion   **4.** direction

4 CONVERSATION

A ▶ LISTEN AND READ. Then practice the conversation with a partner.

A: So, I'm looking for a chef. Can you tell me about your restaurant experience?

B: Sure. I've been a line cook at El Norte restaurant for the last five years. I also owned my own café in Mexico City. And before that, I worked in a couple of restaurants in Mexico for several years.

A: So why do you want to leave El Norte?

B: Well, I've worked there for five years. It's a very good restaurant, but I'm ready for a change. And your restaurant has a great reputation.

B ROLE-PLAY. Imagine you are at a job interview. Make a similar conversation.

A: You own a Singular cell phone store. You are interviewing someone for a job as a store manager. Ask questions.

B: You are an assistant manager in a Horizon cell phone store. You worked there for six years. Before that, you were a sales associate for two years.

I can describe my work history. ■

I need more practice. ■

For more practice, go to MyEnglishLab.

Subject		Verb		*for/since*	
He	**has**	**been**	a chef	**for**	four years.
We	**have**	**lived**	here	**since**	January.

Questions				
How long	**have**	you	**worked**	at that restaurant?
	has	he		

Grammar Watch

- Use the present perfect with *for* or *since* to describe an activity that began in the past and continues into the present.
- Use *for* to talk about a length of time.
- Use *since* to talk about a specific point in time.

A **INVESTIGATE.** Underline the present perfect verbs. Then read the statements. Write *T* (true) or *F* (false).

A: I <u>haven't seen</u> Akim for a long time. Is he still living in East Hollywood?

B: You probably haven't seen him because he has been very busy. He's a manager at Embassy Limousine Warehouse.

A: No kidding? I thought he was just driving for them. How long has he been a manager?

B: He's been a manager for six months. He was a driver for two years, and then they promoted him to manager. He's making more money now, and he has been living in a bigger apartment since last month.

_____ **1.** Akim became a manager six months ago.

_____ **2.** Akim is working a lot of hours right now.

_____ **3.** Akim has a lot of free time.

_____ **4.** Akim moved to a new apartment last month.

B **PRACTICE.** Complete the sentences with *for* or *since*.

1. Mark has worked at H&B Electronics _____*for*_____ six months.

2. I haven't heard from them _____ May.

3. We've been out of town _____ three weeks.

4. Soo Jin has been a sales manager _____ many years.

5. They have helped us _____ the beginning of the year.

6. We haven't taken a vacation _____ 2016.

Grammar

C COMPLETE. Use the present perfect form of the verbs in parentheses.

1. Awa _____has waited on_____ tables in a restaurant for the last year.
   (wait on)

2. Edgar _____ his own business since 2015.
   (own)

3. How long _____ you _____ as a computer programmer?
   (work)

4. You _____ a manager for two years, right?
   (be)

5. I _____ a vacation since 2015.
   (not / take)

6. How long _____ Riko _____ at St. Vincent Hospital?
   (help out)

D COLLABORATE. Look at part of Luis's résumé. Write four questions. Ask and answer your questions.

1. _How long has Luis been a caterer?_____

2. _____

3. _____

4. _____

Work Experience

2014–present	Line cook El Norte restaurant Tucson, Arizona
2012–present	Caterer: part time Tucson, Arizona
2005–2011	Owner Luis's Café Mexico City (sold business and moved to the U.S. in 2011)
2001–2005	Line cook Casa Hidalgo restaurant Mexico City

Show what you know!

1. **ROLE-PLAY.** Imagine you are at a job interview. Use your own résumé or the résumé on this page.

   A: How long have you worked in an office?
   B: I have worked in an office for five years.

2. **WRITE.** Summarize your work experience. Use the present perfect with *for* and *since*.

   I have worked . . .

I can use the present perfect with *for* and *since*. ☐   I need more practice. ☐

For more practice, go to MyEnglishLab.

1 BEFORE YOU READ

RECALL. Have you ever had a job interview? What questions did the interviewer ask you?

2 READ

▶ Listen and read.

> **Academic Skill: Make inferences**
>
> In an article, some ideas are not stated directly. Readers must guess or infer these ideas as they read.

Legal and Illegal Interview Questions

The interview is an important part of a job search. Most employers conduct an interview before they offer someone a job. During an interview, employers can ask many questions. But they are not allowed to
5 ask certain kinds of questions.

Legal Questions
What questions can interviewers ask? They can ask questions about an applicant's qualifications. This means they can ask about his or her skills and work
10 experience. Different jobs need different kinds of employees. For example, nursing assistants need to be patient and kind. They also need to be strong. The interviewer needs to know if an applicant can do the job well. He or she is allowed to ask questions
15 to figure that out.

Illegal Questions
What kinds of questions are not allowed? Interviewers may not discriminate against applicants. They can't treat them unfairly. Some kinds of questions might
20 do this, so these questions are illegal. For example, in the U.S., some people have certain ideas about old people. They think that old people aren't good workers. They don't have much energy. They can't

Interview Questions	Legal	Illegal
What job skills do you have?	✓	
What work experience do you have?	✓	
How old are you?		✓
Do you have children?		✓
Where were you born?		✓
Are you a patient person?	✓	
What is your religion?		✓

learn new things. Some employers don't want to
25 hire them. However, many older people *are* good workers. That is why interviewers may not ask about an applicant's age.

Some employers don't want to hire people with young children. They think these workers will call
30 in sick or come in late too much. Some employers may also not want to hire people of certain races or religions. This is unfair to these people. That's why questions about an applicant's family, race, and religion are all illegal.

35 Remember, in an interview, legal questions ask for information about your qualifications. Illegal questions could help employers discriminate against you.

3 CLOSE READING

A **IDENTIFY.** What is the main idea of the article?

a. Most employers conduct an interview before they offer someone a job.
b. Interviewers can ask questions about an applicant's skills and experience.
c. Some interview questions are legal, but other questions are illegal.

Reading

B **CITE EVIDENCE. Complete the sentences. Where is the information? Write the line numbers.**

Lines

1. Job applicants _____ answer illegal interview questions.
   a. have to   **b.** don't have to   _____

2. An interviewer _____ ask, "Do you know how to use a computer?"
   a. can   **b.** can't   _____

3. Interviewers are _____ to ask, "How old are you?"
   a. allowed   **b.** not allowed   _____

4. It is often _____ for an older worker to find a job.
   a. easy   **b.** hard   _____

5. The question "Are you married?" is _____.
   a. legal   **b.** illegal   _____

C **INTERPRET GRAPHICS. Complete the sentences about the chart.**

1. The chart includes examples of _____ during an interview.
   a. questions that can be asked
   b. questions that cannot be asked
   c. questions that both can and cannot be asked

2. According to the chart, asking about an applicant's age _____.
   a. is legal
   b. is illegal
   c. can be legal or illegal, depending on the situation

4 SUMMARIZE

What are the most important ideas in the article? Write three sentences in your notebook.

Show what you know!

1. **COLLABORATE. List the legal and illegal interview questions from the reading. Then think of one more example of each.**

2. **WRITE. Explain why some interview questions are legal and some are illegal. Give examples.**

   It is legal to ask the question "Where did you work last year?" This is because the employer needs to know about the applicant's work experience. It is illegal to ask...

I can make inferences while reading. ■   I need more practice. ■

To read more, go to MyEnglishLab.

Write a cover letter

1 STUDY THE MODEL

ANALYZE. Read the model and Writing Skill. Then answer the questions.

To: Donna Willis
From: Ana Dominic
Subject: Spanish Tutor

Dear Ms. Willis:

I am writing to apply for the Spanish tutor position at Central School. I am qualified for this position. I am a native Spanish speaker with a lot of teaching experience. I was a Spanish teacher in Colombia for 12 years. Since I moved to the U.S. three years ago, I have been a private Spanish tutor for several students.

Thank you for considering me for this position. I look forward to hearing from you.

Sincerely,
Ana Dominic

Writing Skill:
Add specific details

Add specific details to your writing. To do this, answer the questions *Who, Where, What, When, How*, and *Why* in your paragraph.

1. What job is the writer applying for?
2. Which questions does the writer answer?

2 PLAN YOUR WRITING

A BRAINSTORM. Ask and answer the questions.

What job do you want to apply for? Why do you think you are qualified for the job?

B OUTLINE. Answer the questions.

Who are you writing to? _____

What job are you applying for? _____

Why are you qualified for this position? _____

Where did you work before? _____

3 WRITE

EXPLAIN. Write a cover letter. Add specific details to explain why you are qualified for the job. Use the model, the Writing Skill, and your ideas from Exercise 2 to help you.

4 CHECK YOUR WRITING

COLLABORATE. Read the checklist. Read your writing together. Revise your writing.

WRITING CHECKLIST

☐ Does the cover letter begin with an introduction, such as "Dear Ms. Willis"?

☐ Does the cover letter include specific details about the writer's experience?

☐ Does the cover letter answer important questions?

I can add specific details to writing. ■   I need more practice. ■

For more practice, go to MyEnglishLab.

Lesson 9

Talk about the past and the present

1 BEFORE YOU LISTEN

A **IDENTIFY.** Look at the picture of the culinary school. A culinary school teaches the art and science of cooking and food preparation. What are some other kinds of specialty schools?

culinary school

2 LISTEN

This is a podcast about different kinds of jobs and the people who have them. The host interviews a local chef, Sana Solano.

Sana

A ▶ **LISTEN FOR MAIN IDEA.** Circle the answer.

When did Sana become interested in cooking?
   a. when she was a young girl
   b. when she was a teenager
   c. when she graduated from high school

B ▶ **LISTEN FOR DETAILS.** Did Sana do these things in the past, or does she do them now? Write *past* or *present* in the blanks.

_____ **1.** She is organized.

_____ **2.** She owns a restaurant.

_____ **3.** She cooks with her grandmothers.

_____ **4.** She makes Japanese-style fish tacos for her friends.

C ▶ **EXPAND.** Listen to the rest of the interview. Write *T* (true) or *F* (false).

_____ **1.** Sana used to own a restaurant, but now she teaches full-time at a culinary school.

_____ **2.** Sana teaches cooking classes three days a week.

_____ **3.** Sana feels motivated because she enjoys her job.

_____ **4.** Sana teaches people how to make desserts.

_____ **5.** It is not important for restaurant owners to be flexible.

I can talk about the past and the present. ■   I need more practice. ■

For more practice, go to MyEnglishLab.

The past with *used to*

Subject	used to	Verb	
I		**work**	at a restaurant.
She	**used to**	**play**	soccer.
They		**drive**	to work.

Subject	used to	Verb	
I		**work**,	but now I stay home with my children.
She	**used to**	**play**,	but she doesn't anymore.
They		**drive**,	but now they take the bus.

Grammar Watch

- Talk about past habits with *used to*.
- Use *used to* to contrast past habits with present situations. Use a comma to separate the two ideas.
- *Used to* is usually pronounced "useta."

A **INVESTIGATE.** Read the conversation. Underline *used to* and the verb that follows.

Myra   Aziz

A: Hi, I'm Myra.

B: Nice to meet you. I'm Aziz.

A: Today is your first day, right?

B: Yes, it is. How about you? Have you worked here long?

A: No, I just started last week. I <u>used to work</u> in a doctor's office, but the hours weren't very flexible. It was hard to get my kids to school and be on time for work.

B: That's funny. I used to work at a doctor's office, too. Where did you work?

A: I used to be a receptionist at the Children's Allergy Clinic.

B: Wow! I used to live across the street from there!

A: What a small world!

B **PRACTICE.** Complete the sentences with *used to* and the verb in parentheses.

1. He ___*used to be*___ in college, but he graduated last year.
   (be)

2. I _____ at Rita's Café on Main Street.
   (work)

3. My supervisor _____ lunch at the office, but now she goes out to a restaurant.
   (eat)

4. We _____ at the library together, but we're too busy now.
   (study)

Grammar

C MATCH. What did each person do in the past? What does each person do now? Connect the sentence parts. Write new sentences.

Justin used to live in Seattle,   but now he drives his own car.

Nadia used to work for an electronics company,   but now he lives in Boston.

Ben used to take the bus to work,   but now her desk is a mess.

Teresa used to go shopping at the mall,   but now she buys everything online.

Fatima used to be very organized,   but now she owns her own company.

1. _Justin used to live in Seattle, but now he lives in Boston._____

2. _____

3. _____

4. _____

5. _____

D COMPLETE. Finish each sentence with real or imagined information.

1. I used to live _____.

2. I used to work _____.

3. I used to eat _____.

4. I used to play _____.

5. _____

6. _____

Show what you know!

1. COLLABORATE. Talk about a job you used to have or a place you used to live.

A: I used to live in Miami before I moved here.
B: What did you do there?
A: I worked in a restaurant. I used to be a chef.

2. WRITE. Compare your life five years ago and your life now. Use *used to*.

I used to . . .

I can talk about the past with *used to*. ■   I need more practice. ■

For more practice, go to MyEnglishLab.

Soft Skills at Work

Be positive

1 MEET EMMA

Read about one of her workplace skills.

> I have a positive attitude. For example, when someone is complaining about something, I try to point out something good about the situation.

2 EMMA'S PROBLEM

A READ. Write *T* (true) or *F* (false).

Emma works at Hotel Magnum. She and her co-workers are usually very hardworking. They greet and help hotel guests all day, and they get along well with one another. Today, however, her co-workers are complaining about the 2% raise they all received. They were expecting a larger pay increase. They are upset and want to talk to their manager.

Emma doesn't think everyone should be complaining so much. She wants to be positive about the situation.

_____ **1.** The employees at Hotel Magnum are usually happy at work.
_____ **2.** Everyone is excited about the 2% raise.
_____ **3.** Emma agrees that a 2% raise is a big problem.

B ANALYZE. What is Emma's problem? Write your response in your notebook.

3 EMMA'S SOLUTION

A COLLABORATE. Emma has a positive attitude. She tries to be positive about every situation. What should she do? Explain your answer.

1. Emma talks to the hotel manager and explains why she and her co-workers deserve a larger raise.
2. Emma tells her co-workers to stay positive, work hard, and ask for a bonus at the end of the year.
3. Emma reminds her co-workers that their salaries are already higher than many other hotels in the area.
4. Emma _____.

B ROLE-PLAY. Act out Emma's solution with your partner.

Show what you know!

1. **REFLECT.** When have you demonstrated a positive attitude at work? Give an example.

2. **WRITE.** Now write your example in your Skills Log.

   I have a positive attitude. When something bad happens, I try to be positive about the situation. For example, when my computer was broken, I used that time to clean up my workspace.

3. **PRESENT.** Give a short presentation to show how you are positive.

I can give an example of how I am positive at work. ■

Unit Review: Go back to page 65. Which unit goals can you check off?

5 Traveling

PREVIEW

How often do you take buses, trains, or planes?
Where do you go?

UNIT GOALS

- [ ] Talk about air travel
- [ ] Follow instructions at an airport
- [ ] Read instructions and maps
- [ ] Make travel arrangements

- [ ] Talk about travel delays and cancellations
- [ ] **Academic skill:** Get meaning from context
- [ ] **Writing skill:** Use time-order words
- [ ] **Workplace soft skill:** Find creative solutions

A **PREDICT.** Look at the picture of the air terminal. What do you see? What are the people doing? What are they preparing to do?

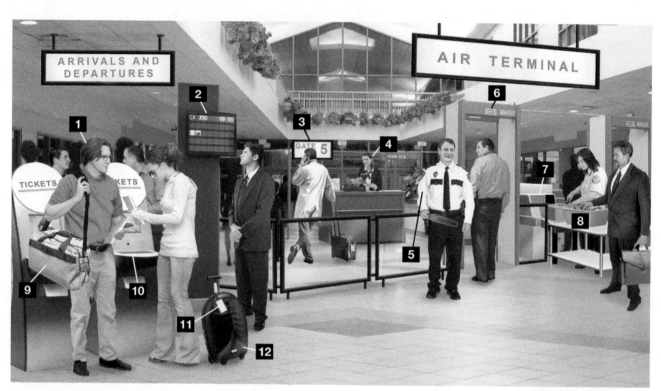

AIR BLUE

COSTA/MICHAEL

FLIGHT	DATE	CLASS	ORIGIN
#9031	03DEC	B	SAN DIEGO
OPERATED BY		COACH	DESTINATION
AIR BLUE			LOS ANGELES

DEPARTURE GATE B26 **SUBJECT TO CHANGE

13 BOARDING PASS
ELECTRONIC TICKET
0 012 1239658783 2

DEPARTS
4:30 PM

SEAT
28C
ZONE 6

14 BOARDING PASS
***********ET***********

COSTA/MICHAEL

SEAT
28C
ZONE 6

FLIGHT	DATE
#9031	03DEC

ORIGIN
SAN DIEGO
DESTINATION
LOS ANGELES
OPERATED BY AIR BLUE

DJ0254/03DEC/SAN-LAX

SND935C35/121

Vocabulary

Look at the picture on page 86.

B MATCH. Look at the picture on page 86. **Write the numbers.**

_____ arrivals and departures display   _____ luggage

_____ bins   _____ luggage tags

_____ boarding pass   _____ metal detector

_____ carry-on bag   _____ passenger

_____ e-ticket   _____ security agent

_____ gate   _____ ticket agent

_____ kiosk   _____ X-ray machine

Study Tip

Use Pictures

Make cards for five words. Write the word on the front of the card. Print a picture of the word from the internet. Cut it out and attach it to the back of the card.

C ▶ LISTEN AND POINT. Check your answers. Then listen and repeat.

D COLLABORATE. Complete the sentences with the vocabulary words.

1. To go through airport security, you need to walk through a _____.

2. We need _____ for our suitcases.

3. You are allowed to take one _____ with you on the plane.

4. Check the _____ to make sure your flight is on time.

5. You need a _____ to get on the plane.

6. You can purchase your _____ online and print it at a _____ in the airport.

7. You need to take off your shoes and put them in the _____. Then they will go through the _____.

8. You need to go to baggage claim to pick up your _____.

Show what you know!

1. **DISCUSS.** Talk about your last trip. Did you travel by airplane? Did you have any problems on your trip? What happened?

   I took a trip to Las Vegas with my family. We took a plane. The airline lost our luggage! They found it and called me the next day.

2. **WRITE.** Describe your last trip.

   Last year, I took a trip to . . .

I can talk about air travel. ☐   I need more practice. ☐

For more practice, go to MyEnglishLab.

Lesson 2 Follow instructions at an airport

1 BEFORE YOU LISTEN

MATCH. Look at the pictures. Write the correct letters.

A

B

C

_____ **1.** board

_____ **2.** mechanical problem

_____ **3.** check in

2 LISTEN

Airport announcements give travelers information.

A ▶ **LISTEN FOR MAIN IDEA.** Are the four announcements about the same flight or about different flights?

B ▶ **LISTEN FOR DETAILS.** Answer the questions.

1. Announcement 1: What is the situation with Flight 385?
   a. It's boarding.
   b. It's taking off.
   c. It's landing.

2. Announcement 2: What is the situation with Flight 289?
   a. Passengers can now check in.
   b. It has been delayed.
   c. It has been canceled.

3. Announcement 3: Which gate is Flight 870 to Caracas departing from?
   a. Gate 2
   b. Gate 8
   c. Gate 22

4. Announcement 4: What is the problem with Flight 901?
   a. a mechanical problem
   b. a cancellation
   c. a gate change

Listening and Speaking

3 PRONUNCIATION

A ▶ **PRACTICE. Listen. Then listen and repeat.**

You can check it.
You can buy a drink on the plane.
Why can't I take it on the plane?
You can't take this through security.

B ▶ **APPLY. Listen. Circle the words you hear.**

1. You **can / can't** park here.
2. We **can / can't** take the bus there.
3. We **can / can't** board the plane now.
4. You **can / can't** use your cell phone.
5. I **can / can't** take this bag.
6. I **can / can't** get another flight.

4 CONVERSATION

A ▶ **LISTEN AND READ. Then practice the conversation with a partner.**

A: Excuse me. Could you please step over to the side?
B: Is there a problem?
A: Something in your bag is showing up on the X-ray machine. Could you please open your bag? Hmm. You can't take this bottle of water. You either have to drink it all now or throw it away.

B **ROLE-PLAY. Pretend a passenger is going through airport security.**

A: You are the passenger. The security agent has found a problem with an item in your bag.
B: You are the security agent. Explain the problem to the passenger. Use one of the items from the box.

moisturizer   peanut butter   yogurt

I can follow instructions at an airport. ☐   I need more practice. ☐

For more practice, go to MyEnglishLab.

Lesson 3

Can / Could for possibility and ability, *be able to* for ability

Can / Could: Affirmative and Negative			
We	can can't		
		hear	the announcement.
I	could couldn't		

Be able to: Affirmative and Negative			
She	was wasn't		
They	were weren't	able to	fly	home.
We	will be won't be		

Grammar Watch

- Use *can* for present ability and present or future possibility.
- Use *could* for past ability.
- Use *will be able to* for future ability.
- Use *was / were able to* for past ability.
- Use *am / is / are able to* for present ability.

A INVESTIGATE. Underline *can, could,* and *be able to* and the verb that follows.

Jack's flight was scheduled for 6:00 this morning, but the plane wasn't able to depart due to bad weather. He couldn't find another flight until later this afternoon. He won't be able to have lunch with us, but we can have dinner together this evening.

B MATCH. Write the correct letters.

_____ 1. You won't be able to reach him.

_____ 2. Vic didn't have his passport.

_____ 3. You can't take that bag on board.

_____ 4. My brother missed the flight.

a. You have to check it.

b. He won't arrive tonight.

c. He couldn't get through security.

d. His phone is turned off.

Grammar

C **CHOOSE.** Cross out the incorrect words.

1. You **can't / ~~couldn't~~** bring that bottle of moisturizer on this flight.

2. My flight was canceled, so I **couldn't / was able to** go to my uncle's funeral.

3. I **can't / couldn't** hear the announcement. There was too much noise.

4. Flight 380 **will be able to / wasn't able to** land on time due to bad weather.

5. Our flight **will be able to / won't be able to** take off for another ten minutes.

6. We **wasn't able to / weren't able to** catch our flight.

7. You **aren't able to / weren't able to** use your cell phone until the plane lands.

D **COMPLETE.** Use the correct form of the verb in parentheses.

We had a lot of problems when my family flew to San Diego. First, at the airport, I

_____*couldn't*_____ find my passport. I had to drive back home and get it, so we missed our
    (not / could)

flight. We _____ get onto another plane, but it was very full. There was almost no
    (be able to)

room for our carry-on bags, but finally the airline attendant _____ fit them in the
    (be able to)

overhead compartment. Then we sat on the plane and waited. There was a storm, so the plane

_____ take off. After a half hour, the attendant announced, "Due to bad weather, we
    (not / could)

_____ take off. All passengers must exit the plane and wait inside the terminal." We
    (not / be able to)

_____ believe our bad luck!
    (not / could)

Show what you know!

1. **COLLABORATE.** How is air travel different today from how it was in the past?

> A: In the past, you could smoke on planes. Now you can't smoke on planes or in airports.
> B: You can use e-tickets now. You couldn't in the past.

2. **WRITE.** Compare how air travel today is different from how it was in the past.
Use *can / could* and *be able to.*

> In the past, you could . . .
> Today, you aren't able to . . .

I can use *can, could,* and *be able to.* ☐   I need more practice. ☐

For more practice, go to MyEnglishLab.

Lesson **4**

1 READ INSTRUCTIONS

A **DISCUSS.** Do you have trouble reading instructions or maps when you travel? Talk about a time you bought tickets from a machine. Was it easy or difficult?

B **READ.** Look at the instructions on this ticket machine.

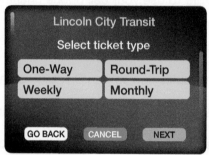
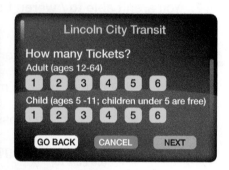
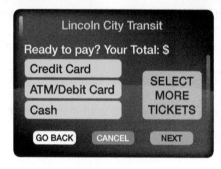
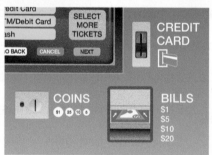

C **APPLY.** Answer the questions. There may be more than one correct answer.

1. You want to buy a monthly ticket. You tapped One-Way by mistake. Which button should you tap?
   a. CANCEL
   b. GO BACK
   c. NEXT

2. You are traveling with your 6-year-old son and 3 year-old daughter. What kind of tickets do you need?
   a. 1 adult and 2 children
   b. 1 adult and 1 child
   c. only one adult

3. You start to buy a ticket and then realize you don't have enough money. Which button should you tap?
   a. GO BACK
   b. CANCEL
   c. NEXT

4. You are ready to pay for a ticket for yourself, but your friend needs one, too. Which button should you tap?
   a. CASH
   b. SELECT MORE TICKETS
   c. CANCEL

Workplace, Life, and Community Skills

2 READ A MAP

A **INTERPRET.** Look at the map of Union Station in Los Angeles, California.

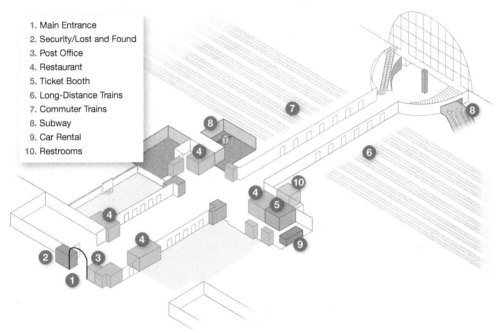

1. Main Entrance
2. Security/Lost and Found
3. Post Office
4. Restaurant
5. Ticket Booth
6. Long-Distance Trains
7. Commuter Trains
8. Subway
9. Car Rental
10. Restrooms

B **APPLY.** You are looking at the map on your phone. Read each situation and decide where to tap to get more information.

1. I lost my wallet somewhere in the station.

   _____

2. I need to get to downtown Los Angeles.

   _____

3. I want to mail a postcard before I get on the train.

   _____

4. I need to change my train ticket for a later time.

   _____

5. I want to get a car and drive to the beach.

   _____

6. I just arrived and need something to eat.

   _____

C **GO ONLINE.** Find an app for buying train or bus tickets in your area.

I can read instructions and maps. ■   I need more practice. ■

For more practice, go to MyEnglishLab.

Lesson 5

Make travel arrangements

1 BEFORE YOU LISTEN

DISCUSS. Do you have public transportation in your city?
What kinds? Is the public transportation good or bad?

2 LISTEN

Ken is calling his friend Amy from the subway.

Ken   Amy

A ▶ **LISTEN FOR MAIN IDEA. Circle the answer.**

Why is Ken late?
    a. He missed the train.
    b. His train was delayed.

B ▶ **LISTEN FOR DETAILS. Write *T* (true) or *F* (false).**

_____ **1.** Ken expects to arrive around 3:30.

_____ **2.** Amy is meeting Ken at 24th Street.

_____ **3.** Amy is driving Ken home in her car.

_____ **4.** Amy can't park her car at the station.

C ▶ **EXPAND. Listen to the second part of the conversation.**

What is Ken's problem?
    a. He took the wrong train.
    b. He got off at the wrong station.
    c. He took the wrong bag.

Listening and Speaking

3 PRONUNCIATION

A ▶ **PRACTICE. Listen. Then listen and repeat.**

I **missed** the **bus.**

When are you arri**ving**?

I'll **meet** you at the **ter**minal.

Are you **tak**ing me **home** in your **car**?

B ▶ **APPLY. Listen. Mark (•) the stressed syllables.**

1. I'm taking the bus.
2. It leaves at seven.
3. It arrives at eight fifteen.
4. Can you pick me up?
5. See you soon.
6. Call me when you get there.

4 CONVERSATION

A ▶ **LISTEN AND READ. Then practice the conversation with a partner.**

A: Hey, Amy. It's me, Ken. I'm on the subway. Sorry, I'm running late. There was a 30-minute delay. A train got stuck at 24th Street.

B: That's too bad. So, what time are you arriving then?

A: I think about 3:30. Which station should I get off at?

B: Lake Merritt Station. Call me when you get there. My car isn't running, but my mom will let me borrow hers. I'll park and come meet you.

A: Great. See you soon.

B **DISCUSS. Have you ever visited a friend who lived in a different city? How did you get there? What was the experience like?**

I can make travel arrangements. ■   I need more practice. ■

For more practice, go to MyEnglishLab.

Grammar

Possessive adjectives and possessive pronouns

Possessive Adjective	Possessive Pronoun
This is **my** bag.	This is **mine**.
That is **your** bag.	That is **yours**.
Is this **his** luggage?	No. **His** is on the bus.
Is that **her** luggage?	No. **Hers** is at home.
This is not **our** car.	**Ours** is on the second level.
That is not **their** car.	**Theirs** is in the shop.

Grammar Watch

- A noun never follows a possessive pronoun.
- The verb after a possessive pronoun agrees with the noun it replaces.
  *Her bag **is** heavy. = Hers **is** heavy.*
  *Her bags **are** heavy. = Hers **are** heavy.*

A INVESTIGATE. Underline the possessive adjectives. Circle the possessive pronouns.

Yesterday, I took a bus to Dallas. I left <u>my</u> phone on the bus. Luckily, the bus driver found it. We were leaving the gate when the driver ran up with the phone and asked if it was ours. One passenger thought it was her phone. But then I felt in my jacket, and my phone was missing. I told the bus driver I thought I had lost mine, so he showed it to us. We knew it was mine, not hers, because it had all my photos and contacts in it.

B CHOOSE. Cross out the incorrect words.

1. We almost left **our / ~~ours~~** tickets at home.
2. That's not my suitcase. **My / Mine** is bigger.
3. Aren't these **your / yours** keys?
4. His car is parked on this level, but **her / hers** must be on a different level.
5. The keys don't open this car because it's not **our / ours** car.
6. Is that my drink or **your / yours**?

Grammar

C **APPLY.** Change the underlined words to possessive pronouns.

1. **A:** Did you leave this water bottle on the seat?

   B: No. ~~My water bottle~~ ^{Mine} is in my bag.

2. **A:** Is that her suitcase?

   B: No, it's <u>his suitcase</u>. <u>Her suitcase</u> is in the overhead compartment.

3. **A:** Who left this bag?

   B: It's <u>his bag</u>. I'm watching it for him while he gets some coffee.

4. **A:** Are these your boarding passes?

   B: No, they're not. I have <u>our boarding passes</u> in my pocket.

5. **A:** Is that their bus?

   B: No. <u>Their bus</u> is at the next gate.

D **COMPLETE.** Write *is* or *are.*

1. These are my bags. His _____*are*_____ over there.

2. Whose ticket is this? _____ it yours?

3. Is this our gate, or _____ ours over there?

4. Dan, my ticket is missing. _____ yours missing, too?

5. My relatives are here. _____ yours here, too?

6. These boarding passes _____ hers.

Show what you know!

1. **ROLE-PLAY. You are at a lost and found at a bus terminal. Tell the clerk what you lost. Use possessive pronouns. Then switch roles.**

   A: You lost your umbrella and phone.
   B: Ask questions. You see a silver phone, a pair of brown gloves, and a blue umbrella.

2. **WRITE. Describe something you lost. Where did you lose it? Did you find it later? Use possessive adjectives and possessive pronouns.**

   I lost my . . .

I can use possessive adjectives and possessive pronouns. ■   I need more practice. ■

For more practice, go to MyEnglishLab.

1 BEFORE YOU READ

RECALL. Have you flown on an airplane recently? Did you have to wait in line to go through security at the airport? What did you have to do?

2 READ

▶ **Listen and read.**

> **Academic Skill: Get meaning from context**
>
> You can sometimes guess the meaning of a word from the words or sentences around it.

AIRPORT SAFETY

Have you been to an airport lately? You probably had to wait in a long line. Nobody enjoys that. Unfortunately, though, the lines are necessary. Why? Air travel can be dangerous. Passengers face threats of different kinds.

5 The Transportation Security Administration (TSA) fights against these threats. It tries to keep passengers secure. It performs safety checks on every passenger. These security screenings take time. They are the reason for the long lines.

10 What kinds of security screenings does the TSA perform?

Baggage Screening
Travelers are allowed to carry small bags on the plane. The TSA screens all of these bags. Passengers have to

wait in line for this. They have to take laptops and other
15 electronics out of their bags. They also have to remove medicines and water bottles. TSA officers open some bags. They pass all of the bags through X-ray machines. They are looking for dangerous items.

Passenger Screening
20 TSA officers also need to check the passengers. A few passengers try to carry weapons under their clothes. The TSA wants to stop them. Each passenger has to walk through a metal detector. The TSA also checks passengers with advanced technology. This technology
25 works like an X-ray machine, but it is safer. TSA officers can only see an outline of the passenger's body. However, they can see dangerous items clearly.

Sometimes, TSA officers check passengers more carefully. They "pat down" the person's body with their
30 hands. Female officers check female passengers. Male officers check male passengers.

The next time you have to wait in a long line at an airport, don't get upset. It's the price we pay to stay safe!

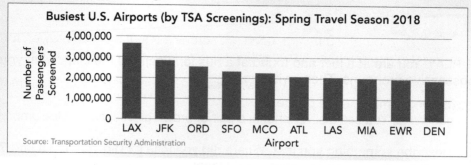

Busiest U.S. Airports (by TSA Screenings): Spring Travel Season 2018

Number of Passengers Screened — Airport: LAX, JFK, ORD, SFO, MCO, ATL, LAS, MIA, EWR, DEN

Source: Transportation Security Administration

3 CLOSE READING

A **IDENTIFY.** What is the main idea of the article?

a. The TSA performs different security screenings on passengers at the airport.
b. Airline passengers don't like waiting in long lines, but it's necessary.
c. TSA officers use advanced technology to check passengers' bodies.

Reading

B **CITE EVIDENCE. Answer the questions. Where is the information? Write the line numbers.**

Lines

1. Why do passengers have to go through security screenings at the airport?

_____   _____

2. How do TSA officers check bags?

_____   _____

3. How do TSA officers check passengers?

_____   _____

4. Why do TSA officers use advanced technology during screenings?

_____   _____

C **INTERPRET GRAPHICS. Complete the sentences about the bar graph.**

1. During the spring travel season, the TSA screened more than 3 million passengers at _____.
   a. Los Angeles International (LAX)
   b. John F. Kennedy International (JFK)
   c. Chicago-O'Hare International (ORD)
2. The TSA screened more than 2 million passengers at _____ of the 10 busiest U.S. airports.
   a. 7
   b. 8
   c. 10

4 SUMMARIZE

What are the most important ideas in the article? Write three sentences in your notebook.

Show what you know!

1. **EVALUATE.** Talk about the different kinds of security screenings that are performed at the airport. Do you think these screenings are necessary? Why or why not?

2. **WRITE.** Describe two different security screenings that passengers go through at the airport.

   Passengers have to go through baggage screening. The TSA officers ...

I can get meaning from context while reading. ☐   I need more practice. ☐

To read more, go to MyEnglishLab.

Explain how to use a transportation app

1 STUDY THE MODEL

ANALYZE. Read the model and Writing Skill. Then answer the questions.

How to Use a Ride-Sharing App

This is how to use a ride-sharing service. First, create an account on the service's website or through an app on your phone. Type in your name, phone number, email address, and credit card number. Then, when you want to get a driver, tap on the app on your phone. Type in your pick-up location and your destination. Choose the type of car you want and the number of seats you need. The app shows you the price of the ride. Next, request the ride. After that, go outside and wait for the ride. Finally, when the ride is over, the payment is charged to your credit card. You can also rate the driver. Give the driver one to five stars. The driver can also rate you as a passenger.

Writing Skill: Use time-order words

Supporting sentences sometimes describe the steps in a process. Put the steps in order from first to last. Use time-order words and phrases such as *first, then,* and *after that.*

1. What time-order words does the author use?
2. What are the different steps in this process?

2 PLAN YOUR WRITING

A **BRAINSTORM. Ask and answer the questions.**

What is an app you use to get around? Do you use a map, transportation, or ride-sharing app? How do you use it? What are the steps?

B **OUTLINE. Write three or four steps.**

Process: _____

Step 1:	Step 2:	Step 3:	Step 4:

3 WRITE

EXPLAIN. Write about how to use the app. Explain the process. Use the model, the Writing Skill, and your ideas from Exercise 2 to help you.

4 CHECK YOUR WRITING

COLLABORATE. Read the checklist. Read your writing together. Revise your writing.

WRITING CHECKLIST

☐ Does the paragraph describe how to use an app?

☐ Does the paragraph include each step in the process, from first to last?

☐ Does the paragraph include time-order words to introduce the steps?

I can use time-order words. ■

I need more practice. ■

For more practice, go to MyEnglishLab.

Lesson 9

Talk about travel delays and cancellations

1 BEFORE YOU LISTEN

DISCUSS. Were you ever at a bus station or an airport when your trip was delayed or canceled? What was the reason? How long did you have to wait? How did you feel?

2 LISTEN

This is an announcement at a bus station.

Carlos

A ▶ **LISTEN FOR MAIN IDEA.** Circle the answer.

The announcement is about a bus that

was _____.

    a. delayed
    b. canceled
    c. repaired

B ▶ **LISTEN FOR DETAILS.** Carlos tells his mother he has bad news and good news.

What is the bad news? _____

What is the good news? _____

C ▶ **EXPAND.** Circle the correct answers.

1. The announcement is for people going to _____.
    a. Miami   **b.** Jacksonville   **c.** Georgia

2. What time is the next bus leaving for Miami?
    a. at 9:08   **b.** at 3:24   **c.** at 3:30

3. What's the number of the next bus to Miami?
    a. 908   **b.** 980   **c.** 918

4. How old will Carlos's mother be on her birthday?
    a. 77   **b.** 70   **c.** She won't say.

5. When will Carlos be back?
    a. next month   **b.** this month   **c.** in 7 months

I can talk about travel delays and cancellations. ■   I need more practice. ■

For more practice, go to MyEnglishLab.

Making polite requests

Polite Requests with *would / will / could / can*				Answers
Would **Will** **Could** **Can**	you (please)	**do**	me a favor?	Sure. Of course. No problem.

Requests for Permission				Answers
Can **Could** **May**	I (please)	**sit**	here?	Yes, you can. / Sure. No, you can't. Yes, you may. No, you may not.

Grammar Watch

- Do not use *could* in short answers.
- When making a request, *may* is more formal than *can* or *could*.
- To say *no* to a request, say "Sorry" and give a reason.

A **INVESTIGATE. Underline the requests.**

A: Hi, could you tell me when bus 20 leaves?
B: Sure. It leaves in ten minutes.
A: Thanks. Can I bring food on the bus?
B: Yes, you can.

B **CHOOSE. Cross out the incorrect response to each request.**

1. **A:** Could I look at your bus schedule?

   B: Yes, you can. / Yes, you could.

2. **A:** May I please have a transfer ticket?

   B: Yes, you may. / Yes, you would.

3. **A:** Could you switch seats with me?

   B: No, you could. / No problem.

4. **A:** Would you please turn off your phone?

   B: Yes, I would. / Sure.

Grammar

C COMPLETE. Use the words in the box and *can, could, may,* or *would.* There may be more than one correct answer.

get	give	have	help	put	~~watch~~

A: Hey, Bob. _____*Can*_____ you _____*watch*_____ my things? I'm getting a drink.

B: No problem. _____ you _____ me a coffee?

A: Sure. I'll be right back.

C: _____ I _____ you?

A: Yes. _____ I _____ a large orange juice and a coffee?

C: Here you go.

A: Oh. _____ you also _____ me a small bag of pretzels and an apple?

C: OK. Anything else?

A: No, thanks. But _____ you _____ everything in a bag?

D APPLY. Rewrite the requests using the words in parentheses.

1. Is it OK to bring food on the bus? (May) _May I bring food on the bus?_____

2. Please watch my luggage. (Could) _____

3. Is it OK to smoke on the bus? (Can) _____

4. Is it OK to sit here? (Can) _____

Show what you know!

1. **ROLE-PLAY.** You are traveling. Make polite requests and ask for permission. Use the ideas below or your own ideas.

   get a bus schedule   move that bag off the seat
   get a transfer   switch seats

2. **WRITE.** In an email, make polite requests and ask a friend for a favor. Use *would, could, will, can,* or *may.*

   Dear Sam,
   Would you do me a favor? Can you . . .

I can make polite requests. ■   I need more practice. ■

For more practice, go to MyEnglishLab.

Soft Skills at Work

Find creative solutions

1 MEET HUGO

Read about one of his workplace skills.

> I find creative solutions to problems. I'm always thinking of new ideas. For example, when I face a challenge, I find a way to solve it.

2 HUGO'S PROBLEM

A READ. Write *T* (true) or *F* (false).

Hugo owns a small business with two partners. They are responsible and understand the need to fix appliances immediately when someone calls. That's why Hugo and his partners are available any time of day or night.

A restaurant owner calls Hugo late on Friday night with an emergency. His refrigerator has stopped working, and there will be a wedding at the restaurant on Saturday. There is a lot of food in the refrigerator. Hugo rushes to the restaurant. He knows it will not be an easy fix.

_____ 1. Appliances usually need to be fixed as soon as possible.

_____ 2. The refrigerator breaks down before a wedding.

_____ 3. It won't be a problem to fix the refrigerator quickly.

B ANALYZE. What is Hugo's problem? Write your response in your notebook.

3 HUGO'S SOLUTION

A COLLABORATE. Hugo finds creative solutions. He can find a way to solve any problem. What should he do? Explain your answer.

1. Hugo tells the restaurant owner that he should have a back-up refrigerator.
2. Hugo says, "I'm sorry, but this will take a long time to fix. Can you store the food somewhere else while I work?"
3. Hugo says, "I have two older refrigerators in storage. I'll have my partners bring them here to store your food while I fix your refrigerator."
4. Hugo _____.

B ROLE-PLAY. Act out Hugo's solution with your partner.

Show what you know!

1. **REFLECT.** How have you creatively solved a problem at work? Give an example.

2. **WRITE.** Now write your example in your Skills Log.

   I find creative solutions no matter what problem I face. For example, one night the power went out at the restaurant where I work. I lit candles for every table. The customers loved it!

3. **PRESENT.** Give a short presentation to show how you find creative solutions.

I can give an example of how I find creative solutions at work. ■

Unit Review: Go back to page 85. Which unit goals can you check off?

6 Getting a Good Deal

PREVIEW

When you buy appliances, electronics, or cell phones, what is most difficult? Making a decision? Getting a good price? Getting a refund?

UNIT GOALS

- [ ] Identify and discuss problems with purchases
- [ ] Identify product defects
- [ ] Discuss problems with cell phone service
- [ ] Understand rebates
- [ ] Analyze a rebate application
- [ ] Make an exchange at a store

- [ ] **Academic skill:** Understand formatting clues
- [ ] **Writing skill:** Use details to compare and contrast
- [ ] **Workplace soft skill:** Respond to customer needs

Vocabulary

Problems with purchases

A **PREDICT.** Look at the vocabulary. The words describe problems with purchases (things you buy). Which words do you know?

Problems with purchases

1. bent   **2.** broken   **3.** cracked
4. damaged   **5.** dented   **6.** defective
7. incompatible **8.** leaking   **9.** scratched

B ▶ **LISTEN AND POINT.** Then listen and repeat.

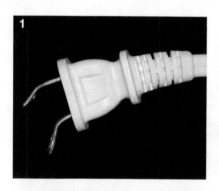

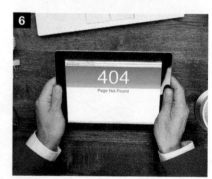

Study Tip

Make Connections

Make cards for five words. Write the problem on the front of the card. Write two things you buy that can have the problem on the back of the card.

Vocabulary

C **MATCH. Write the correct letter.**

_____ **1.** You got a package, but it's dented.

_____ **2.** Do you have a screen protector for your phone?

_____ **3.** Why did that company ask us to send back the toy?

_____ **4.** What's wrong with the refrigerator?

_____ **5.** My phone's battery is still dead.

_____ **6.** Why are you returning this TV?

a. No, but I really need one. It's already scratched.

b. I'm not sure, but it's leaking from the bottom.

c. Look inside and see if the merchandise is broken.

d. It's defective and dangerous for children.

e. The remote is broken.

f. You need a different charger. This one is incompatible with your phone.

Show what you know!

1. **INTERPRET. When you buy a product, it sometimes comes with a warranty. This is a written guarantee. If the product is defective, the company will fix or replace it under certain conditions. Read the warranty below. How long does it last? What are the conditions?**

CANA **Digital Camera™ Limited Warranty**   USA, Canada only

This Cana digital camera is under warranty for 1 year from the date of purchase. NOTE the following conditions:

- The camera must be in new condition at time of purchase.

- Cana will replace a defective camera with new parts or a new camera.

- This warranty does not cover cameras scratched or dented from regular, everyday use.

2. **WRITE. Explain product warranties. Why is it important to get a warranty? Do you have a warranty for any products you own? What are they?**

Product warranties are important because . . .

I can identify and discuss problems with purchases. ☐   I need more practice. ☐

For more practice, go to MyEnglishLab.

Identify product defects

1 BEFORE YOU LISTEN

A **DISCUSS. Look at the pictures. What types of defects could these products have?**

vacuum cleaner

car seat

treadmill

coffee maker

B **MAKE CONNECTIONS. What do you do when you buy a defective product?**

2 LISTEN

Emilio and Ana are talking about their vacuum cleaner.

A ▶ **LISTEN FOR MAIN IDEA. Circle the answer.**

What's wrong with the vacuum cleaner?
- **a.** It won't turn on.
- **b.** It doesn't pick up dirt.
- **c.** It sounds and smells strange.

B ▶ **LISTEN FOR DETAILS. Write *T* (true) or *F* (false).**

_____ **1.** Emilio thinks the vacuum cleaner sounds and smells strange.

_____ **2.** The filter is dirty.

_____ **3.** The warranty on the vacuum is still good.

_____ **4.** The vacuum is less than five years old.

_____ **5.** Ana is happy that the vacuum is damaged.

Listening and Speaking

3 PRONUNCIATION

A ► **PRACTICE. Listen. Then listen and repeat.**

this	When did we buy this?
the	What's the matter?
think	I think it's broken.
three	The model number is 3223.

B ► **APPLY. Listen. Is the _th_ sound voiced or voiceless? Check (✓) the correct column.**

	Voiced	Voiceless
1. thing		
2. then		
3. that		
4. throw		

4 CONVERSATION

A ► **LISTEN AND READ. Then practice the conversation with a partner.**

A: Ana, stop the vacuum.

B: What's the matter?

A: Something is wrong. The vacuum sounds strange, and it smells funny, too. Maybe we need to change the filter or clean the brush. What do you think?

B: The filter isn't dirty, and the brush isn't, either. The vacuum always sounds like that. It's just old.

B **ROLE-PLAY. Make a similar conversation.**

A: Tell your partner to turn off the air conditioner. You smell something burning. You think the air conditioner is dirty or broken. Ask your partner if he or she changed the air filter.

B: You changed the air filter. You think the air conditioner is broken.

| I can identify product defects. ■ | I need more practice. ■ |

For more practice, go to MyEnglishLab.

Grammar

Additions with *too* and *either*

Affirmative Statement		Addition
		I am, **too**.
Claire is busy,	and	they are, **too**.
		he is, **too**.

Negative Statement		Addition
		I'm not, **either**.
John isn't home,	and	you aren't, **either**.
		she isn't, **either**.

Grammar Watch

- Use an addition as a way to avoid repeating information in a sentence.
- Use *too* for affirmative sentences.
- Use *either* for negative sentences.
- Use a comma before *too* or *either*.

A INVESTIGATE. Underline the sentences that have additions.

A: Continental Home Warranty service. How may I help you?

B: Hi. <u>My refrigerator is broken, and my microwave is, too.</u> The cord on the microwave is damaged. Oh, and I almost forgot! Our toaster isn't working, either.

A: I see. Is the microwave built in?

B: No, it's a countertop microwave.

A: I'm sorry. The microwave isn't covered under your warranty, and the toaster isn't, either. We don't cover countertop appliances. But I can help you with the fridge. What seems to be the problem?

B: Well, the refrigerator isn't very cold inside, and the ice maker doesn't work. It just makes a strange buzzing sound when we try to use it.

A: I see. We can send a technician to your home first thing tomorrow morning.

B: Oh, that won't work. I'm not going to be home tomorrow, and my husband isn't, either.

A: What days and times are you available?

B: Let me see. Tuesday evening is good, and Thursday is, too.

A: How about Thursday afternoon between 4:00 and 7:00?

B: Yes, that works.

A: OK. Our technician will call you on his way to your home.

B: Great. Thanks!

B MATCH. Write the correct letters.

_b_	**1.** My computer isn't connecting to the internet,	**a.**	and the refrigerator is, too.
____	**2.** The dishwasher is leaking,	**b.**	and my phone isn't, either.
____	**3.** Customer service wasn't available,	**c.**	and my old one was, too.
____	**4.** My new phone is defective,	**d.**	and these headphones aren't, either.
____	**5.** This charger isn't compatible with my phone,	**e.**	and tech support wasn't, either.

Grammar

C **COMPLETE. Use the correct form of *be* and *too* or *either*.**

1. My cell phone's screen is scratched, and my tablet's screen _____*is, too*_____.
2. Maya wasn't home yesterday, and her sisters _____.
3. The air conditioner is making strange sounds, and the heater _____.
4. The soda machine is out of order, and the vending machines _____.
5. The TV display isn't working, and the sound _____.
6. The bank isn't open today, and the schools _____.

D **APPLY. Put the words in the correct order. Add commas where necessary.**

1. These headphones / isn't / aren't / with my phone / compatible / and / the charger / either
   These headphones aren't compatible with my phone, and the charger isn't, either.

2. The plumber isn't available today / the electrician / either / isn't / and
   _____

3. The stove is broken / and / too / is / the microwave
   _____

4. I / for a refund / am asking / are / too / and / my parents
   _____

5. My computer wasn't working / either / and / my printer / wasn't
   _____

Show what you know!

1. **COLLABORATE. Do you have similar problems with two appliances or devices? What is wrong with them? Use *too* and *either*.**

   A: *My toaster isn't working well, and my vacuum cleaner isn't, either.*
   B: *My camera lens is scratched, and my phone's screen is, too.*

2. **WRITE. Report on problems you've had with two different appliances and devices. What did you do to fix or replace them?**

   My . . . is broken, and my . . . is, too.
   I had to . . .

Lesson 4

Read about warranties and service agreements

1 BEFORE YOU READ

DEFINE. Products such as cell phones, TVs, and washing machines often come with warranties or service agreements. What is a warranty? What is a service agreement?

2 READ

▶ Listen and read.

> **Academic Skill: Understand formatting clues**
>
> Authors sometimes use formatting such as boldface type, bullets, and color to help readers find the main points of an article.

Warranties and Service Agreements

Caveat emptor means "buyer beware." What does that mean? When you buy something, you should be careful. Some products are low quality. They break easily. Nobody wants to buy a product like this. Sometimes, though, it's
5 hard to tell how good a product is. You should do one important thing before you buy a product. Check its warranty or service agreement. This will protect you if the product breaks. This is even more important when you buy an expensive product.

10 **Warranties**
A **warranty** is a promise from the product's manufacturer. The manufacturer promises to repair the product if it breaks. Cars, appliances, and computers usually come with warranties. They are **included in the price** of the
15 product. The warranty usually lasts for a year. You should always read it carefully.

Service Agreements
These are also called "service contracts" or "extended warranties." Warranties and **service agreements** are
20 both promises to fix a product if it breaks. The difference is the price. A service agreement **costs extra**. Before you pay, study the service agreement. Make sure it isn't a waste of money.

Don't pay extra for a service agreement in these
25 situations:

- The product is high quality. This means it probably won't break. It won't need repairs.

30 - It doesn't cost much to repair the product. You can just pay someone to make the repairs. It doesn't make sense to pay extra for a service agreement.

35 - The service agreement only covers part of the product. Another part might break. Then you will have to pay for the repairs.

40 Before you buy a product, protect yourself. Always check the warranty and service agreement.

> **How likely is it that a product will break?**
> Some products break more often than others. After three years, TVs have a 3% failure rate. Cameras have a 10% failure rate. Laptops have a 43% failure rate! (*Source: Consumer Reports*)

3 CLOSE READING

A IDENTIFY. What is the main idea of the article?
a. Some products break easily, so buyers should be careful.
b. Before you buy a product, always check the warranty and service agreement.
c. Sometimes you shouldn't pay extra for a service agreement.

Reading

B **CITE EVIDENCE. Complete the sentences. Where is the information? Write the line numbers.**

Lines

1. With warranties and service agreements, manufacturers promise to _____.
   a. fix a product
   b. give the buyer a different product
   _____

2. A warranty lasts _____.
   a. forever
   b. for a period of time
   _____

3. A service agreement _____.
   a. is included in the price of a product
   b. costs extra
   _____

4. You shouldn't pay for a service agreement when _____.
   a. repairs for the product cost a lot
   b. the product probably won't break
   _____

5. If a service agreement only covers a refrigerator's motor, and the door breaks, _____ pay for the repair of the door.
   a. you have to
   b. the manufacturer has to
   _____

C **INTERPRET VOCABULARY. Circle the correct answers.**

1. The word *manufacturer* in line 11 means _____.
   a. the company that makes a product
   b. the store that sells a product
   c. the person who buys a product

2. The word *appliances* in line 13 means _____.
   a. small products
   b. large pieces of equipment for the home
   c. phones or computers

3. The phrase *included in* in line 14 means _____.
   a. more than
   b. less than
   c. part of

4. The word *repair* in line 30 means _____.
   a. buy
   b. sell
   c. fix

5. The word *covers* in line 36 means _____.
   a. promises
   b. pays for
   c. explains

4 SUMMARIZE

What are the most important ideas in the article? Write three sentences in your notebook.

Show what you know!

1. **COLLABORATE.** Compare your experiences with warranties and service agreements. What did you buy that required one? Was it worth the money? Why or why not?

2. **WRITE.** Describe the differences between warranties and service agreements. When is it a good idea to pay extra for a service agreement? Give examples in a paragraph.

   Warranties and service agreements are both promises to . . .

I can understand formatting clues while reading. ■   I need more practice. ■

To read more, go to MyEnglishLab.

Lesson 5
Discuss problems with cell phone service

1 BEFORE YOU LISTEN

DISCUSS. Have you ever gotten a bill that was much higher than you expected? What did you do?

2 LISTEN

Lucas is telling Yonas about a surprising phone bill.

A ▶ **LISTEN FOR MAIN IDEA.** Circle the answer.

What is the problem?
- **a.** Lucas's phone bill is too high.
- **b.** Lucas's phone isn't working.
- **c.** Lucas got a good deal with a new phone carrier.

> *carrier:* a telecommunications company
>
> *unlimited talk:* as many minutes to talk as you want
>
> *unlimited text:* as many texts as you want to send
>
> *unlimited data:* as much internet access as you want

B ▶ **LISTEN FOR DETAILS.** Answer the questions.

1. How much is Lucas's bill?
   - **a.** $100
   - **b.** $640
   - **c.** $614

2. When did Lucas switch carriers?
   - **a.** last month
   - **b.** last week
   - **c.** today

3. What was the main reason Lucas switched carriers?
   - **a.** unlimited talk, text, and data
   - **b.** unlimited calls to Brazil
   - **c.** $640 plan

C ▶ **EXPAND.** Listen to the rest of the conversation. Write *T* (true) or *F* (false).

_____ **1.** Lucas's contract says he has unlimited international calls.

_____ **2.** Lucas didn't call the cell phone carrier about the problem.

_____ **3.** Yonas thinks Lucas should cancel his plan.

_____ **4.** Horizon has good international plans.

Listening and Speaking

3 CONVERSATION

A ▶ **LISTEN AND READ.** Then practice the conversation with a partner.

A: What's wrong, Lucas?

B: I just got my phone bill today. It was $640!

A: What? How did that happen?

B: Last month I switched to a new phone carrier. The plan was for unlimited talk, text, and data for $100 a month.

A: That sounds like a good deal.

B: I thought so, too. And best of all, the salesperson said I could make unlimited calls to Brazil. That's the main reason I switched carriers.

A: So what happened?

B: Look at this bill. They charged me $2 a minute for calls to Brazil.

B **PROBLEM SOLVE.** Read the situations and possible solutions. Which of the solutions will work best? Discuss.

Situation 1

Vera bought a prepaid phone card for $10 to call Egypt. The phone card promised 1,000 minutes. She used only 600 minutes, and now her card doesn't work.

Situation 2

Sergio just signed a contract with a cell phone company. He found out that he lives on a street with bad cell phone reception. When he makes or gets a call, the signal often fails.

Possible Solutions:

- Ask the company for a refund.
- Cancel the plan.
- Change cell phone carriers.
- File a complaint against the company.
- Find someone to take over your plan.

I can discuss problems with cell phone service. ■   I need more practice. ■

For more practice, go to MyEnglishLab.

Grammar

Comparing with adjectives

	Adjective		Grammar Watch
My new phone plan is	cheaper more convenient less convenient	than my old plan.	• Use the comparative form of an adjective + *than* to compare two people, places, or things. • The comparative forms of *good*, *bad*, and *far* are irregular: *good–better, bad–worse, far–farther*. • See page 262 for rules when comparing with adjectives.
Our old TV is	bigger smaller heavier	than our new TV.	

A INVESTIGATE. Read the ad. Underline the adjectives that compare.

PACIFIC The cell phone provider you've been looking for.

Are you tired of expensive monthly fees? Poor reception? Bad customer service?

Sign up with Pacific today. We offer <u>cheaper</u> monthly rates; no hidden fees; clearer reception; and faster, more efficient customer service. Make your life more convenient and spend less money with our unlimited talk, text, and data plans. Call Pacific today and get a second line free for your first year of service.

B COMPLETE. Use the correct comparative form of the adjectives in parentheses.

My family used to have a phone with T-M cell phone company. We signed up for the plan because

we thought T-M had a _____lower_____ price. But we ran out of data quickly and had to pay extra
(low)

data fees, so the plan wasn't really _____. The reception was bad, so we had a lot of
(cheap)

dropped calls. Now we have a Pacific plan. We have unlimited data, so it's _____ than
(convenient)

my old plan. The reception is also _____, and we haven't had any dropped calls. We're
(clear)

_____ with Pacific. It's a much _____ cell phone provider.
(happy)   (good)

Grammar

C COMPARE. Look at the TV ads. Write the correct form of the adjectives in parentheses.

Viza 39" LED TV
1080p resolution full HD
Superfast
120 hertz refresh rate
$349.99

Polara 32" LCD TV
$199.99
720p resolution
60 hertz refresh rate

1. The Viza is _____*faster*_____ than the Polara.
   (fast)

2. The Viza has _____ resolution than the Polara.
   (good)

3. The Viza's screen is _____ than the Polara's screen.
   (big)

4. The Polara is _____ than the Viza.
   (expensive)

5. The Polara is _____ than the Viza.
   (small)

6. The Polara's refresh rate is _____ than the Viza's refresh rate.
   (slow)

7. The Polara is _____ than the Viza.
   (cheap)

8. The Polara has _____ resolution than the Viza.
   (bad)

Show what you know!

1. **COMPARE.** Read the ads and discuss the vacuum cleaners. Use the comparative forms of *cheap, expensive, good, heavy, light,* and *powerful.*

Dirt Angel
good performance
2-year warranty
15 lbs.
$99.99

HABER
POWERFUL PERFORMANCE
5-YEAR WARRANTY
25 LBS.
$149.99

2. **WRITE.** Analyze the two vacuum cleaners. Which do you want to buy? Why?

I want to buy the Dirt Angel because it is cheaper and lighter. I don't want to carry a heavy vacuum. Smaller vacuums are easier to use.

I can use adjectives to compare. ■   I need more practice. ■

For more practice, go to MyEnglishLab.

Understand rebates

1 READ ABOUT REBATES

A READ. Learn about rebates.

Everyone likes to save money. That's why it's a good idea to search for special offers, such as rebates, before making a major purchase. A rebate is an amount of money given back to someone who has bought an item. Rebates are offered by manufacturers and stores to try to increase sales of their products.

For example, stores may offer rebates on large appliances, such as stoves or refrigerators. Utility (electric or gas) companies might offer rebates on household items that are energy efficient.

Look for advertisements for rebates online, but be careful. Rebates usually have an expiration date, so the forms need to be completed and sent in promptly.

B INTERPRET. Write *T* (true) or *F* (false).

_____ **1.** You need to complete the rebate form before you purchase an item.

_____ **2.** You can only find rebates in stores.

_____ **3.** People can save money by using rebates.

_____ **4.** Some products that reduce energy usage offer rebates.

_____ **5.** It doesn't matter when you send the rebate application back.

BUCK'S

11% Rebate

via Buck's gift card by mail or email

Make a purchase from a participating Buck's store between 2/8/20 and 2/14/20 to be eligible to receive an 11% Rebate in the form of a Buck's gift card.

Consumers who purchase between 2/8/20 and 2/14/20 will be eligible to receive 11% rebate on a Buck's gift card based on the purchase prices of eligible items. Buck's gift card will be delivered via a physical card by mail or virtual card by email. In-store only based on participating store list. See a Buck's store associate for details.

C GO ONLINE. Search for special offers and rebates. Search by ZIP code to see what is available in your area.

Workplace, Life, and Community Skills

2 ANALYZE A REBATE APPLICATION

A READ. Look at the advertisement.

Kenvore 4.5 Cu. Ft. High-Efficiency Front-Load Washer

Item #79054   Model #WM65812
SAVE through 12/31/2020

~~$899~~   **$809**

Plus up to $200 in rebates
(Click to learn more)

B ANALYZE. Look at the rebate application for the washing machine.

To receive your Kenvore rebate:

1. Purchase a qualifying washing machine from a participating store between 10/01/2020 and 12/31/2020. Requests must be made by 1/31/2021. Claims posted after this date will not be honored.
2. Limit (1) per household.
3. Please allow 6–8 weeks for processing. If you do not receive your rebate after 8 weeks, visit Kenvorerebates.com or call (877) 555-1223.
4. Keep a copy of all materials submitted for your records.
5. Upload a copy of your cash register receipt showing purchase of qualifying product(s).
6. Complete the information below.

Name   Andrew Gomez

Address   10 Gavin Avenue   Apt.   3B

City   Long Beach   State   CA   Zip Code   90813

Cell Phone   (562) 555-2098   Email Address   gavina@rmail.com

ADD SCANNED DOCUMENTS HERE

Answer the questions. Circle *Yes* or *No*.

1. Mr. Gomez bought this washing machine on September 16. Is he eligible for a rebate?   Yes   No
2. Mr. Gomez lost his receipt. Can he still get a rebate?   Yes   No
3. Mr. Gomez emailed his application on January 30. Will he get the rebate?   Yes   No
4. Mr. Gomez waited 9 weeks and still hasn't received the rebate. Should he contact Kenvore?   Yes   No

C DISCUSS. Stores sometimes offer rebates to improve their sales. What are other ways stores can improve sales?

I can understand and analyze a rebate application. ☐   I need more practice. ☐

For more practice, go to MyEnglishLab.

Make an exchange at a store

1 BEFORE YOU LISTEN

A READ.

A manufacturer's warranty is a promise from a company to fix or replace defective products under certain conditions. It is usually included in the price of a product.

A store protection plan is an extra warranty offered by the store that sells the product. It is sometimes called a service agreement, a service contract, or an extended warranty. It costs extra money.

B **MAKE CONNECTIONS.** Do you think it's necessary to purchase a store protection plan? What types of products have this option? Have you ever purchased one?

2 LISTEN

Rahel is returning a phone to the store.

A ▶ **LISTEN FOR MAIN IDEA.** Circle the answer.

Why is Rahel returning the merchandise?
- **a.** It doesn't take good pictures.
- **b.** It's not easy to use.
- **c.** It's slow.

B ▶ **LISTEN FOR DETAILS.** Write *T* (true) or *F* (false).

_____ **1.** Rahel has to pay $35 because she returned the phone after 15 days.

_____ **2.** Customers can return items up to 30 days after the purchase.

_____ **3.** Rahel thinks her phone is defective.

_____ **4.** Rahel lost her receipt.

_____ **5.** Rahel didn't purchase a protection plan.

_____ **6.** Rahel wants a refund.

Listening and Speaking

3 PRONUNCIATION

A ▶ PRACTICE. Listen. Then listen and repeat.

I'll take it.

Here it is.

There's a restocking fee for opened boxes.

Can I exchange it for another phone?

Linking Words

We link words in a phrase together. We do not stop between each word. We usually link a consonant sound at the end of a word to a vowel sound at the beginning of the next word.

B ▶ APPLY. Listen and repeat. Draw lines to show where the sounds in two words link together.

1. Do you have any newer phones?

2. This isn't as expensive.

3. Is there anything wrong with it?

4. Can I exchange it for that phone?

4 CONVERSATION

A ▶ LISTEN AND READ. Then practice the conversation with a partner.

A: Do you want a refund or an exchange?

B: I'd like an exchange, please. Can I exchange it for this Simsung?

A: Sure, but that's $50 more. We have other models that aren't as expensive as that one.

B: How about this LTC phone?

A: That one is on sale today. It isn't as expensive as the Simsung, but it has all the same features.

B: I'll take it.

B ROLE-PLAY. Pretend you and your partner are a customer and a sales clerk. Make a similar conversation.

A: You're returning a T-M phone. It doesn't have a good camera. You want to exchange it for a Simsung phone.

B: You are the clerk. The Simsung costs $50 more.

I can talk about making an exchange at a store. ■   I need more practice. ■

For more practice, go to MyEnglishLab.

Comparing with *as . . . as*

	as	Adjective	*as*	
This store is This store isn't	**as**	clean	**as**	that store.
That book is That book isn't	**as**	expensive	**as**	this book.

Grammar Watch

- Use *as . . . as* to say how two things, places, or people are like each other.
- Use *not as . . . as* to say how two things, places, or people are not like each other.
- Leave out the second part of an *as . . . as* phrase when the meaning is clear from context. For example, *That TV isn't as big (as this TV).*

A INVESTIGATE. Underline the *as . . . as* phrase. Then read the statements about the two stores. Write *T* (true) or *F* (false).

The Trego store is as clean as the Archway store.

The Archway store is not as big as the Trego store.

The lines at Archway are not as long as the lines at Trego.

_____ **1.** The Archway store is cleaner.

_____ **2.** The Trego store is bigger.

_____ **3.** The lines at Archway are shorter.

B APPLY. Complete each sentence with a verb and an *as . . . as* phrase. Use the adjective in parentheses.

1. Customer service at aro.com __*is not as good as*__ it is at acb.com.

(not / good)

2. Deliveries _____ they are at acb.com.

(fast)

3. The merchandise at aro.com _____ it is at acb.com.

(not / good)

4. Shopping on aro.com _____ it is on acb.com.

(easy)

5. Prices at aro.com _____ they are on acb.com.

(not / high)

Show what you know!

1. DISCUSS. Is shopping for a large purchase in your native country similar to shopping in the U.S.? Are items the same price and quality?

2. WRITE. Compare shopping in your native country with shopping in the U.S. Use *as . . . as*.

   Many stores in Jordan do not take credit cards. Shopping in Jordan is not as easy as it is in the U.S.

I can use *as . . . as* to compare two things, places, or people. ■   I need more practice. ■

For more practice, go to MyEnglishLab.

Writing

Compare two stores

1 STUDY THE MODEL

ANALYZE. Read the model and Writing Skill. Then answer the questions.

Arcadia or Dollarmart?

Arcadia and Dollarmart are both supermarkets in my neighborhood. Each store is located only a few blocks from my home. I can walk to both of them. They're very convenient. Their prices are about the same, too. I do a lot of shopping at both stores. However, I think Arcadia is a better store than Dollarmart. The employees are friendlier. It's more organized so you can find things right away. The merchandise is much better quality, too. At Dollarmart, the employees are less helpful, and they don't know where things are. The store isn't very clean, either. For these reasons, I prefer to shop at Arcadia.

Writing Skill: Use details to compare and contrast

When you compare two things, you find similarities between them. When you contrast, you find differences. You should organize similarities and differences together in your writing and include supporting details.

1. What are some similarities between the two stores?
2. What are some differences between the two stores?

2 PLAN YOUR WRITING

A **BRAINSTORM. Ask and answer the questions. Use a Venn diagram to compare and contrast.**

What are two stores in your neighborhood that sell the same thing? What is similar about them? What is different? Which store do you like better? Why?

B **OUTLINE. Add supporting details.**

Compare and Contrast: _____ and _____

Topic Sentence: _____

Similarities: _____

    Supporting Details: _____

Differences: _____

    Supporting Details: _____

3 WRITE

COMPARE. Compare and contrast two stores. Use the model, the Writing Skill, and your ideas from Exercise 2 to help you.

4 CHECK YOUR WRITING

COLLABORATE. Read the checklist. Read your writing together. Revise your writing.

WRITING CHECKLIST

☐ Does the paragraph compare and contrast two stores?

☐ Does the paragraph identify similarities between the stores?

☐ Does the paragraph identify differences between the stores?

☐ Does the paragraph include supporting details?

I can use details to compare and contrast. ■   I need more practice. ■

For more practice, go to MyEnglishLab.

Respond to customer needs

1 MEET JESSA

Read about one of her workplace skills.

> I am creative and helpful when working with customers. For example, if a customer is unhappy about something, I always try to find a solution.

2 JESSA'S PROBLEM

A READ. Write *T* (true) or *F* (false).

Jessa works in a large department store. She is helping a customer who is buying many items. The customer wants to use a coupon to save money. Unfortunately, the coupon isn't good until the following week. The customer can't use it today.

She gets upset and starts complaining loudly. She asks to speak to the manager, and she says she will go online to complain.

_____ 1. The coupon is expired.
_____ 2. The customer is very upset.
_____ 3. It's Jessa's fault the customer can't use the coupon.

B ANALYZE. What is Jessa's problem? Write your response in your notebook.

3 JESSA'S SOLUTION

A COLLABORATE. Jessa responds to customers' needs. She tries to find solutions to keep them happy. What should she do? Explain your answer.

1. Jessa says, "I'm really sorry, but you should read the coupon more carefully."
2. Jessa says, "Why don't you come back next week when you can use the coupon?"
3. Jessa says, "I can give you a 20% discount if you give me your email to register with the store."
4. Jessa _____.

B ROLE-PLAY. Act out Jessa's solution with your partner.

Show what you know!

1. **REFLECT.** Have you ever had to respond to a customer's needs? When do you need to be creative and helpful to solve a problem at work? Give an example.

2. **WRITE.** Now write your example in your Skills Log.

   I am creative and helpful when a customer needs something from me. For example, I always have suggestions when a customer can't decide what to buy.

3. **PRESENT.** Give a short presentation to show how you respond to customer needs.

I can give an example of how I respond to customer needs. ☐

Unit Review: Go back to page 105. Which unit goals can you check off?

7 Getting There Safely

PREVIEW

Is it important to have a car where you live?
What problems do car owners have?

UNIT GOALS

- [ ] Talk about driving and traffic
- [ ] Talk about car maintenance
- [ ] Identify car parts and dashboard icons
- [ ] Discuss traffic accidents
- [ ] Identify steps to take after an accident

- [ ] **Academic skill:** Interpret charts
- [ ] **Writing skill:** Present two different opinions when arguing
- [ ] **Workplace soft skill:** Be flexible

125

A **DESCRIBE.** Look at the picture. What do you see?

Vocabulary

B IDENTIFY. Match the pictures with the words. Write the numbers.

Driving and traffic

_____ construction

_____ entrance ramp/on ramp

_____ exit

_____ freeway/highway

_____ lane

_____ overpass

_____ shoulder

_____ toll booth

_____ tow truck

_____ traffic jam

_____ vehicle

C ▶ LISTEN AND POINT. Then listen and repeat.

D ▶ PRACTICE. Listen to the traffic report. Circle the correct answers.

1. On the 110 South, there has just been _____.
   a. construction   **b.** an accident   **c.** a traffic jam

2. On Slauson Avenue East, there is _____.
   a. a traffic jam   **b.** a delay of 25 minutes   **c.** construction

3. On the 105 East, _____.
   a. there are no delays   **b.** there is construction   **c.** there is a blocked lane

4. On the 405 South, _____.
   a. the right lane is closed   **b.** an accident has just happened   **c.** an accident is almost cleared

Show what you know!

1. **DISCUSS.** Compare traffic conditions where you live now to traffic in your native country. Is the traffic better or worse? Are the roads safer or less safe?

2. **WRITE.** Analyze traffic where you live. Is traffic heavier in certain parts of town? What is traffic like at different times of day?

   Where I live, traffic is very slow during rush hour. It is bad from 6:00 to 8:30 in the morning and from 5:00 to 6:00 in the evening. The highways are more crowded than the small side streets, but the side streets have a lot of traffic lights. Traffic downtown is always slow.

I can talk about driving and traffic. ■	I need more practice. ■

For more practice, go to MyEnglishLab.

Lesson 2 Listening and Speaking

Talk about car maintenance

1 BEFORE YOU LISTEN

A **EXPLAIN.** What are common car problems? What can you do to keep a car in good condition?

B **IDENTIFY.** Look at the pictures. Match the pictures with the words.

_____ **1.** change the oil

_____ **2.** replace the brakes

_____ **3.** rotate the tires

2 LISTEN

Li is talking to a mechanic about his car.

A ▶ **LISTEN FOR MAIN IDEA.** Circle the answer.

What does Li want?
  a. an oil change
  b. a new tire
  c. new brakes

B ▶ **LISTEN FOR DETAILS.** Write _T_ (true) or _F_ (false).

_____ **1.** An oil change costs $25.

_____ **2.** An oil change takes 15 minutes.

_____ **3.** Li needs new brakes.

_____ **4.** Li needs new front tires.

_____ **5.** The mechanic is going to rotate Li's tires.

_____ **6.** Li is going to fix the dent in his car.

Listening and Speaking

3 PRONUNCIATION

A ▶ PRACTICE. Listen. Then listen and repeat.

a new battery	You need a new battery.
an oil change	I'd like an oil change.
the tires	We should rotate the tires.

B ▶ APPLY. Listen. Write the article you hear. Use *a, an,* or *the.*

1. There's _____ major traffic jam on _____ freeway.

2. _____ vehicle is blocking _____ left lane.

3. When's _____ last time you got _____ oil change?

4. Take _____ first exit after you go through _____ toll booth.

4 CONVERSATION

A ▶ LISTEN AND READ. Then practice the conversation with a partner.

A: So, what can I do for you?
B: I'd like an oil change.
A: No problem.
B: How much will that be?
A: $29.95.
B: OK. How long will that take?
A: About half an hour.

B ROLE-PLAY. Look at the information below and make a similar conversation.

A: You are a car owner. Tell the mechanic what you need. Ask how much it will cost.
B: You are a mechanic. Answer the questions.

New battery
Cost: $75
Time to fix: 15 minutes

New tire
Cost: $120
Time to replace: 30 minutes

New air conditioning coolant
Cost: $15
Time to put in: 5 minutes

I can talk about car maintenance. ■   I need more practice. ■

For more practice, go to MyEnglishLab.

Grammar

Articles

A, An, The

The car needs **a** battery and **an** air filter.

The battery is weak, and **the** air filter is dirty.

Today is **a** warm day, and **the** sun is shining.

Grammar Watch

- Use the article *a* or *an* the first time you talk about something. Use *a* before consonant sounds. Use *an* before vowel sounds.
- Use the article *the* when you talk about something for the second time.
- Use *the* for things that are known to both you and the listener.
- Use *the* when there is only one of something.

A **INVESTIGATE. Read sentence (a) and underline the articles. Then cross out the incorrect article in sentence (b).**

1. (a) Alex told Claudia about a used car he liked.
   (b) Claudia asked Alex if he bought **a / the** car.

2. (a) Alex told Claudia that he bought the car.
   (b) Claudia asked if it had **a / the** warranty.

3. (a) Claudia asked if the car needed repairs.
   (b) Alex said it didn't, but **a / the** turn signal wasn't working.

4. (a) Claudia asked Alex if he fixed the turn signal.
   (b) He told her that he bought **a / the** new light bulb and installed it.

B **PRACTICE. Use *a*, *an*, or *the* to complete the paragraph.**

Two months ago, I bought _____*an*_____ old car for very little money. _____ car had problems. _____ air conditioner and _____ heater didn't work well. I also had to buy _____ air filter. There was _____ noise coming from _____ engine. There was also _____ hole on _____ floor of _____ car. I covered _____ hole and got used to _____ noise. _____ car gets me to work and that saves me time. I hope _____ car lasts until _____ summer. Then I'll have enough money for _____ better car.

Grammar

C ▶ **APPLY. Complete the conversations with *a*, *an*, or *the*. Then listen and check your answers.**

1. **A:** My car won't start. ___The___ battery must be dead.

   B: Let me jump-start your car. I have jumper cables in my car.

2. **A:** I think there's _____ oil leak under _____ car.

   B: I'll take _____ look.

3. **A:** After the accident, he called for _____ tow truck.

   B: Did it take long for _____ tow truck to come?

   A: It finally came after _____ hour.

4. **A:** We have _____ flat tire.

   B: Oh, no. I hope we have _____ spare tire in the trunk.

5. **A:** Is there _____ good auto repair shop nearby?

   B: I always go to _____ garage on East 4th Street. _____ mechanics there are excellent, and _____ prices are fair.

6. **A:** What's _____ problem with your car?

   B: There's _____ noise in the engine.

   A: Is it _____ same noise you complained about last month?

   B: No. It's _____ different noise.

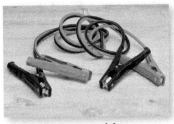

jumper cables

oil leak

flat tire

spare tire

D **COLLABORATE. Practice the conversations.**

Show what you know!

1. **DISCUSS. Talk about an experience or problem you have had with a car, a mechanic, or getting to work or school.**

2. **WRITE. Explain how to fix or take care of a car. Choose a specific topic. Use articles.**

   - How to change a flat tire
   - How to change the oil
   - How to wash a car
   - How to jump-start a car
   - How to choose a good mechanic

I can use the articles *a*, *an*, and *the*. ☐   I need more practice. ☐

For more practice, go to MyEnglishLab.

Workplace, Life, and Community Skills

Identify car parts and dashboard icons

1 IDENTIFY CAR PARTS

A READ. Look at the picture. Which parts of the car do you know?

1. hood
2. windshield
3. trunk
4. engine
5. sideview mirror
6. bumper
7. headlights
8. license plate
9. turn signal

B APPLY. Complete the sentences.

1. You always need to have a ____license plate____ on the back of your car.

2. _____ help the driver see the road at night.

3. It's a good idea to keep a spare tire in the _____ of your car.

4. Check the _____ before you change lanes.

5. The _____ protects your car if you have a minor accident.

6. The _____ is located under the _____ of the car.

7. The _____ lets people know you are making a turn.

8. The _____ should be cleaned frequently so you can see clearly.

Workplace, Life, and Community Skills

2 IDENTIFY DASHBOARD ICONS

A **READ.** Look at the pictures. Which parts of the car and symbols do you know?

1. rearview mirror
2. steering wheel
3. horn
4. GPS
5. brakes
6. accelerator/gas pedal
7. glove compartment

a. emergency brake
b. low tire pressure
c. door open
d. low fuel
e. seatbelt not on
f. oil pressure low
g. temperature warning
h. engine warning

B **IDENTIFY.** Write the name of the correct car part next to each instruction.

1. Turn this to move the car to the right or left: _____
2. Step on this to go faster: _____
3. Keep your insurance card inside here: _____
4. Step on this to stop the car: _____
5. Use this before backing up the car: _____
6. Program this when traveling to an unknown place: _____

C ▶ **LISTEN.** Look at the icons. Listen to the conversations and choose the correct icon.

1. _____   2. _____   3. _____

D GO ONLINE. Look up different types of cars, such as sedans, SUVs, crossovers, and hybrids. Learn about the differences.

I can identify car parts and dashboard icons. ☐   I need more practice. ☐

For more practice, go to MyEnglishLab.

Discuss traffic accidents

1 BEFORE YOU LISTEN

A IDENTIFY. Look at the pictures. What are the drivers doing?

B MAKE CONNECTIONS. What are some things that can distract drivers?

2 LISTEN

A police officer is talking to two drivers after an accident.

A PREDICT. What do you think caused the accident?

a. speeding and cell phone use
b. broken traffic light
c. tired driver

B ▶ LISTEN FOR DETAILS. Write *T* (true) or *F* (false).

_____ 1. Mr. Desmond needs an ambulance.

_____ 2. Mr. Desmond has a serious injury.

_____ 3. Mr. Desmond thinks the other car was going too fast.

_____ 4. Mr. Desmond was talking on his cell phone.

C ▶ EXPAND. Listen to the conversation. Circle the correct answers.

1. The officer asks to see Mr. Ortiz's license, registration, and _____.
   a. car insurance   b. social security card

2. Mr. Ortiz was driving in the _____.
   a. left-hand lane   b. right-hand lane

3. The police officer asks if Mr. Ortiz was _____ on his phone.
   a. talking   b. texting

4. Talking on a cell phone in California is _____.
   a. legal   b. illegal

Listening and Speaking

3 PRONUNCIATION

A ▶ **PRACTICE. Listen. Then listen and repeat.**

hap•pen   in•sur•ance   ac•cident   con•struc•tion

Stressed Syllables

In words with more than one syllable, one syllable is stressed. Other syllables are unstressed. The vowel in an unstressed syllable often has a very short, quiet sound.

B ▶ **APPLY. Listen. Mark (•) the stressed syllable.**

1. license   **2.** about   **3.** statement   **4.** engine   **5.** ambulance

4 CONVERSATION

A ▶ **LISTEN AND READ. Then practice the conversation with a partner.**

A: Are you hurt, sir?

B: No, I'm all right, Officer.

A: Okay. May I see your license, registration, and insurance please? . . . Well, Mr. Ortiz, can you explain what happened?

B: Yes, Officer. I was driving in the right-hand lane. There was nothing in front of me. Suddenly, this car came out of nowhere—I think it came from the left lane. It was slowing down in front of me to turn onto Martine Avenue. There wasn't time for me to stop.

B **ROLE-PLAY. Make a similar conversation.**

A: You are the officer. Ask questions.

B: You are the driver. You were exiting the freeway. It was raining. You lost control and hit the car in front of you.

I can discuss traffic accidents. ☐   I need more practice. ☐

For more practice, go to MyEnglishLab.

Grammar

Past continuous

Subject	was / were		Verb		Grammar Watch
I He She You We They	**was** **were**	(not)	**driving** **playing** **watching**	fast. baseball. TV.	• Past continuous verbs end in *-ing*. • Use the past continuous for activities that were happening at a specific time in the past. • *was not* = *wasn't* • *were not* = *weren't*

A INVESTIGATE. Underline examples of the past continuous.

There was an accident on Route 4 just before the bridge yesterday afternoon. It <u>was raining</u>, and one car hit another car. The driver of the car in front was slightly injured. He wasn't wearing a seat belt. Other cars were slowing down to see what happened. They weren't driving at the regular speed. They were "rubbernecking." As a result, there was a big traffic jam.

B PRACTICE. Unscramble the sentences. Write the words in the correct order.

1. the car / stopping / at any red lights / not / was

   The car was not stopping at any red lights.

2. the child / wearing / not / was / a seat belt

   _____

3. was / the woman / speeding / on the highway

   _____

4. the drivers / were / paying attention / not

   _____

5. texting and / the teenager / driving / was

   _____

Grammar

C PRACTICE. Cross out the incorrect words.

They ~~was doing~~ / **were doing** construction on the highway, so we drove through the city. It took a long time because it **was raining** / **were raining** and traffic was heavy. It often floods on that highway, but we were lucky. It **didn't flooding** / **wasn't flooding** that day. Later, my car broke down on 14th Street. Fortunately, it **wasn't raining** / **not raining** when that happened. The sun **was shine** / **was shining**, and it **is getting** / **was getting** warm. I **was becoming** / **were becoming** impatient, but at last the tow truck arrived.

D APPLY. Use the past continuous form of the verbs in parentheses.

Dear Mayor Gordon:

I'm writing to share my concern about traffic accidents in our city. There aren't enough traffic lights downtown. This week, there was another accident on West Adams Street and North 19th Avenue.

I ____was sitting____ on a bench on 19th Avenue. I _____ for the Number 4 bus,
      (sit)   (wait)

and I saw the accident. A taxi _____ down 19th Avenue when a bus hit it. The
                                (drive)

bus driver didn't see the taxi coming. Fortunately, the drivers _____, and they
                                      (not / speed)

_____ their seat belts. No one was hurt, but we need a traffic light at that intersection.
     (wear)

Thank you for your attention,

Mary Ann Watson

Show what you know!

1. **MAKE CONNECTIONS.** Talk about an accident you were in, saw, or heard about.

2. **WRITE.** Report on an accident or a difficult situation you know about. Use the past continuous to talk about actions that were happening when the accident occurred.

> I was taking my kids to school last week. I was driving, and my kids were sitting in the back seat. I wasn't paying attention to my speed. We were listening to music and singing. Then we heard a police siren. I looked in my rearview mirror and saw a police car behind me. The officer said I was going 15 miles per hour over the speed limit. She didn't give me a ticket, but she gave me a warning.

I can use the past continuous. ■   I need more practice. ■

For more practice, go to MyEnglishLab.

Read about safety on the road

1 BEFORE YOU READ

DISCUSS. Where do you think most car accidents happen? When do you think they happen?

2 READ

▶ Listen and read.

> **Academic Skill: Interpret charts**
>
> Charts show important information in an article. They show this information in a visual format that is easy to see and understand.

Safety on the Road

Car accidents cause thousands of injuries and deaths every year. In the U.S., a car accident happens every few seconds. Where and when do all of these accidents happen? What can drivers do to stay safe on the road?

5 **Where Do Most Accidents Happen?**
Many people believe that most car accidents occur on major roads when drivers are far from their homes. Many serious, fatal accidents do happen in these places. But research shows that the majority of car accidents happen close to drivers' homes. In fact,
10 52 percent of collisions happen five minutes or less from home.

Why do drivers crash more often when they are close to home? Researchers think that people feel comfortable in their own neighborhoods. They are familiar
15 with the area, so they stop paying attention. They don't drive safely. They text while driving. They don't put on their seat belts. The result? More accidents.

20 Accidents also happen more often at certain types of locations. For example, they often occur at intersections, at stoplights, and on busy roads. Many accidents happen in parking lots. These are all places where cars come together.

When Do Most Accidents Happen?
25 The most dangerous time of day to drive is from 3 p.m. to 6 p.m. Many people are driving home from school or work at that time. They are tired. They make mistakes. Lots of accidents also occur on the weekend. That's when more people drive drunk and speed. Many more serious accidents happen on Saturdays than
30 on Tuesdays or Wednesdays.

How can drivers protect themselves from accidents? Knowing when and where accidents are likely to happen can help a lot. Drivers should stay focused. They should
35 drive extra safely in risky places and at risky times. That will help reduce the number of car accidents and keep
40 drivers safe on the road.

Where Most Accidents Happen

One mile or less from home	23%
2–5 miles from home	29%
6–10 miles from home	17%
11–15 miles from home	8%
16–20 miles from home	6%
More than 20 miles from home	17%

Source: Progressive .com

3 CLOSE READING

A IDENTIFY. What is the main idea of the article?

a. Drivers can prevent car accidents if they know when and where accidents often happen.
b. Research shows that most car accidents happen close to drivers' homes.
c. Many more serious accidents happen on Saturdays than on Tuesdays or Wednesdays.

Reading

B CITE EVIDENCE. Complete the sentences. Where is the information? Write the line numbers.

Lines

1. _____ percent of accidents happen five minutes or less from home.
   a. 23　　　　　　　**b.** 52　　　　　　　**c.** 17　　　　　_____

2. Drivers have more accidents when they are close to home because _____.
   a. they are often speeding
   b. they stop paying attention
   c. there are many intersections　　_____

3. Most accidents happen from _____.
   a. 3–6 p.m.　　　　　**b.** 9–11 a.m.　　　　　**c.** 9–11 p.m.　　　_____

4. Most serious car accidents happen on _____.
   a. Tuesdays　　　　　**b.** Wednesdays　　　　　**c.** Saturdays　　　_____

C INTERPRET GRAPHICS. Complete the sentences about the bar graph.

1. The bar graph shows _____.
   a. places where car accidents happen
   b. the distances from drivers' homes to places where car accidents happen
   c. the types of drivers who cause accidents

2. According to the graph, most accidents happen _____.
   a. one mile or less from home
   b. more than 20 miles from home
   c. 2–5 miles from home

3. Which statement from the article does the chart support?
   a. The most dangerous time of day to drive is from 3 p.m. to 6 p.m.
   b. Research shows that the majority of car accidents happen close to drivers' homes.
   c. In the U.S., a car accident happens every few seconds.

4 SUMMARIZE

What are the most important ideas in the article? Write three sentences in your notebook.

Show what you know!

1. **COLLABORATE.** Discuss what you know and have learned about car accidents. Does the information in the article about when and where accidents happen make sense? Why or why not?

2. **WRITE.** Describe where and when most car accidents happen.

   Most car accidents happen close to drivers' homes. They happen . . .

I can interpret charts while reading. ■　　　　　　　　　I need more practice. ■

To read more, go to MyEnglishLab.

Write about an accident

1 STUDY THE MODEL

ANALYZE. Read the model and Writing Skill. Then answer the questions.

Who Caused the Accident?

There was an accident on my street yesterday at 2 p.m. I was waiting to cross the street at a pedestrian crossing. A woman in a blue car stopped for me. Then an SUV crashed into the back of the car.

The SUV driver, a teenaged boy, thought the woman caused the accident. He said, "You stopped in the middle of the road for no reason!" But the woman thought the boy caused the accident. She said, "I stopped at a pedestrian crossing! Why didn't you stop, too? I think it's because you weren't paying attention!"

I think the woman was right. Cars should always stop at pedestrian crossings. The boy clearly wasn't paying attention. I think he was probably texting because he was holding a phone. I think the accident was the boy's fault.

Writing Skill: Present two different opinions when arguing

Argue for or against something by presenting two different opinions. Then clearly state which opinion is yours. Support your opinion with reasons.

1. What is the writer's opinion about the accident?
2. What is another opinion about the accident?

2 PLAN YOUR WRITING

A **BRAINSTORM. Ask and answer the questions.**

Think about an accident that happened at home, school, or work. Who caused the accident? Why do you think that person caused it?

B **OUTLINE. Include your opinion about an accident and an opposing view.**

Accident: _____
Opinion 1: _____
    Supporting Sentence: _____
Opinion 2: _____
    Supporting Sentence: _____
Your Opinion: _____
    Reason: _____

3 WRITE

EXPLAIN. Write about an accident and who caused it. Use the model, the Writing Skill, and your ideas from Exercise 2 to help you.

4 CHECK YOUR WRITING

COLLABORATE. Read the checklist. Read your writing together. Revise your writing.

WRITING CHECKLIST

☐ Does the paragraph describe an accident?

☐ Does the paragraph present two opinions about who caused the accident?

☐ Does the paragraph clearly state an opinion and include reasons?

I can present two different opinions when arguing. ■   I need more practice. ■

For more practice, go to MyEnglishLab.

Listening and Speaking

Identify steps to take after an accident

1 BEFORE YOU LISTEN

EXPLAIN. What should you do after an accident with another moving car?

2 LISTEN

This is a radio show about what to do after a car accident.

A ▶ **LISTEN FOR MAIN IDEA.** Write *T* (true) or *F* (false).

_____ **1.** You should stop after you have an accident with a moving car, parked car, or pedestrian.

_____ **2.** It is illegal to hit and run.

_____ **3.** If you hit something and don't stop, you can go to jail.

_____ **4.** If you hit something and don't stop, you can lose your license.

_____ **5.** If you hit a parked car and can't find the owner, you do not need to report the accident.

_____ **6.** You don't need to wait for the police to arrive.

_____ **7.** Your insurance company might need a copy of the police report.

B ▶ **LISTEN FOR DETAILS.** Circle the correct answers.

1. What should you do if you hit a parked car and cannot find the owner?
 a. nothing **b.** leave a note on the car

2. If someone is hurt in an accident, you should _____.
 a. move the person **b.** call 911 for an ambulance

3. After a car accident, you should get the other driver's name, address, driver's license number, license plate number, and _____.
 a. date of birth **b.** insurance information

4. When the police come, they will want to see proof of insurance and your _____.
 a. driver's license **b.** proof of citizenship

I can identify steps to take after an accident. ■   I need more practice. ■

For more practice, go to MyEnglishLab.

Grammar

Time clauses

Time Clause	Main Clause
Before you buy a car,	you should compare prices at different dealers.
When you have a car,	you need car insurance.
After you get an oil change,	your car gets better gas mileage.

Grammar Watch

- The main clause can come before the time clause.
- When the main clause comes first, do not use a comma (*You need car insurance when you have a car*).

A INVESTIGATE. Circle the main clause in each sentence. Underline the time clause.

1. <u>When you drive a car,</u> (you need a license, registration, and insurance).
2. Before you buy car insurance, you should compare different companies' rates.
3. People pay more for car insurance when they have a bad driving record.
4. Drivers break the law when they drive without car insurance.
5. When people drive without car insurance, they can get a fine, lose their license, or go to jail.

B PRACTICE. Unscramble the sentences. Remember to capitalize and add commas where necessary.

1. you should look for coupons online / to an auto repair shop / before you go

   Before you go to an auto repair shop, you should look for coupons online.

2. before you / make a list of all the problems / take your car to the garage

   _____

3. describe the problems to the mechanic / bring your car in / when you

   _____

4. a mechanic works on your car / before / you should ask how much it will cost

   _____

5. after / you should take it for a test drive / the mechanic works on your car

   _____

Grammar

C **PRACTICE.** Rewrite the sentences. Switch the order of the clauses. Add a comma when the time clause comes first.

1. When you go to Tom's Automotive, you get great service.

   You get great service when you go to Tom's Automotive.

2. Tom gives you a written estimate before he works on your car.

   _____

3. Tom always shows you exactly what is wrong when he finds problems.

   _____

4. After he replaces a car part, Tom returns the old part.

   _____

D **APPLY.** Combine the sentences into one sentence. Use the words in parentheses.

1. You fill up your car with gas. Don't fill it to the top. (when)

   When you fill up your car with gas, don't fill it to the top.

2. You save gas. You get regular tune-ups. (when)

   _____

3. You buy gas. Check for good deals online. (before)

   _____

4. You get gas. Look for the gas station with the lowest price. (before)

   _____

5. You leave the gas station. Check your tire pressure. (before)

   _____

Show what you know!

1. **MAKE CONNECTIONS.** How do you save money on gas and car maintenance?

2. **WRITE.** Give advice to a friend about buying and maintaining a car. Use time clauses.

   When you buy a car, be sure to compare prices at different dealers. When you choose a dealer, look online for special deals or promotions. After you buy your car, you need to get insurance. Have the information about the car ready before you call the insurance company.

I can use time clauses. ☐   I need more practice. ☐

For more practice, go to MyEnglishLab.

Be flexible

1 MEET KOKI

Read about one of his workplace skills.

> I am flexible. I believe change is an opportunity to learn. For example, I enjoy learning new things and having new experiences.

2 KOKI'S PROBLEM

A READ. Write *T* (true) or *F* (false).

Koki is a nurse in a small hospital. He normally works during the day. One of the other nurses just broke her leg and won't be at work for two months. As a result, everyone's schedule changed. All of the nurses have to work more. Several people are unhappy with the changes.

Koki has to work on a different floor of the hospital, and he has been given two night shifts. The head nurse wants to meet with Koki to go over his new schedule.

_____ **1.** Koki has been in a serious accident.
_____ **2.** Every nurse's schedule had to change.
_____ **3.** Koki normally does not work the night shift.

B ANALYZE. What is Koki's problem? Write your response in your notebook.

3 KOKI'S SOLUTION

A COLLABORATE. Koki is flexible. He adapts to changes easily. What should he do? Explain your answer.

1. Koki says, "I'll help however I can, but I can't work the night shift. I don't work well at night."
2. Koki says, "Can I switch with another nurse? I don't think I'll work well with the new schedule."
3. Koki says, "This is a big change with new responsibilities. I'm excited for the challenge!"
4. Koki _____.

B ROLE-PLAY. Act out Koki's solution with your partner.

Show what you know!

1. **REFLECT.** When have you been flexible at work? Give an example.

2. **WRITE.** Now write your example in your Skills Log.

   I am flexible. When something comes up, I can adapt to the situation. For example, I had to train a new employee last week. I wasn't expecting it, but it was a fun challenge.

3. **PRESENT.** Give a short presentation to show how you are flexible.

I can give an example of how I am flexible at work. ■

Unit Review: Go back to page 125. Which unit goals can you check off?

8 Staying Healthy

PREVIEW

What foods do you eat every day?
What did you eat in your native country?
Do you have healthy eating habits?

UNIT GOALS

- [ ] Identify different eating habits
- [ ] Identify healthy eating habits
- [ ] Read nutritional labels
- [ ] Talk about diets and food allergies
- [ ] Talk about family health

- [ ] Talk about dental health
- [ ] **Academic skill:** Understand facts and opinions
- [ ] **Writing skill:** Support an opinion with facts
- [ ] **Workplace soft skill:** Take initiative

Vocabulary

Eating habits

A **PREDICT.** Look at the pictures and phrases. They describe eating and shopping habits. Which words do you know?

B ▶ **LISTEN AND POINT.** Then listen and repeat.

1 have a snack

2 cook homemade meals

3 buy frozen dinners

4 drink sugary beverages

5 eat fast food

6 buy fresh fruits and vegetables

7 be on a diet

8 buy junk food

9 eat fatty foods

10 get takeout

Vocabulary

C **IDENTIFY.** Look at the phrases on page 146. Are the habits healthy or unhealthy? Can they be both? Write them in the diagram.

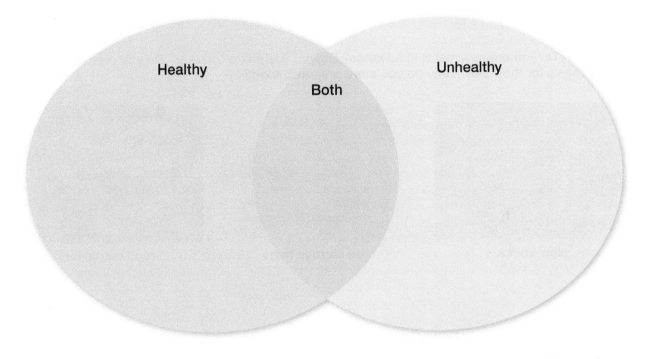

Healthy   Both   Unhealthy

Study Tip

Make Connections

Make cards for five phrases. Write each phrase on the front of a card. Write three examples of the phrase on the back.

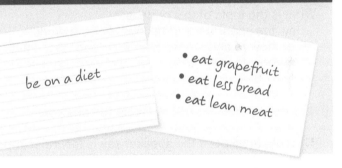

be on a diet

- eat grapefruit
- eat less bread
- eat lean meat

Show what you know!

1. **COLLABORATE.** Compare your answers from Exercise C. If a habit can be both healthy and unhealthy, give examples.

2. **WRITE.** Make a list of healthy eating habits.

   1. Eat fresh fruits and vegetables every day.
   2. Avoid fatty foods.
   3. Drink plenty of water.

I can identify different eating habits. ☐   I need more practice. ☐

For more practice, go to MyEnglishLab.

1 BEFORE YOU LISTEN

DISCUSS. Do you prepare meals in advance? Do you use a slow cooker? Do you prepare and freeze meals for the week? How do you store prepared food?

slow cooker

food storage bags

food containers

2 LISTEN

This is a podcast about having a healthy lifestyle.

A ▶ **LISTEN FOR MAIN IDEA.** Circle the answer.

What is the topic of this podcast?
- **a.** the importance of taking breaks at work
- **b.** how to choose the best fast-food restaurants
- **c.** how to stay healthy with a busy schedule

B ▶ **LISTEN FOR DETAILS.** Circle the answers.

1. What meal does the speaker say is the most important?
   a. breakfast   **b.** lunch   **c.** dinner

2. What is the problem with food from vending machines?
   a. It's too expensive.   **b.** It's often unhealthy.   **c.** It's easy.

3. What is one way to prepare food in advance?
   a. Use a slow cooker.   **b.** Use a vending machine.   **c.** Buy food from restaurants.

4. What should you order instead of fries?
   a. onion rings   **b.** chips   **c.** soup or salad

5. What is a good way to stay hydrated at work?
   a. Take coffee breaks.   **b.** Take a water bottle.   **c.** Drink caffeinated beverages.

Listening and Speaking

3 PRONUNCIATION

A ▶ **PRACTICE. Listen. Then listen and repeat.**

1. It's one of the best things you can do.
2. Breakfast is one of the most important meals of the day.
3. Those are some of the most common items on the menu.
4. This is one of the easiest ways to prepare food.
5. Some of the healthiest choices include vegetables.

B ▶ **APPLY. Listen. Mark (•) the stressed word.**

1. This is one of the best dishes I've ever had

2. She's one of the youngest new chefs in the city.

3. Peppers are some of the spiciest foods in the world.

4. Deb's Diner is in one of the oldest buildings in town.

5. Some of the hardest dishes to cook have more than 20 ingredients!

> **Stress with Superlatives**
>
> The words *one of the* and *some of the* are pronounced quickly, and the vowels have a weak pronunciation. The superlative that follows is stressed.

4 CONVERSATION

A ▶ **LISTEN AND READ. Then practice the conversation with a partner.**

A: How was your weekend? Did you have time to relax?

B: I had a nice weekend, but it wasn't relaxing. Saturday is one of the busiest days of the week for me. My kids have sports and music lessons, and I usually cook all day.

A: Why do you cook so much on Saturday?

B: I prepare all of our food for the week in advance.

A: Really? I prepare my food in advance, too, but I use a slow cooker each morning.

B: I don't have time to prepare food in the morning, and I don't know much about slow cookers. What do you make?

A: Some of the easiest dishes are soups and stews. I'll give you some of my best recipes.

B: I would like that. Thanks!

B **MAKE CONNECTIONS. Do you usually eat out or make homemade food for dinner? Do you prepare food each night or make food in advance?**

A: I'm not very good at cooking, so I usually grab some takeout. There's a good Chinese place right across the street from my apartment.
B: I always cook dinner. I like to cook.
C: I don't have time to cook every night, so I prepare food in advance on Saturday or Sunday.

I can identify healthy eating habits. ■	I need more practice. ■

For more practice, go to MyEnglishLab.

Grammar

Superlatives

Superlatives

It is	the	**cheapest**	item	on the menu.
	the most	**expensive**		
	the least	**healthy**		
	one of the	**best**	items	

Grammar Watch

- *Good, bad,* and *far* have irregular forms of the superlative: *good–best, bad–worst, far–farthest.*
- We often use *one / some of the* with a superlative: *It is one of the healthiest options.*
- For adjectives that end in *-y*, change the *y* to *i* and add *est*: *healthy–healthiest.*
- For more spelling rules with the superlative, see page 262.

A INVESTIGATE. Underline *one / some of the* plus the superlative form of the adjective that follows.

Fiber is <u>one of the most important</u> parts of a healthy diet. Fiber can help prevent weight gain, heart disease, diabetes, and other health problems. Many people don't get enough fiber. Some of the best sources of fiber include whole grains. Eating whole-wheat bread and pasta will add a lot of fiber to your diet. Beans are also one of the most common fiber sources. One of the easiest ways to consume fiber is by eating whole fruits and vegetables. But don't peel your apples and potatoes! One of the best ways to get fiber from fruits and vegetables is to eat the skin, if possible.

high fiber foods

B PRACTICE. Write the superlative form of the word in italics.

1. I'm looking for a *large* grocery store. What is the _____*largest*_____ grocery store in the city?
2. Main Street Café offers *healthy* menu options. It is the _____ restaurant in my neighborhood.
3. That seafood dish is very *expensive*. It is the _____ item on the menu.
4. Oranges are a *good* source of vitamin C. In fact, they are one of the _____ sources of vitamin C.
5. I need an *easy* recipe for dinner tonight. Please give me your _____ recipe.

Grammar

C APPLY. Complete the conversation with the words in parentheses. Use the superlative form.

A: I've made some bad mistakes, but eating fast food every day was _____*one of the worst*_____
(one of / bad)

mistakes I've ever made.

B: Why don't you change your diet? That is _____ way to lose weight.
(good)

A: I'm trying, but it's _____ things for me to do right now.
(one of / difficult)

B: Why is it so difficult?

A: I always eat fast food. It's the _____ and _____
(cheap)   (easy)

option because I'm not good at cooking.

B: I can teach you how to cook. I'll show you _____ recipes I know.
(some of / simple and healthy)

A: That's great, but can you also show me _____ recipes you know?
(some of / delicious)

Show what you know!

1. **COLLABORATE. Make questions with the following words and the superlative form. Then interview a classmate.**

   What / bad dish / you have ever tried
   Where / good restaurant to eat / around here
   What / one of / easy recipe / you know
   What / some of / healthy foods / you like

   A: *What is the worst dish you have ever tried?*
   B: *For me, the worst dish was alligator soup. I really didn't like it.*
   A: *Really? I think it's one of the most delicious dishes I've ever tried.*

2. **WRITE. Draft a short summary of your partner's responses.**

   The worst dish Omar ever tried was . . .

| I can use superlatives. ■ | I need more practice. ■ |

Lesson 4

Read nutritional labels and talk about diets and food allergies

1 READ NUTRITIONAL LABELS

A DISCUSS. When you buy food, do you look at the nutritional labels?

B LOCATE. Find the following words in each nutritional label and circle them.

calories	fat	servings	sodium

Fiesta Chips

Nutrition Facts
3 servings per container
Serving size: 1 oz. (28g/about 32 chips)

Amount per serving
Calories   160

	% Daily Value*
Total Fat 10g	**16%**
Saturated Fat 1.5g	**7%**
Trans Fat 0g	**0%**
Cholesterol 0g	**0%**
Sodium 170 mg	**7%**
Total Carbohydrate 15g	**5%**
Dietary Fiber 1g	**4%**
Total Sugars 3g	
Includes 2g added sugars	**8%**
Protein 3g	
Vitamin D 2mcg	2%
Calcium 100mg	3%
Iron 0mg	0%
Potassium 120mg	4%

*The % Daily Value (DV) tells you how much a nutrient in a serving of food contributes to a daily diet. 2,000 calories a day is used for general nutrition advice.

Ingredients: Corn, corn oil, and salt. No preservatives. May contain traces of peanuts.

Cara Chips

Nutrition Facts
4 servings per container
Serving size: 1 oz. (28g/about 32 chips)

Amount per serving
Calories   130

	% Daily Value*
Total Fat 5g	**8%**
Saturated Fat 1g	**2%**
Trans Fat 0g	**0%**
Cholesterol 0g	**0%**
Sodium 150 mg	**6%**
Total Carbohydrate 18g	**6%**
Dietary Fiber 1g	**4%**
Total Sugars 0g	
Includes 0g added sugars	**0%**
Protein 2g	
Vitamin D 4mcg	3%
Calcium 120mg	4%
Iron 0mg	0%
Potassium 80mg	3%

*The % Daily Value (DV) tells you how much a nutrient in a serving of food contributes to a daily diet. 2,000 calories a day is used for general nutrition advice.

Ingredients: Corn meal, rice, rice and/or sunflower oil, aged cheddar cheese (nonfat milk, salt, cheese cultures, enzymes), whey, and lowfat buttermilk. Contains dairy ingredients.

C INTERPRET. Complete the sentences. Use the nutritional labels above.

1. There are _____ servings in Fiesta Chips and _____ servings in Cara Chips.

2. There are 520 calories in a whole bag of _____ Chips.

3. Fiesta Chips have _____ calories per serving. Cara Chips have _____ calories.

4. Fiesta Chips have _____ more calories than Cara Chips per serving.

5. _____ Chips contain more fat than _____ Chips.

6. _____ Chips contain more sodium than _____ Chips.

Workplace, Life, and Community Skills

2 TALK ABOUT DIETS

A **EVALUATE.** Read the situations. Which snacks from page 152 can each person eat?

Situation	Fiesta Chips	Cara Chips	Neither
1. Marta needs to reduce the amount of fat in her diet.			
2. Calvin has high blood pressure. He's on a salt-restricted diet.			
3. Eric has type 2 diabetes. He should not have any sugar.			
4. Tara is allergic to milk.			
5. Maya is allergic to peanuts.			

B **APPLY.** Which snack is healthier for you? Explain why.

3 TALK ABOUT FOOD ALLERGIES

A ▶ **LISTEN FOR MAIN IDEA.** What do new employees at Karla's Café need to learn about?

B ▶ **LISTEN FOR DETAILS.** Listen again. Read the sentences. Write *T* (true) or *F* (false).

_____ **1.** About 15 million Americans have food allergies.

_____ **2.** Only children have food allergies.

_____ **3.** Some common food allergies are to milk, peanuts, and chicken.

_____ **4.** It's important to understand what a guest says about allergies.

_____ **5.** The manager needs to know when guests have food allergies.

_____ **6.** The kitchen staff has a list of the ingredients in every dish.

C GO ONLINE. Find the nutritional information for two foods you like to eat. Compare the ingredients.

I can read nutritional labels and talk about diets and food allergies. ■   I need more practice. ■

For more practice, go to MyEnglishLab.

Lesson 5

Talk about family health

1 BEFORE YOU LISTEN

DISCUSS. What can parents do to help their children have a healthy lifestyle?

2 LISTEN

This is a podcast about family health.

A ▶ LISTEN FOR MAIN IDEA. Circle the answer.

What is the speaker's purpose?
   a. He is explaining why being overweight can cause health problems.
   b. He is offering advice for parents to help prevent children from becoming overweight.
   c. He is comparing the eating habits of children and adults.

B ▶ LISTEN FOR DETAILS. Circle the answers.

1. How many American children in the study were overweight?
   a. about 17 percent
   b. about 19 percent
   c. about 10 percent

2. What problems can being overweight cause?
   a. heart problems
   b. type 2 diabetes
   c. both a and b

3. Why are so many children overweight?
   a. family health history
   b. fast food and takeout
   c. bad eating habits and lack of exercise

C ▶ EXPAND. Listen. Write _T_ (true) or _F_ (false).

_____ **1.** You should give children whole grains like wheat bread.

_____ **2.** Children should eat high-fat dairy products.

_____ **3.** Children need 60 minutes of activity once a week.

_____ **4.** Parents' eating habits and physical activity are important for children to have a healthy lifestyle.

3 CONVERSATION

A ▶ **LISTEN AND READ. Then practice the conversation with a partner.**

A: The doctor said that my son needs to lose weight. What can I do to help him? He doesn't like dieting.

B: Well, you can change the way you cook.

A: What do you mean?

B: You can use low-fat ingredients. For example, get low-fat milk instead of whole milk. It has less fat and still tastes good.

B **ROLE-PLAY. Make similar conversations.**

A: Someone in your family needs to go on a diet.

B: Talk about healthy substitutes. Use the ideas below or your own ideas.

lard: white fat from pigs that is used in cooking

C **MAKE CONNECTIONS. In small groups, make a list of other foods or ingredients you think are not healthy. Make a list of healthy substitutes. Then compare ideas with a different group.**

I can talk about family health. ■ I need more practice. ■

For more practice, go to MyEnglishLab.

Grammar

Lesson 6

Verb + gerund as object

Subject	Verb	Gerund	
He	**enjoys**	**buying**	snacks from vending machines.
They	**like**	**eating**	lunch from a food truck.

Grammar Watch

These verbs can also be followed by a gerund: *can't stand, consider, dislike, don't mind, keep, practice, think about,* and *try.*

A **INVESTIGATE.** Underline the examples of verb + gerund in the paragraph.

Lu Yi is 65 years old and lives in Cleveland, Ohio. Her doctor told her to exercise. Lu Yi doesn't <u>like exercising</u> too much, but she doesn't mind doing tai chi. She used to do it outdoors in China. The problem is Cleveland is too cold in the winter to do tai chi outside. Lu Yi can't stand being out in the cold very long. Then she learned that the senior center near her home has a free indoor tai chi class. She goes twice a week and enjoys exercising all winter.

tai chi, **a martial art**

B **PRACTICE.** Complete the sentences with the gerund form of the verbs in the box.

buy	cook	dance	exercise
~~practice~~	prepare	watch	

1. For exercise, try ____practicing____ martial arts or _____.
2. You should try _____ dishes with whole grains.
3. At the supermarket, avoid _____ white bread and potato chips.
4. When you cook, think about _____ more fish and lean meat.
5. Spend time _____ outside with your children.
6. Stop _____ TV and do other activities instead.

Grammar

C **COMPLETE. Use the correct form of verbs in parentheses.**

1. **A:** My children just want to sit around and watch TV.

   B: ___Try taking___ them to the park on weekends. They'll probably _____
   (try / take)   (start / run)

   around and forget about TV.

2. **A:** My doctor told me to exercise, but I don't have time or extra money.

   B: There are ways to exercise that don't take too much time and are free. _____
   (try / walk)

   around the mall.

3. **A:** My son _____ vegetables.
   (can't stand / eat)

   B: Give him raw carrots and peppers. Many children _____ them.
   (don't mind / eat)

4. **A:** We eat a lot of canned soup.

   B: We eat a lot of soup, too, but I _____ my own soup. It has a lot less salt.
   (prefer / make)

5. **A:** How can I get my family to eat more fruit?

   B: _____ smoothies. Most children _____ them. You just mix
   (try / make)   (love / drink)

   together fruit, yogurt, juice, and ice in a blender.

Show what you know!

1. **COLLABORATE. How can different habits make a family's lifestyle healthy or unhealthy? Discuss the topics below. Make suggestions for a healthy lifestyle.**

   food choices   physical activity
   meal portion size   TV/computer habits

   A: My children love eating junk food. I can't get them to stop.
   B: Stop buying potato chips. Try making snacks like low-fat dip and carrots.

2. **WRITE. Describe some healthy changes you can make in your life. Use verb + gerund as object.**

   My family loves eating fried chicken, but I'm going to try baking it instead.

I can use verbs with gerunds as objects. ■   I need more practice. ■

For more practice, go to MyEnglishLab.

Read about school lunches

1 BEFORE YOU READ

DISCUSS. Look at the pictures of school lunches in the article below. Which lunch do you think looks better? Why?

2 READ

▶ Listen and read.

> **Academic Skill: Understand facts and opinions**
>
> When you read, look carefully at the information. Is it a fact (something you can prove) or an opinion (a person's idea or belief)? Identifying facts and opinions when you read helps you make better judgments about what you are reading.

SCHOOL LUNCHES

A hungry child can't learn well. That's why schools don't want their students to be hungry. Everyone agrees that schools should feed children. But what kinds of food should children eat at school? Over the years, that question has been answered in different ways.

5 In 1946, the U.S. government started the National School Lunch Program. It served free or low-cost lunches. Every school day, it fed more than 30 million children. The lunches were usually hot cooked meals. Some experts worried that the lunches were not nutritious. Schools often served foods such as pizza, French fries, and hamburgers. These foods are high in fat, sugar, salt, carbohydrates, and cholesterol. They can make children gain too much weight. Overweight children have a bigger risk for health problems.

10 In 2010, the government passed the Healthy Hunger-Free Kids Act. This act tried to make school lunches healthier. It made new rules for fat and sugar levels. Because of this act, many schools stopped serving pizza, French fries, and hamburgers. Instead, they began to serve more nutritious meals with fruits and vegetables. Many teachers, parents, and children welcomed these healthy new meals. Others complained. They said that the new rules were
15 too strict. Students didn't want to eat the meals. Some officials also objected that the healthy meals cost too much.

It seems obvious that schools should serve nutritious, cheap meals. Kids should also actually want to eat these meals. Nowadays, some schools are finding their own ways to achieve these goals. Many schools have introduced salad bars. They also have "make your own meal"
20 stations. These innovations are popular. They make cafeterias feel more like restaurants. They give students more choice. Some schools also have organic gardens. They grow fruits and vegetables for the school lunches. Students and their families help take care of the gardens. More and more schools are serving meals that are healthy, affordable, and delicious.

3 CLOSE READING

A IDENTIFY. What is the main idea of the article?

a. The National School Lunch Program serves free or low-cost lunches to more than 30 million children each school day.
b. The Healthy Hunger-Free Kids Act made new rules for fat and sugar levels in foods and beverages.
c. Schools should serve meals that are healthy, affordable, and delicious, and many schools are trying to do this.

Reading

B **CITE EVIDENCE. Are these statements facts or opinions? Circle the answer. Then write the line number that supports your response.**

Lines

1. In 1946, the U.S. government started a National School Lunch Program.
   a. Fact   **b.** Opinion   _____

2. In the past, National School Lunch Program meals were not nutritious.
   a. Fact   **b.** Opinion   _____

3. Pizza, French fries, and hamburgers are high in fat, sugar, and salt.
   a. Fact   **b.** Opinion   _____

4. It seems obvious that schools should serve healthy meals kids want to eat.
   a. Fact   **b.** Opinion   _____

5. Many schools have introduced salad bars as a lunch option.
   a. Fact   **b.** Opinion   _____

C **INTERPRET VOCABULARY. Answer the questions.**

1. The word *nutritious* in line 6 means _____.
   a. healthy   **b.** unhealthy   **c.** delicious

2. When people *complain* (line 14) about something, they _____.
   a. are happy about it   **b.** are unhappy about it   **c.** explain what it means

3. When people *object* (line 15) to something, they _____.
   a. ask questions about it   **b.** say they agree with it   **c.** say they disagree with it

4. The word *innovations* in line 20 means _____.
   a. old ways of doing   **b.** new ways of doing   **c.** easy ways of doing
   something   something   something

5. The word *affordable* in line 23 means _____.
   a. cheap   **b.** expensive   **c.** delicious

4 SUMMARIZE

What are the most important ideas in the article? Write three sentences in your notebook.

Show what you know!

1. **RECALL.** What kinds of school lunches have you eaten? How were your lunches similar to or different from the lunches described in the article? Did you like them?

2. **WRITE.** Describe school lunches and the kinds of food children are eating at school now.

   Children are eating nutritious foods at school nowadays. They are eating . . .

I can understand facts and opinions while reading. ■   I need more practice. ■

To read more, go to MyEnglishLab.

1 ▸ BEFORE YOU LISTEN

MATCH. Look at the pictures. Write the correct letters.

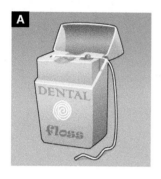
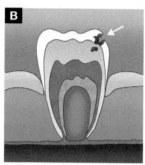
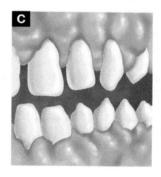

_____ **1.** cavity

_____ **2.** X-ray

_____ **3.** floss

_____ **4.** gum disease

2 LISTEN

David is at the dentist's office. He just got a cleaning.

(A) ▸ **LISTEN FOR MAIN IDEA.** Circle the answer.

What are David and the dentist talking about?
   a. checkups
   b. flossing and brushing
   c. X-rays

(B) ▸ **LISTEN FOR DETAILS.** Write _T_ (true) or _F_ (false).

_____ **1.** David flosses often.

_____ **2.** David does not brush his teeth often.

_____ **3.** The dentist says flossing is more important than brushing.

_____ **4.** If you don't floss enough, you can get cavities or gum disease.

_____ **5.** The dentist says a soft toothbrush is better for teeth than a hard toothbrush.

_____ **6.** David will probably brush and floss more carefully in the future.

David

Listening and Speaking

3 PRONUNCIATION

A ▶ **PRACTICE. Listen. Then listen and repeat.**

Do you floss every day?

Is it important?

How often do you floss?

What is a cavity?

Tone in Questions

- In a *yes / no* question, your voice goes up at the end.
- In *wh-* questions, your voice goes up on the most important word and then falls at the end of the sentence.

B ▶ **APPLY. Listen. Does the voice go up or down at the end? Draw arrows, ↗ or ↘, over the last word.**

1. How often do I need to get a checkup?

2. How long should I brush my teeth?

3. What is fluoride?

4. Is it important to use fluoride?

4 CONVERSATION

A ▶ **LISTEN AND READ. Then practice the conversation with a partner.**

A: You probably need to floss more. Do you floss?

B: Well, not that much.

A: Try flossing more. Flossing keeps your gums healthy.

B: Isn't brushing my teeth enough?

A: Brushing after every meal is important, too. But you can't always get your teeth clean unless you floss.

B **ROLE-PLAY. Pretend you are at a dentist's office.**

A: You are the dental assistant. Ask the patient if he or she brushes and flosses every day.

B: You are the patient. Ask the dental assistant for more information about dental hygiene.

I can talk about dental health. ☐   I need more practice. ☐

For more practice, go to MyEnglishLab.

Grammar

Gerunds as subjects

Gerunds as subjects		
Going to the dentist regularly	is	important for good dental health.
Brushing and **flossing** your teeth	are	

Grammar Watch

- Use a singular verb with one gerund. (*Brushing is important.*)
- Use a plural verb with two or more gerunds. (*Brushing and flossing are important.*)

A INVESTIGATE. Read about dental care for children. Underline the gerunds.

<u>Starting</u> dental care at a very early age is necessary in order for children to have healthy teeth. Wiping babies' gums with a soft, damp cloth will help keep their mouths clean. Make sure not to leave a baby with a bottle in the crib, since this can damage teeth. Later, when children are preschool age, help them brush their teeth. Showing them how to brush their teeth is important. Brush each tooth in circles, one at a time. Giving your children more milk and serving them less juice will also keep their teeth strong.

B APPLY. Rewrite each sentence. Start with a gerund.

1. It's bad for your teeth to eat candy and drink soda.
   Eating candy and drinking soda is bad for your teeth.

2. It's important to brush your teeth after meals.
   _____

3. It's hard to get some kids to brush and floss.
   _____

4. It's a good idea to get a cleaning twice a year.
   _____

5. It's important to use toothpaste with fluoride.
   _____

Show what you know!

1. **COLLABORATE.** Talk about how you keep your teeth healthy. What things should you do? What things should you not do?

2. **WRITE.** Make a list of rules for good dental health. Use gerunds as subjects.
   Getting regular dental checkups is necessary.
   Using a soft toothbrush is good for your teeth.

I can use gerunds as subjects. ☐   I need more practice. ☐

For more practice, go to MyEnglishLab.

Writing

Write about a food

1 STUDY THE MODEL

ANALYZE. Read the model and Writing Skill. Then answer the questions.

Chocolate Chip Cookies

Chocolate chip cookies taste good, but they aren't good for you. You can see this when you read the nutritional label for a package of chocolate chip cookies. One cookie is 90 calories. It contains 5 grams of fat and 6 grams of sugar. People shouldn't eat a lot of fat and sugar because they are not nutritious, and they can make you gain weight. That's why chocolate chip cookies are not a healthy choice.

Writing Skill: Support an opinion with facts

When you state an opinion, support your opinion with facts. Do research to find facts that support your opinion.

1. What is the writer's opinion?
2. Which facts support the writer's opinion?

2 PLAN YOUR WRITING

A **BRAINSTORM. Ask and answer the questions. Look at a nutritional label for research.**

What is one food you like to eat? Is it healthy? Why or why not?

B **OUTLINE. Use facts from a nutritional label.**

Food: _____

    Fact 1: _____

    Fact 2: _____

    Fact 3: _____

    Fact 4: _____

3 WRITE

DESCRIBE. Write about a food. Use the model, the Writing Skill, and your ideas from Exercise 2 to help you.

4 CHECK YOUR WRITING

COLLABORATE. Read the checklist. Read your writing together. Revise your writing.

WRITING CHECKLIST

☐ Does the paragraph give an opinion about a food?

☐ Does the paragraph support the opinion with facts?

I can support an opinion with facts. ■   I need more practice. ■

For more practice, go to MyEnglishLab.

11 Soft Skills at Work

Take initiative

1 MEET REGINA

Read about one of her workplace skills.

> I take initiative. When I see a way to make something better, I do it. For example, I keep my workplace neat and clean every day. I don't wait for my manager to say something.

2 REGINA'S PROBLEM

A **READ.** Write *T* (true) or *F* (false).

Regina works at Myersville High School. Students, teachers, and employees all eat in the cafeteria. Regina serves food, and she gets along well with her customers. She has been an employee at the school for three years. Regina is friendly and knows everyone's name. She even knows their favorite foods.

Recently, people have started complaining about the food selections. They want more healthy options. For example, they are asking for more grilled meat and vegetables. Regina wants her customers to be happy.

_____ 1. Regina has a good relationship with her customers.

_____ 2. The cafeteria has many healthy food options.

_____ 3. Regina doesn't care about her customers' complaints.

B **ANALYZE.** What is Regina's problem? Write your response in your notebook.

3 REGINA'S SOLUTION

A **COLLABORATE.** Regina takes initiative. She does things without being told. What should she do? Explain your answer.

1. Regina apologizes and tells people the salad bar is a healthy option.
2. Regina tells people to go online and give feedback on the cafeteria website.
3. Regina makes a list of foods customers want to eat, and she gives the list to her supervisor.
4. Regina _____.

B **ROLE-PLAY.** Act out Regina's solution with your partner.

Show what you know!

1. **REFLECT.** When have you taken initiative at work? Give an example.

2. **WRITE.** Now write your example in your Skills Log.

   I take initiative. I do things without being told. For example, I check the paper in the copy machine every morning to make sure we have enough.

3. **PRESENT.** Give a short presentation to show how you take initiative.

I can give an example of how I take initiative at work. ◼

Unit Review: Go back to page 145. Which unit goals can you check off?

9 Doing Your Job

PREVIEW

What skills are important for most jobs in the U.S.?

UNIT GOALS

- [ ] Identify important job skills
- [ ] Ask for clarification
- [ ] Identify expectations on the job
- [ ] Identify safety hazards at work
- [ ] Respond appropriately to correction
- [ ] **Academic skill:** Skim
- [ ] **Writing skill:** Define new words and acronyms
- [ ] **Workplace soft skill:** Listen actively

A **PREDICT.** Look at the pictures and the phrases that describe important job skills. Which phrases do you know?

B ▶ **LISTEN AND POINT.** Then listen and repeat.

be part of a team

be responsible for something

deal with complaints

follow instructions

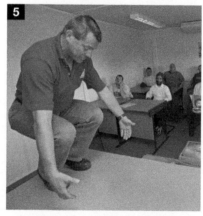

attend a training session

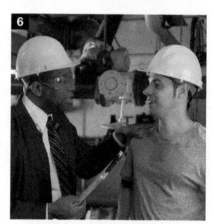

give someone feedback

discuss a problem

train other employees

give instructions

Vocabulary

C **MAKE CONNECTIONS.** Think about yourself. How good are your skills in these areas? Write *1* for excellent, *2* for good, or *3* for needs work.

Job skills

_____ be part of a team	_____ be responsible for something	_____ deal with complaints
_____ follow instructions	_____ attend a training session	_____ give someone feedback
_____ discuss a problem	_____ train other employees	_____ give instructions

Study Tip

Give Examples

Make five cards for job skills. Write the job skill on the front of the card. Write a job that uses that skill on the back.

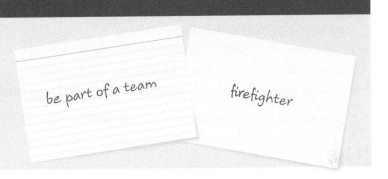

be part of a team

firefighter

Show what you know!

1. **COLLABORATE.** Talk about your best job skills. Give examples.

   I work part-time at Blooms. I think I'm good at dealing with customers, even when they complain. I know how to talk to them.

2. **WRITE.** What are your biggest problems on the job? Which job skills do you need to improve? How can you improve those skills?

   A problem I have at work is . . .

I can identify important job skills. ☐   I need more practice. ☐

For more practice, go to MyEnglishLab.

Listening and Speaking

Ask for clarification

1 BEFORE YOU LISTEN

A **IDENTIFY.** Look at the words and definitions. Do you know any of these words?

inventory: a list of all the things in a place

quantity: how much you have of something

supplies: something you use for daily life or work, such as paper, tape, or boxes

vendor: a person who sells something

B **MAKE CONNECTIONS.** What can you do if you have trouble understanding an employer's instructions?

2 LISTEN

Margo is training her assistant, Jason, to order supplies for the office kitchen.

A ▶ **LISTEN FOR MAIN IDEA.** Does Jason understand Margo's instructions?

B ▶ **LISTEN FOR DETAILS.** Write *T* (true) or *F* (false).

_____ **1.** Jason needs to do inventory before he orders supplies.

_____ **2.** Doing inventory means throwing out old supplies.

_____ **3.** Jason needs to use an inventory sheet to order supplies.

_____ **4.** Jason needs to email the inventory sheet.

_____ **5.** Jason needs to call the vendor and talk about the order.

_____ **6.** Jason does not need to check the quantity in a box.

Listening and Speaking

3 PRONUNCIATION

Stress for Clarification

We use stress to clarify which thing(s) we are talking about.

A ▶ PRACTICE. Listen. Then listen and repeat.

A: Please lift this **box**.

B: **Which** box? **This** one?

A: No, **that** one. The **green** one.

B ▶ APPLY. Listen. Mark (•) the stressed words.

1. Please bring me that folder.

2. Which folder? The blue one or the red one?

3. No, not those folders. The black one.

4. The one by the phone?

5. No, not that black folder. The one on my desk.

4 CONVERSATION

A ▶ LISTEN AND READ. Then practice the conversation with a partner.

A: OK, you need to be sure there are enough supplies in the kitchen. First, you do inventory. Start with the things on the counter. See if there are enough paper cups and paper towels. If something is missing, check in the cabinets and drawers.

B: OK.

A: If we don't have enough, you need to order more.

B: How do I do that?

A: You fill out an inventory sheet. Write down what you need under *item.* Then write the quantity or amount.

B: Which box shows quantity?

A: This one.

B: OK. Then what do I do?

B ROLE-PLAY. Make up a conversation.

A: You are a new school bus driver. Ask what you should do if there isn't a parent at the bus stop when you drop off a child.

B: You are the supervisor. Tell what steps to take:
- Never let a child off the bus alone without the written permission of a parent.
- If you don't have permission, don't drop off the child. Call the school and transportation office, and then drop off the other children.
- If the child's parent is still not at the bus stop, take the child back to school.

I can ask for clarification. ■   I need more practice. ■

For more practice, go to MyEnglishLab.

One / ones

A: Please lift this box.
B: Which **one**? This **one**?
A: No, that **one**. The green **one**.

A: Please help me move these boxes.
B: Which **ones**? These?
A: No, those. The big **ones**.

A INVESTIGATE. Underline *ones*, *this one*, *those*, and *which one*.

A: Hi, may I help you?

B: I'm looking for a T-Moby phone. Which one do you recommend?

A: They're all good, but this one has a lot more features.

B: Are the silver ones on sale?

A: No, those aren't. But the black ones are.

B: I'll take this one then.

B CHOOSE. Cross out the incorrect words.

A: Could you please take those tablets out of the boxes?

B: Which ~~one~~ / **ones**?

A: The 10-inch **one / ones**. We need to display them.

B: OK. Where should I put them?

A: Put them up front near the cash register.

B: Sure. Oh, wait, Tony. This **one / ones** is scratched.

A: Which **one / ones**? Show me. Oh, you're right. OK. Put it back in the box. We'll send it back. But put the other **one / ones** out. And put up the sale sign.

B: Which **one / ones** are on sale?

A: The Simsung tablets. The Galactic **one / ones** aren't on sale this week.

Grammar

C **PRACTICE. Cross out the underlined words and write *one* or *ones*.**

1. We have three orders. Which ~~order~~ *one* should I start with?

2. All of those customers are waiting for a table. Which <u>customers</u> should I seat first?

3. I need some mixing bowls. Would you give me the big <u>mixing bowls</u>?

4. Excuse me, this glass is dirty. Can you give me a new <u>glass</u>?

5. This towel is wet. Can you give me a dry <u>towel</u>?

6. I need two more cups. This <u>cup</u> is broken and that <u>cup</u> has lipstick on it.

D **COMPLETE. Use *one* or *ones*.**

1. There are a lot of pharmacies in Atlanta. I work at the _____*one*_____ on Buford Highway.

2. We keep batteries next to the cash register so people can grab the _____ they need when they are checking out.

3. There are so many batteries to choose from. People often ask me which _____ are the best.

4. People also want to know which _____ last longer.

5. Some batteries can be recycled. The closest recycling center is the _____ on Adamson Street.

Show what you know!

1. **COLLABORATE. Use *this*, *that*, *these*, or *those* in the following conversation.**

   A: You are a supermarket manager. You received new inventory. Tell your employee where to put the boxes.

   B: You are an employee. Ask questions. Find out which boxes go in which aisles.

2. **WRITE. Describe a purchase you made. What brands, colors, sizes, or models did you have to choose from? Which ones were the most expensive? Which ones were the best quality? How did you make your choice? Use *one* and *ones*.**

   When I bought a new TV, I had to make a choice between two different models. One was bigger and had a nicer picture. The other one was smaller and cheaper.

I can use *one* and *ones*. ■   I need more practice. ■

For more practice, go to MyEnglishLab.

Lesson 4 Read about working the late shift

1 BEFORE YOU READ

PREDICT. Skim the article. What do you think the article will be about?

2 READ

▶ Listen and read.

> **Academic Skill: Skim**
>
> Skimming means to look quickly over an article. You should pay attention to headings, pictures, and graphics. Skimming helps you guess what the article will be about.

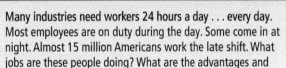  

Working the Late Shift

Many industries need workers 24 hours a day . . . every day. Most employees are on duty during the day. Some come in at night. Almost 15 million Americans work the late shift. What jobs are these people doing? What are the advantages and
5 disadvantages of working the late shift?

Advantages
Why do some people choose to work when most people are asleep? The late shift offers some advantages. Late-shift workers have
10 free time during the day. They can shop or go to the doctor when everyone else is at work. They can work a second job. They can go to school. They also have easier commutes.

There are other advantages. At work, there are few other people
15 around. That means that there are fewer distractions. Late-shift workers often experience less stress. Each worker also has more

> Workers with these common jobs often work the late shift:
> • Police officers
> • Nurses and home health aides
> • Computer operators
> • Cooks and servers

responsibilities. This makes the job more interesting. The worker can learn new job skills. Finally, companies usually pay late-shift workers more. These workers also get more vacation time.

20 **Disadvantages**
There are some disadvantages to working this shift. Late-shift workers often feel exhausted. It's hard to get enough sleep during the day. Over time, this can lead to insomnia, depression, and anxiety. These
25 health problems are known as "shift-work sleep disorder." In addition, late-shift workers can't spend much time with their families and friends. Their relationships may suffer.

Working the late shift has both advantages and disadvantages.
30 However, it is the right decision for many people. Workers can be successful on the late shift. They just need to get enough sleep. They should also try to spend enough time with family and friends.

3 CLOSE READING

A **IDENTIFY. What is the main idea of the article?**

a. Police officers and nurses often work the late shift.
b. Working the late shift has both advantages and disadvantages.
c. To be successful on the late shift, workers need to get enough sleep.

Reading

B **CITE EVIDENCE. Answer the questions. Where is the information? Write the line numbers.**

Lines

1. When do workers work the late shift?

   _____   _____

2. What are advantages of working the late shift?

   _____   _____

3. What are disadvantages of working the late shift?

   _____   _____

4. What do late-shift workers have to do to be successful?

   _____   _____

5. Look at the list of jobs. Why do you think these jobs have late shifts?

   _____

C **INTERPRET VOCABULARY. Complete the sentences.**

1. The words *on duty* in line 2 mean _____.
   a. working   **b.** sleeping   **c.** relaxing

2. The word *advantages* in line 4 means _____.
   a. good things   **b.** bad things   **c.** reasons

3. The word *disadvantages* in line 5 means _____.
   a. good things   **b.** bad things   **c.** ideas

4. The word *exhausted* in line 22 means _____.
   a. unhappy   **b.** angry   **c.** tired

5. The word *insomnia* in line 24 means _____.
   a. sickness   **b.** stress   **c.** an inability to sleep

4 SUMMARIZE

What are the most important ideas in the article? Write three sentences in your notebook.

Show what you know!

1. **COLLABORATE.** Talk about people you know who work the late shift. What do they like about it? What do they not like? How are their experiences similar to the experiences described in the article? How are they different?

2. **WRITE.** Describe the advantages and disadvantages of working the late shift.

   The advantages of working the late shift are . . .

I can skim for information while reading. ☐   I need more practice. ☐

To read more, go to MyEnglishLab.

Writing

Describe a job

1 STUDY THE MODEL

ANALYZE. Read the model and Writing Skill. Then answer the questions.

EMTs

EMTs (emergency medical technicians) help people who are sick or injured. When there is an emergency and someone needs medical assistance, EMTs drive to the emergency in an ambulance. They give the person medical treatment if they can. They put the person in the ambulance and take him or her to the ER. This means they take them to an emergency room in a hospital for treatment. EMTs save people's lives.

Writing Skill: Define new words and acronyms

Give definitions when you introduce new words or acronyms (for example, EMT). Introduce the definitions with a defining verb, such as *means* or *refers to*, or with parentheses ( ).

1. What are the new words or acronyms in the paragraph?
2. What do the words or acronyms mean?

2 PLAN YOUR WRITING

A **BRAINSTORM. Ask and answer the questions.**

Think of a job that uses an acronym (for example, FBI agent, NASA scientist, or HVAC technician). Research the job. What does the acronym mean? What are the duties of the job? What is good or bad about the job?

B **OUTLINE. Make sure to define any acronyms. Include the duties of the job.**

Job: _____

Acronym: _____

Duties: _____

3 WRITE

DESCRIBE. Write about a job. Use the model, the Writing Skill, and your ideas from Exercise 2 to help you.

WRITING CHECKLIST

☐ Is the paragraph about a job and its duties?

☐ Does the paragraph include and define new words or acronyms?

4 CHECK YOUR WRITING

COLLABORATE. Read the checklist. Read your writing together. Revise your writing.

I can define new words and acronyms. ■   I need more practice. ■

For more practice, go to MyEnglishLab.

Lesson 6

Identify expectations on the job

1 BEFORE YOU LISTEN

DISCUSS. What do employers expect from employees? What do employees expect? What is most important to you at a job?

2 LISTEN

Carl works for a real-estate agency. He is speaking with his manager, Bill.

Bill   Carl

A **PREDICT.** Do you think Carl and his manager have a good relationship? Why or why not?

B ► **LISTEN FOR DETAILS.** Write *T* (true) or *F* (false).

_____ **1.** Tony didn't have time to finish a job.

_____ **2.** Carl can't get to the building.

_____ **3.** Tony will take photographs of a building.

_____ **4.** Carl is going to finish Tony's report.

_____ **5.** The report is due by Friday.

C ► **LISTEN FOR DETAILS.** Circle the correct answers.

1. What does Carl want to do next Friday?
   a. He wants to take the day off.   **b.** He wants to leave early.

2. Why does Carl make the request?
   a. It's his son's birthday.   **b.** It's his son's graduation.

3. What does Bill mean when he says, "I don't see why not"?
   a. It's OK.   **b.** It's not OK.

D **EXPAND.** In the U.S., many employers want employees to call them by their first name. Is it the same in your native country? Which way is more comfortable for you?

I can identify expectations on the job. ■   I need more practice. ☐

For more practice, go to MyEnglishLab.

Grammar

Verb + object + infinitive

	Subject	Verb	Object	Infinitive	
	Bill	**needs**	**Carl**	**to do**	this job.
	He	**would like**	**me**	**to finish**	the job today.
	She	**expects**	**us**	**not to come**	late.
Do	you	**want**	**her**	**to call you**	when she gets home?
Can	you	**ask**	**them**	**to stop**	making so much noise?

Grammar Watch

With verb + object + infinitive, the object can be a noun or pronoun.

A INVESTIGATE. Underline the examples of verb + object + infinitive.

A: John, I'd <u>like you to work</u> late tonight. Is that OK? Of course, you'll get paid overtime.

B: I think so, but let me call my sister first. I need her to pick me up. We share a car. Do you want me to work late tomorrow night, too?

A: No, just tonight. Lena had an emergency and can't come in tonight, so I need you to cover her shift.

B PRACTICE. Complete the conversation. Unscramble the words in parentheses.

A: Joe, I need a favor. _____*I need someone to work*_____ for me on June 14th. My sister is
(to work / someone / need / I)

getting married. Can you work then?

B: Sure. _____ for you any other day?
(do / me / to cover / need / you)

A: Just then. _____ for you sometime?
(to work / like / me / you / would)

B: How about Friday the 21st? I want to go away for the weekend. Can you work then?

A: Oh no, I'm sorry, I can't. _____ her parents from the airport
(to pick up / needs / me / my wife)

that day.

Grammar

C COMPLETE. Read the complaints from restaurant servers. Then complete the sentences.

Tanya: We have to wear a uniform in my restaurant. I really don't like it, but my supervisor says we all have to look alike. Do you have to wear one?

Renata: No, but we sing when it's a customer's birthday. I have a terrible voice, and I don't like to sing.

Rob: We have to work on holidays because that's when the restaurant is the busiest.

Anaya: I have to work on Friday and Saturday nights.

1. Tanya's employer expects _____

   _____

2. Renata's employer wants _____

   _____

3. Rob's employer expects _____

   _____

4. Anaya's employer expects _____

   _____

Show what you know!

1. **PROBLEM SOLVE. Discuss the situations. What should the people do?**

   A: My manager expects me to stay late almost every day. He doesn't pay me for the overtime. When I complain, he seems angry.

   B: My manager expects us to work as a team. I'm better and faster than the other employees. I don't want to work with a team. I want to work alone.

2. **WRITE. Report about the job expectations where you work now or at a place where you worked in the past. Use verb + object + infinitive.**

   I work at the front desk of a hotel. My manager expects me to arrive on time every day. She gets very upset when workers are late. She expects us to wear nice clothes, but she doesn't require us to wear a uniform. My manager wants all employees to smile and be friendly to the hotel guests. She expects us not to text or talk on our phones during our shift.

I can use verb + object + infinitive. ☐   I need more practice. ☐

For more practice, go to MyEnglishLab.

1 READ SAFETY INSTRUCTIONS

A **EVALUATE.** Read the list of safety rules. Talk about words you don't know.

Blackman Company Safety Rules

Attention employees: Be aware of safety hazards. Follow the safety procedures.

Prevent slips, trips, and falls.
- Always clean up your work area.
- Make sure wires and equipment are kept out of the way.
- Use caution when walking on wet or slippery floors.
- Wear non-slip shoes when working in machine areas.
- Never stand on an office chair to reach for something.
- Don't lean back too far in an office chair.

Operate machinery carefully.
- Turn off machinery before cleaning or repairing.
- Turn off machinery when not in use.
- Wear eye protection (goggles) or a face shield.
- Keep your hands at a safe distance from machinery.
- Do not wear loose-fitting clothes or long sleeves when operating machines.

B **ANALYZE.** What is the main idea of the workplace sign?

a. Be careful of machinery.
b. Put away all equipment.
c. Prevent accidents and injuries.

C **APPLY.** Answer the questions. Write *T* (true) or *F* (false).

_____ 1. Workers can stand on office chairs if they need to reach something high.

_____ 2. When workers take breaks, they should turn off the machinery.

_____ 3. Machines need to be turned off when they are being cleaned.

_____ 4. Workers need to protect their eyes.

_____ 5. Loose-fitting pants are acceptable clothing.

Workplace, Life, and Community Skills

2 IDENTIFY SAFETY HAZARDS

A MATCH. Connect the danger with an accident it might cause.

_____ **1.** There's a wire on the floor.

_____ **2.** A can of paint has spilled on the floor.

_____ **3.** There are too many boxes on a high shelf.

_____ **4.** A large knife has been left on a worktable.

_____ **5.** Workers are using a table saw without goggles.

_____ **6.** A worker using a machine has loose clothing.

a. You could cut yourself with it.

b. It might get caught in the machine.

c. You might trip over it.

d. They might fall on someone.

e. You might slip and fall.

f. They could injure their eyes.

B GIVE EXAMPLES. Talk about the safety signs. What do they mean? Have you ever seen them at work? Where did you see them?

C DISCUSS. Look at the workplaces in the box. What safety hazards do you think you might find at each?

construction site	factory	hospital
hotel	office	restaurant

D GO ONLINE. Look up safety hazards for machinery you use at work or at home.

I can identify safety hazards at work. ☐   I need more practice. ☐

For more practice, go to MyEnglishLab.

Lesson 9

Respond appropriately to correction

1 BEFORE YOU LISTEN

MAKE CONNECTIONS. Have you ever made a mistake at work? What happened? Why did it happen? What did your supervisor say to you? How did you answer?

2 LISTEN

Margo, an office manager, is talking to Jason, a new office assistant.

A ▶ **LISTEN FOR MAIN IDEA.** What is the problem?

B ▶ **LISTEN FOR DETAILS.** Write *T* (true) or *F* (false).

_____ **1.** The copy machine next to Mr. Yang's office is not working.

_____ **2.** Jason checked all of the copy machines in the morning.

_____ **3.** Margo did not tell Jason to check the copy machines.

_____ **4.** When the copy machines are broken, Margo can always fix them.

_____ **5.** Jason apologizes to Margo.

C **EXPAND.** Did Margo correct Jason in a positive way? Did Jason respond appropriately? Why or why not?

Listening and Speaking

3 CONVERSATION

A ▶ **LISTEN AND READ.** Then practice the conversation with a partner.

A: Jason, Mr. Yang just called me. He told me that the copy machine next to his office isn't working.

B: It isn't?

A: That's right. Did you check all the copy machines and printers this morning?

B: Well, I checked almost all of them, but maybe I forgot about that one. I'm sorry.

A: OK, Jason. I know you're new here. But remember: You need to check all of the copy machines and printers first thing when you come in. We need to make sure they're working. If there's a problem, we need to fix it. If we can't fix it, we have to call service repair.

B: I understand, Margo. I'll make sure it doesn't happen again.

A: OK, very good.

B **ROLE-PLAY.** Make conversations based on the situations.

A: You are the employer. Tell the employee something he or she did wrong. Use the situations or your own ideas.

B: You are the employee. Use one of the apologies.

Situations

Your employee forgot to give you a message.
Your employee made too many personal calls at work.
Your employee completed a task incorrectly.

Apologies

I'm sorry. I'll do better next time.
I'm sorry. It won't happen again.
I'm sorry. I'll do it over.

I can respond appropriately to correction. ■

I need more practice. ■

For more practice, go to MyEnglishLab.

Grammar

Reported speech

Direct Speech		Reported Speech	Grammar Watch
Check the printers.	→	The manager **told me to check the printers**.	
Please call service repair.	→	Margo **asked me to call service repair**.	
Don't come late again.	→	She **told him not to come late again**.	

Grammar Watch

When you change direct speech to reported speech, make sure to change pronouns and possessives.

A ▶ **INVESTIGATE. Read and listen to the voicemail message.**

> Hello, Boris. This is Richard. Listen, I left a phone number on the pad on my desk in the back. Could you check if it's there and get me the number? Thanks. My number here is 890-555-4567.

What does the caller want?
  a. Boris asked Richard to leave a number for him.
  b. Richard asked Boris to give him his phone number.
  c. Richard asked Boris to call him and give him a phone number.

B **PRACTICE. Unscramble the sentences.**

1. Mr. Kwang / the employees / to set up the display / told

   Mr. Kwang told the employees to set up the display.

2. asked / to check that all items have prices / them / he

   _____

3. warned / he / not / to come late / them

   _____

4. he / to recycle the papers / them / told

   _____

5. them / expected / he / to work late

   _____

6. they / him / asked / to explain / the time-off policy

   _____

Grammar

C **APPLY.** Read the questions and statements. Rewrite the statements. Use reported speech and pronouns.

1. What did Mr. Lan tell Alex? ("Restock the batteries.")

   Mr. Lan told Alex to restock the batteries.

2. What did Ms. Alvarado ask Marta to do? ("Please check your work.")

   _____

3. What did Ms. Khan tell Joe? ("Replace the products that we sold.")

   _____

4. What did Ms. Rice ask Jen to do? ("Please work the register today.")

   _____

5. What did Mr. Smith say to Bob and Lee? ("Don't worry about the store window.")

   _____

6. What did Mr. Green say to Susan? ("Don't make personal calls at work.")

   _____

Show what you know!

1. **ROLE-PLAY. Choose a workplace you know well. Make a conversation about that workplace.**

   | construction site | hospital | office |
   | restaurant | warehouse | |

   A: You are the manager. Give your employee instructions.
   B: You are the employee. Ask questions to make sure you understand.

2. **WRITE. Explain the instructions your partner gave you in Step 1. Use reported speech.**

   Carla told me to use a pleasant voice with customers. She asked me to make sure the printers
   work and to order new office supplies.

I can use reported speech. ■   I need more practice. ■

For more practice, go to MyEnglishLab.

1 MEET MATEO

Read about one of his workplace skills.

> I listen actively at work. When I don't, somebody could get hurt. For example, I always make sure I understand what my supervisor needs me to do.

2 MATEO'S PROBLEM

A READ. Write *T* (true) or *F* (false).

Mateo is a reliable worker. He does a lot of different jobs. He runs errands, cleans job sites, makes deliveries, and sets up materials and tools.

After a major storm, Mateo has to check on a site that is near his house. His supervisor calls and asks him to check for flooding, downed power lines, or other damage. The phone connection is bad, and it's hard for Mateo to hear everything his supervisor is saying.

_____ **1.** The construction site is close to Mateo's house.

_____ **2.** The problems at the site are caused by a fire.

_____ **3.** Mateo understands everything his supervisor wants him to do.

B ANALYZE. What is Mateo's problem? Write your response in your notebook.

3 MATEO'S SOLUTION

A COLLABORATE. Mateo listens actively. He makes sure he understands what is being told to him. What should he do? Explain your answer.

1. Mateo says, "I can't hear what you're saying. But don't worry. I'll figure it out. I'll quickly walk through and let you know if I see any problems."

2. Mateo says, "I can't hear you very well. I would feel more comfortable if you asked someone else to do this."

3. Mateo says, "We have a bad connection. Let me repeat what you want me to do. You want me to check if there has been any flooding and if any power lines are down. Is that right?"

4. Mateo _____.

B ROLE-PLAY. Act out Mateo's solution with your partner.

Show what you know!

1. **REFLECT.** When have you listened actively at work? Give an example.

2. **WRITE.** Now write your example in your Skills Log.

   I listen actively. I make sure I understand what someone is telling me. For example, I always ask questions and repeat what the person said.

3. **PRESENT.** Give a short presentation to show how you listen actively.

I can give an example of how I listen actively at work. ■

Unit Review: Go back to page 165. Which unit goals can you check off?

10 Going to the Doctor

PREVIEW

Have you ever been to a hospital in the U.S.? What experiences have you or your family had with hospitals or doctors?

UNIT GOALS

- [ ] Recognize places in a hospital
- [ ] Reschedule a doctor's appointment
- [ ] Read and complete a medical history form
- [ ] Talk about symptoms

- [ ] Discuss medical procedures and concerns
- [ ] **Academic skill:** Interpret graphics
- [ ] **Writing skill:** Write a concluding sentence
- [ ] **Workplace soft skill:** Prioritize

Places in a hospital

A **PREDICT.** Look at the pictures. Describe what is happening in each picture.

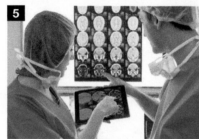

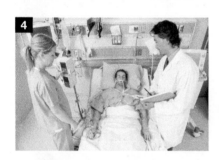
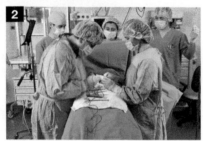

Vocabulary

B IDENTIFY. Match the pictures with the words. Write the numbers.

Places in a hospital

_____ admissions   _____ emergency room (ER)   _____ intensive care unit (ICU)
_____ laboratory   _____ maternity ward   _____ nurse's station
_____ pediatrics   _____ physical therapy   _____ radiology/imaging
_____ surgery

C ▶ LISTEN AND POINT. Then listen and repeat.

D APPLY. Look at the telephone numbers. Then read the situations. Write the telephone numbers you should dial.

ER 7790   ICU................ 9089
Admissions 8790   Laboratory..... 9091
Radiology........7450   Clinic 9087

Study Tip

Make Connections
Make cards for five places in a hospital. Write the place on the front of the card. Write what patients do there on the back.

1. You had surgery and need a follow-up appointment. You dial _____.

2. Your cousin had a heart attack. She's not doing well. You want to find out visiting hours. You dial _____.

3. You want to schedule an appointment for a chest X-ray. You dial _____.

4. You need to schedule some blood tests before an operation. You dial _____.

5. Your uncle went to the emergency room two hours ago. You want to find out if the doctor has seen him yet. You dial _____.

Show what you know!

1. DISCUSS. Which places in a hospital have you been in or visited?

2. WRITE. Explain the purpose of one place or department in a hospital. Who works there? What do they do?

The radiology department is where people go to get X-rays. Radiologists work there. They take X-rays and report the results to doctors and nurses.

I can recognize places in a hospital. ■   I need more practice. ■

For more practice, go to MyEnglishLab.

Reschedule a doctor's appointment

1 BEFORE YOU LISTEN

MAKE CONNECTIONS. What are your biggest problems with making or going to a doctor's appointment? Discuss the ideas in the box.

- inconvenient office hours
- waiting a long time on the phone
- waiting a long time for an appointment
- waiting a long time in the clinic

2 LISTEN

Isabella is a medical receptionist. She is helping patients with their appointments.

Isabella

A ▶ **LISTEN FOR MAIN IDEA.** Circle the answers.

1. Mr. Chen is calling _____.
   a. to make an appointment
   b. to cancel an appointment
   c. to speak to the doctor

2. Mr. Chen wants to see the doctor _____.
   a. on Thursday at 3:00
   b. on Friday at 3:00
   c. today at 4:00

B ▶ **LISTEN FOR DETAILS.** Circle the answers.

1. Ms. Ledesma wants to get an appointment for _____.
   a. today at 4:00
   b. today at 5:00
   c. Thursday at 5:00

2. Ms. Ledesma's problem is that _____.
   a. she's sleeping too much
   b. she can't sleep, and she's tired
   c. she isn't hungry

3. Isabella _____.
   a. gave Mr. Chen an appointment
   b. gave Mr. Chen's appointment to Ms. Ledesma
   c. did not find a good time for Ms. Ledesma to come in

Listening and Speaking

3 PRONUNCIATION

A ▶ **PRACTICE. Listen. Then listen and repeat.**

One syllable	**Extra syllables**
booked = /t/	frustrated = /ɪd/
confused = /d/	reminded = /ɪd/

-ed Endings

We pronounce the -ed ending as an extra syllable only after the sounds /t/ and /d/.

B ▶ **APPLY. Say the words to yourself. Write the words in the correct columns. Then listen and check your answers.**

bored	embarrassed	exhausted	shocked	worried

-ed = /t/	-ed = /d/	-ed = extra syllable / ɪd/

4 CONVERSATION

A ▶ **LISTEN AND READ. Then practice the conversation with a partner.**

A: Hello, Westside Health Center.

B: Hi. This is Yao Chen. I have an appointment with Dr. Barnes for today at 4:00, but I need to cancel.

A: OK, Mr. Chen. Would you like to reschedule?

B: Yes, I would. Can I come in next Thursday at 3:00?

A: Sorry, we're all booked. How about Friday at 3:00?

B: I think that's OK.

B **ROLE-PLAY. Make a similar conversation. Cancel and reschedule an appointment with a doctor.**

I can reschedule a doctor's appointment. ■   I need more practice. ■

For more practice, go to MyEnglishLab.

Unit 10, Lesson 2 **189**

Grammar

Participial adjectives

The instructions are confusing.

The patient is confused.

Grammar Watch

- Participial adjectives end with *-ing* or *-ed*.
- Use *-ing* for someone or something that causes a feeling.
- Use *-ed* for the person who has the feeling.
- Some adjectives do not have an *-ing* form or we do not use the *-ing* form often. For example: *relieved, stressed,* and *worried*.
- See page 263 for a list of common participial adjectives.

A INVESTIGATE. Circle the *-ed* forms. Underline the *-ing* forms.

1. I'm worried about my health because I haven't seen a doctor for a few years.

2. The hospital has so many departments and floors that I get confused and don't know where to go.

3. It's frustrating when you have to wait months for an appointment.

B PRACTICE. Complete the sentences with the correct words from the box.

frightening	frustrating	relieved	~~stressed~~	tiring

1. I'm really _____*stressed*_____. The hospital charged me $1,500 for that operation.

2. I was _____. The clinic didn't charge me for that visit.

3. It's _____ when I try to make a doctor's appointment. The doctor's office is closed evenings so I have trouble calling.

4. My son thinks that doctors are _____. He cries when he sees them.

5. It's _____ to wait a long time for the doctor. Sometimes, I fall asleep in the waiting room.

Grammar

C CHOOSE. Cross out the incorrect word.

1. I had to wait in the ER for hours before the doctor could see me. It was very ~~bored~~ / **boring** to stay there so long.

2. Everyone was **shocked** / **shocking** to hear that Luz's uncle had cancer.

3. Lately, I've been **exhausted** / **exhausting**. I hope I'm not sick.

4. It's really **frustrated** / **frustrating** when I go to Greenville Clinic. The doctors never have time to explain anything.

5. I'm **frustrated** / **frustrating** because the doctors don't seem to understand what I'm saying.

D COMPLETE. Use the *-ed* or *-ing* form of the word in parentheses.

1. Do you feel like doctors are _____*interested*_____ in you and care about your health?
   (interest)

2. Is it _____ for you to make a doctor's appointment?
   (frustrate)

3. Are you often _____ when you talk to doctors?
   (confuse)

4. Do you think hospitals are _____?
   (frighten)

5. Are you often _____ about medical bills?
   (worry)

Show what you know!

1. **DISCUSS. Talk about your experiences with doctors and hospitals in the U.S. Use some of the questions in Exercise D and your own ideas.**

   A: Have you ever been confused by a doctor?
   B: Yes, I have. Once, the doctor said, "Say, 'Ah.'" I didn't understand. It was so confusing. Then he spoke slowly and said, "I want you to open your mouth and say, 'Ah.'" Finally, I understood, and he was able to examine my throat.

2. **WRITE. Describe a time when you went to a doctor's office. How did you feel? How was the experience? Use participial adjectives.**

   My son was very scared when I took him to the doctor's office. He . . .

I can use participial adjectives. ☐   I need more practice. ☐

For more practice, go to MyEnglishLab.

Lesson 4

Read and complete a medical history form

1 READ A MEDICAL HISTORY FORM

A INTERPRET. Look at the medical history form. Discuss new words.

MEDICAL HISTORY FORM   Date: 3/24/19

Patient Name _Rostov, Natasha_   Date of Birth _7/20/67_

Reason for visit today: _difficulty breathing_

How long have you had these symptoms? _one week_

Have you been under a doctor's care in the last two years? ☑ Yes ☐ No

If yes, for what? _heart problems and high blood pressure_

Have you ever been hospitalized, had a major operation, or had a
serious illness? ☐ Yes ☑ No

If yes, for what? _____

Please list any medications you are currently taking: _high blood_

pressure medication

Are you allergic to any medications? ☐ Yes ☑ No

If yes, please list: _____

Do you now or have you ever had:

☑ Heart problems   ☐ Emphysema
☑ High blood pressure   ☐ Tuberculosis
☐ Diabetes   ☐ Hepatitis
☐ Cancer (type)   ☐ Pneumonia
☐ Stroke   ☐ Asthma
☐ HIV/AIDS

In the past month, have you had any of the following symptoms?

☐ Weight gain or loss   ☐ Dizziness
☑ Chest pain   ☐ Nausea
☑ Shortness of breath   ☐ Stomach pain
☐ Fainting   ☐ Vomiting
☐ Headaches

B DISCUSS. Answer the questions.

1. What health problems does Natasha have now?
2. What kind of medication is Natasha taking?
3. Does Natasha have any allergies to medications?
4. What other medical problems has Natasha had?

C GO ONLINE. Find information about one of the conditions listed on the medical history form. What are some symptoms of the condition?

Workplace, Life, and Community Skills

2 COMPLETE A MEDICAL HISTORY FORM

A ▶ **LISTEN FOR MAIN IDEA.** Why does the patient want to see a doctor?

B **APPLY.** Imagine you have a doctor's appointment. Complete this portion of a medical history form.

Reason for visit today: _____

How long have you had these symptoms? _____

I can read and complete a medical history form. ■   I need more practice. ■

For more practice, go to MyEnglishLab.

Lesson 5 | Listening and Speaking

Talk about symptoms

1 BEFORE YOU LISTEN

MAKE CONNECTIONS. When you go to a doctor, what questions does the doctor usually ask you? How much time does he or she spend with you? Do you usually have questions for the doctor?

2 LISTEN

Ms. Ledesma doesn't feel well and is visiting the doctor.

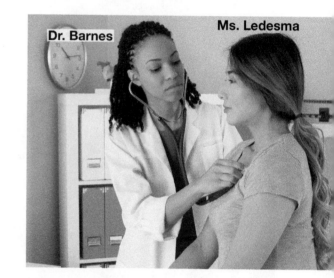
Dr. Barnes   Ms. Ledesma

A ▶ LISTEN FOR MAIN IDEA. Why is the patient visiting the doctor?

B ▶ LISTEN FOR DETAILS. Write *T* (true) or *F* (false).

_____ **1.** She has trouble sleeping at night.

_____ **2.** She has lost some weight.

_____ **3.** When she comes home, she is very tired.

_____ **4.** She is stressed at work.

_____ **5.** She does not like to weigh herself.

C ▶ EXPAND. Listen to the rest of the conversation. Circle the correct answers.

1. Dr. Barnes thinks the problem with Ms. Ledesma is _____.
   a. high blood pressure
   b. heart disease
   c. high cholesterol

2. Dr. Barnes tells Ms. Ledesma to _____.
   a. sleep more
   b. stop taking her medication
   c. eat healthy and exercise

3. Dr. Barnes doesn't like to give medication because it often _____.
   a. makes patients sleep too much
   b. makes patients gain weight
   c. is not necessary

Listening and Speaking

3 PRONUNCIATION

A ▶ PRACTICE. Listen. Then listen and repeat.

Stressed and Unstressed Syllables

Stressed syllables take longer to say than unstressed syllables. The time it takes to say a sentence depends on how many stressed syllables there are.

Work hard.   She's working hard.   She's been working hard.

B ▶ APPLY. Listen. Mark (•) the stressed syllables in each sentence.

1. She hasn't been sleeping well.

2. He's trying to lose weight.

3. The doctor gave him some advice.

4. Is anything bothering you?

4 CONVERSATION

A ▶ LISTEN AND READ. Then practice the conversation with a partner.

A: Good afternoon, Ms. Ledesma. What seems to be the problem?

B: I feel terrible. I haven't been sleeping well. I fall asleep, and I wake up after a couple of hours.

A: Hmm. Anything else?

B: Well, I've been trying to lose weight like you said, but I can't. I come home exhausted, and I eat too much.

A: Is anything bothering you?

B: My job. They fired two people last month, so the rest of us have been working twice as hard.

B MAKE CONNECTIONS. Talk about a time when you were sick. Did you have any of the symptoms in the box? Did you have other symptoms? What did you do? Did you go to the doctor? Did you go to the emergency room?

chest pain or neck pain	loss of appetite
coughing	nausea
fatigue	shortness of breath
high fever	weight loss

I can talk about symptoms. ■

I need more practice. ■

For more practice, go to MyEnglishLab.

Lesson 6

Present perfect continuous

Subject	*have/has*			Verb + *-ing*
He She The medicine	**has**			
		not	**been**	**working**.
I We They	**have**			

Grammar Watch

We use the present perfect continuous to show that an action began in the past and is still continuing.

A **INVESTIGATE.** A nurse is teaching some students about diabetes symptoms. Underline the examples of the present perfect continuous.

My patient is a 40-year-old male. He <u>has been losing</u> weight. He says that lately he's been feeling very tired and thirsty. His wife says he hasn't been watching his diet, and he hasn't been exercising much. I think he may have type 2 diabetes. Fortunately, this can usually be controlled with diet, exercise, or medicine.

B **PRACTICE.** Complete the sentences with the present perfect continuous. Use the verbs in parentheses.

1. My uncle _____*has been having*_____ chest pains.
                    (have)

2. My husband _____ for the past two weeks.
                         (cough)

3. I _____ with sharp pains in my stomach.
           (wake up)

4. My son is 12 years old. For the last week, he _____ about leg pains.
                                      (complain)

5. My sister _____ a high fever.
                  (run)

Grammar

C) COMPLETE. Use the words in parentheses and the present perfect continuous.

A: Good afternoon, Mr. Hu. How _____*have you been doing*_____ since I saw you last?
(you / do)

B: _____ chest pain. And I have trouble breathing when I walk.
(I / feel)

A: Hmm. Well, _____? You said you were going to quit.
(you / smoke)

B: No, _____. I gave it up.
(I / not / smoke)

A: _____ your high blood pressure medication?
(you / take)

B: Yes, I have. Every day. And _____ twice a week.
(I / exercise)

A: Good. But try to exercise four times a week. It's important. And _____
(you / watch)

your diet? _____ salty foods and alcohol?
(you / stay away from)

B: Well, _____ any alcohol, and _____ chips.
(I / not / drink)   (I / not / eat)

Show what you know!

1. **ROLE-PLAY. Pretend you are a doctor and patient.**

   A: You are the doctor. Your patient has high cholesterol. Ask how he or she has been doing. Has the patient been doing any of the following?
   - exercising
   - eating fruits and vegetables
   - eating fewer eggs and less butter
   - eating whole grains
   - taking medication

   B: Answer the doctor's questions.

2. **WRITE. Take notes and report about your patient. Use the present perfect continuous.**

   Awa has high cholesterol. She hasn't been exercising much lately. She has been eating fruits and vegetables, but she has also been eating salty, fatty food. She has been eating eggs and butter. She has not been eating whole grains. She has not been taking any medication.

I can use the present perfect continuous. ☐   I need more practice. ☐

Read about vaccinations

1 BEFORE YOU READ

PREDICT. Skim the article. Read the title and headings. What questions do you think the article will answer?

2 READ

▶ Listen and read.

> **Academic Skill: Interpret graphics**
>
> Looking at graphics, such as pictures and diagrams, helps you understand what an article is about. They show information in a visual format that is easy to see and understand.

Vaccinations

Fifty years ago, measles and polio were serious health problems. Many people got sick or died from them. Today, people in the U.S.
5 almost never get these diseases. Why? They get vaccinated. Vaccinations protect millions of people from deadly illnesses. Most importantly, they protect children.

10 **Why do children get vaccinations?**
Vaccinations keep children safe and healthy. Most children get shots that protect them from 14 different diseases. These include measles, mumps, chicken pox, and polio.

15 **When do children get the vaccines?**
Children get different vaccines at different ages. Children need only one dose, or shot, of some vaccines. Other vaccinations require several doses. Your doctor can give you a schedule for your child's shots.

20 **Do children *have to* get vaccinated?**
All 50 states have vaccination requirements for school children. This means that children must get certain shots before they start school. However, all states allow medical exemptions. Some children have serious
25 medical conditions. Vaccines are dangerous for them. These children don't have to get vaccinated. Some people also refuse to get shots. Their reasons are religious or moral. A few states allow them to do this.

I don't have insurance. Can I get these shots for free?
30 Yes. Vaccines for Children (VFC) gives free vaccines to children. Most family doctors participate in VFC.

What vaccinations should adults get?
Influenza (the flu) makes millions of people sick every year. It makes people miss many days of school and
35 work. It's a good idea to get a flu shot every year. The vaccine may not completely protect you from the flu. However, some protection is better than no protection.

Vaccinations prevent disease. They are important for your health. They are even more important for your
40 child's health. They are also important for the health of your community. That's why you and your children should get them.

VACCINATION SCHEDULE
These are some of the vaccinations children should get during the first year of life:

	Birth	1 month	2 months	4 months	6 months	1 year
Hepatitis B	✓	✓		✓	✓	✓
Diphtheria, Tetanus			✓	✓	✓	✓
Polio			✓	✓	✓	✓
Influenza (Flu)					✓	✓
Measles, Mumps						✓
Hepatitis A						✓

3 CLOSE READING

A **IDENTIFY.** What is the main idea of the article?

a. Children are supposed to get different vaccinations at different ages.
b. All 50 states have vaccination requirements for school children, but they allow medical exemptions.
c. Vaccinations are important for your health, your child's health, and the health of your community.

Reading

B CITE EVIDENCE. Answer the questions. Where is the information? Write the line numbers.

Lines

1. What diseases do most children get vaccines for?

   _____   _____

2. What is a situation where children don't have to get shots?

   _____   _____

3. Do parents always have to pay for shots?

   _____   _____

4. What vaccine should both adults and children get? Why?

   _influenza_____   _____

C INTERPRET GRAPHICS. Complete the sentences about the chart.

1. According to the chart, 6-month-old children should get ___4___ vaccinations.
   a. three
   b. (four)
   c. six

2. During the first year of life, children should get the _____ vaccine five times.
   a. Hepatitis A
   b. (Hepatitis B)
   c. Polio

3. At what age are children supposed to get their first shots?
   a. (birth)
   b. 1 month
   c. 1 year

4 SUMMARIZE

What are the most important ideas in the article? Write three sentences in your notebook.

Show what you know!

1. **DESCRIBE.** Do you, your children, or people you know get vaccinated? Which of the vaccinations described in the article do you have experience with?

2. **WRITE.** Explain which vaccinations children should get and why. What about adults?

   Children should get the measles vaccine because . . .

I can interpret graphics while reading. ■   I need more practice. ■

To read more, go to MyEnglishLab.

Write about a healthy habit

1 STUDY THE MODEL

ANALYZE. Read the model and Writing Skill. Then answer the questions.

Exercising: A Healthy Habit

I think everyone should exercise for at least half an hour every day. First, it helps you lose weight. Second, it helps you prevent serious health problems like heart disease or diabetes. Third, it improves your mood and makes you feel happier. Fourth, it gives you more energy. Fifth, it helps you sleep better at night. Finally, it's a good way to connect with family and friends. In conclusion, exercising is good for your health.

Writing Skill: Write a concluding sentence

End your paragraph with a concluding sentence that summarizes the paragraph or gives an opinion on the topic. Use a concluding word or phrase such as *In conclusion, To conclude, Therefore,* or *To sum up*.

1. What is the concluding sentence of the paragraph?
2. What concluding word or phrase is used?

2 PLAN YOUR WRITING

A BRAINSTORM. Ask and answer the questions.

What is another healthy habit? Why is it healthy?

B OUTLINE. Include reasons why the habit is healthy. Add a conclusion.

Topic Sentence:

Reasons:

Concluding Sentence:

3 WRITE

JUSTIFY. Write about a healthy habit. Use the model, the Writing Skill, and your ideas from Exercise 2 to help you.

WRITING CHECKLIST

☐ Does the paragraph end with a concluding sentence?

☐ Does the concluding sentence summarize the paragraph or give an opinion?

☐ Does the concluding sentence use a concluding word or phrase?

4 CHECK YOUR WRITING

COLLABORATE. Read the checklist. Read your writing together. Revise your writing.

I can write a concluding sentence. ■ | I need more practice. ■

For more practice, go to MyEnglishLab.

Discuss medical procedures and concerns

1 BEFORE YOU LISTEN

DISCUSS. Most people worry before a hospital stay. What are some common worries?

2 LISTEN

Mrs. Garcia is speaking with her doctor.

Mrs. Garcia

A ▶ **LISTEN FOR MAIN IDEA.** Circle the answer.

Why is Mrs. Garcia talking to the doctor?
  a. She wants to lose weight.
  b. She's going to have an operation.
  c. She's been sad and depressed.

B ▶ **LISTEN FOR DETAILS.** Write *T* (true) or *F* (false).

_____ **1.** The doctor is worried about Mrs. Garcia.

_____ **2.** Mrs. Garcia is worried about having an operation.

_____ **3.** Mrs. Garcia is worried her family will have a hard time
         when she is away from home.

_____ **4.** Mrs. Garcia is stressed because she will miss work.

C ▶ **EXPAND.** Listen again. Circle the answers.

1. What does the doctor suggest? Mrs. Garcia should call _____.
    a. a relative or friend   **b.** her neighbor   **c.** her employer

2. Mrs. Garcia is afraid to ask some of her relatives for help because _____.
    a. they aren't healthy   **b.** they're busy   **c.** they don't want to help

3. What is Mrs. Garcia's solution? She is going to ask her _____ for help.
    a. sister   **b.** cousin   **c.** friend

I can discuss medical procedures and concerns. ■   I need more practice. ■

For more practice, go to MyEnglishLab.

Grammar

Preposition + gerund

	Preposition	Gerund Expression
I'm worried	**about**	**missing** work.
Her husband isn't used	**to**	**taking** care of the children.
She's afraid	**of**	**asking** for help.

Grammar Watch

- Prepositions are words like *in, of, to, at, about,* and *on.*
- Common expressions with gerunds: *be afraid of, believe in, complain about, think about.*

A INVESTIGATE. Underline the prepositions + gerunds.

Before a hospital visit, people are often nervous about different things. Most people are nervous <u>about being</u> away from their family. People are often afraid of being in pain, and they are concerned about missing work. Many people are worried about paying for the medication they need after a visit. But these days, hospital stays are often short, doctors are well trained, and there are excellent pain medications.

B PRACTICE. Unscramble the sentences. Write the words in the correct order.

1. not / looking forward / to / that blood test / taking / I'm
   I'm not looking forward to taking that blood test.

2. he's / on / getting / for his family / planning / health insurance
   _____

3. my cousin / is / paying for an operation / worried / about
   _____

4. some people / complaining / are / about / getting sick at that hospital
   _____

5. for my injured shoulder / thinking about / I'm / trying / physical therapy
   _____

6. some people / but I think they're important / don't believe in / checkups / getting
   _____

Grammar

C **COMPLETE.** Add the correct prepositions and gerunds. Use the verbs in parentheses.

Maya Clinic Frequently Asked Questions

Q: I'm afraid _of getting_ heart disease. How do I know if I am at risk?
             (get)

A: Common risk factors for heart disease are high blood pressure, high cholesterol, smoking, and being overweight.

Q: I'm worried _____ heart disease because my father had it. Is it true it runs in families?
               (get)

A: Yes, heart disease can run in families. That does not mean you will get it. You need to watch your diet, exercise, and see a doctor regularly.

Q: I want to make sure I'm healthy and don't get breast cancer. I'm thinking _____ a mammogram. Can I get one for free?
                              (have)

A: Yes, there are some clinics that give them for free. Call 1-800-4-CANCER.

Q: My husband complains _____ tired all the time. I want him to go see the doctor, but he doesn't believe
                (be)

_____ medicine. He's not afraid _____ sick, but I'm afraid for him. We have two little children.
     (take)   (become)

A: Tell him he needs to see the doctor. If he doesn't want to go, tell him it's important for your children.

Show what you know!

1. **COLLABORATE.** Talk about health matters that you worry, think, or complain about.

2. **WRITE.** Summarize your health concerns and plans. Use preposition + gerund combinations.

   I plan on taking better care of my health. I often worry about getting diabetes because it runs in my family. I plan on eating healthy foods and avoiding too much sugar and fat. I believe in getting annual checkups with my family doctor. Sometimes, I complain about going to the gym, but I know exercise is important. I plan on going to the gym more often.

I can use prepositions with gerunds. ■   I need more practice. ■

For more practice, go to MyEnglishLab.

Lesson 11 Prioritize

1 MEET CAMILA

Read about one of her workplace skills.

> I prioritize my responsibilities at work. I do the most important things first. For example, when I have many tasks to complete, I figure out which one is the most important and which is the least important.

2 CAMILA'S PROBLEM

A READ. Write *T* (true) or *F* (false).

Camila works at a busy medical center. She has had this job for three years and knows how to solve several issues at once.

Today, she has four important tasks that need her immediate attention. A patient needs to make an appointment on the phone. She has to get allergy information from another patient before he sees a doctor. She needs to find a replacement for a nurse who called in sick at the last minute. And she must handle a disruptive patient in the waiting room.

_____ **1.** Camila is usually very busy at work.
_____ **2.** She has three things she needs to do right now.
_____ **3.** One of the tasks is ordering lunch for the head doctor.

B ANALYZE. What is Camila's problem? Write your response in your notebook.

3 CAMILA'S SOLUTION

A COLLABORATE. Camila is organized and knows how to prioritize her responsibilities. What should she do? Explain your answer.

1. Camila walks out of the office to calm down before prioritizing the tasks.
2. Camila makes a list to decide what task is most important to do first.
3. Camila deals with the two patients in the office first. She then schedules an appointment for the patient on the phone while she chooses a replacement nurse to call.
4. Camila _____.

B ROLE-PLAY. Act out Camila's solution with your partner.

Show what you know!

1. **REFLECT.** When did you have to prioritize tasks at work? Give an example.

2. **WRITE.** Now write your example in your Skills Log.

   I know how to prioritize. I know how to decide which task is most important. For example, I usually have several customers at once. They all want something, and I have to keep them all happy.

3. **PRESENT.** Give a short presentation to show how you prioritize.

I can give an example of how I prioritize at work. ■

Unit Review: Go back to page 185. Which unit goals can you check off?

11 Spending and Saving Money

PREVIEW

Do you use a bank? Do you use credit cards? How do you usually pay your bills?

UNIT GOALS

- [ ] Discuss money and banking
- [ ] Use bank services wisely
- [ ] Budget expenses
- [ ] Read a utility bill
- [ ] Save money on utilities

- [ ] Ask about appliances and utilities
- [ ] **Academic skill:** Identify author's purpose
- [ ] **Writing skill:** Add specific examples
- [ ] **Workplace soft skill:** Think critically

A PREDICT. Look at the pictures. What do you see?

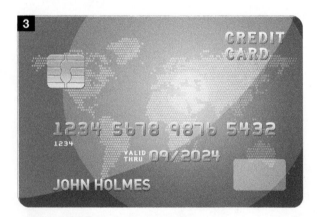

Vocabulary

B **MATCH. Look at the pictures on page 206. Write the numbers.**

Money and Banking

_____ ATM/debit card
_____ ATM withdrawal
_____ balance
_____ bank statement
_____ bank teller
_____ check
_____ credit card

C ▶ **LISTEN AND POINT. Then listen and repeat.**

D **IDENTIFY. Read the bank statement on page 206. Answer the questions.**

1. What was Myra's account balance at the start of the month? _____

2. How much money did Myra spend on debit card purchases? _____

3. How much money did she take out of the ATM? _____

4. How much money did she put into her bank account? _____

5. What was her account balance at the end of the month? _____

Show what you know!

1. **DISCUSS. If you have a bank account, do you read your statements? Why are bank statements useful? What can happen if you don't use them?**

2. **WRITE. Explain how to open a bank account. Explain the difference between a credit card and a debit card.**

   I want to open a bank account. First, I will . . .

I can discuss money and banking. ■   I need more practice. ■

For more practice, go to MyEnglishLab.

Listening and Speaking

Use bank services wisely

1 BEFORE YOU LISTEN

A **DISCUSS.** Do you use direct deposit? Why or why not? What are the advantages and disadvantages?

> When you have *direct deposit,* your employer puts your paycheck in your bank account electronically.

B **INTERPRET.** Read the ad. What is a cash bonus?

Zenith Bank

✔ Free checking account when you bank online or use direct deposit.

✔ Open your account today and get a $50 cash bonus.

✔ Open a free savings account with just $25.

What are you waiting for?
Banking has never been so easy.

2 LISTEN

This is a radio advertisement for Zenith Bank.

A ▶ **LISTEN FOR MAIN IDEA.** Circle the answer.

What is the commercial about?
    a. savings accounts   **b.** checking accounts

B ▶ **LISTEN FOR DETAILS.** Circle the answers.

1. What happens if you have direct deposit?
    a. You get a free checking account.   **b.** You pay fees for an account.

2. To get a cash bonus, when do you need to open an account?
    a. on or before April 3   **b.** on or after April 3

3. What is one way to get a free checking account?
    a. make any deposit   **b.** enroll in mobile banking

4. What are some things you can do with the mobile app?
    a. pay bills and transfer money   **b.** withdraw money and close your account

5. How much is the bonus?
    a. $100   **b.** $50

Listening and Speaking

3 PRONUNCIATION

A ▶ **PRACTICE. Listen. Then listen and repeat.**

1. If you want to open a bank account, you need to show ID.
2. If you want to deposit a check, you need to sign the back of it.
3. If you get the app, you can check your balance on your phone.
4. If you have direct deposit, your employer puts your paycheck in your account.

> **Pausing at Punctuation**
>
> When you start a sentence with the word *if*, your voice should pause at the comma. Your voice should go down at the end of the sentence.

B ▶ **APPLY. Listen. Add a comma where you hear a pause.**

1. If you have any questions please feel free to ask me.

2. If you want to open an account you need to fill out this form.

3. If you have less than $100 in your checking account you will pay a fee.

4. If you lose your debit card you should call this phone number.

4 CONVERSATION

A ▶ **LISTEN AND READ. Then practice the conversation with a partner.**

A: Hi. How may I help you?

B: Hi. I'd like to open a free checking account.

A: Sure. There are a couple of ways to qualify. First of all, if you have direct deposit, you get a free checking account.

B: Hmm. Well, I don't have direct deposit.

A: OK, then there is a second way to qualify. Do you have a smartphone? If you enroll in mobile banking, you can get a free checking account.

B: Oh, sure. I can enroll in mobile banking.

A: Great. To get started, all you have to do is download our app.

B **DISCUSS. Do you use mobile banking? What do you like about it? What don't you like about it?**

I can use bank services wisely. ■	I need more practice. ■

For more practice, go to MyEnglishLab.

Grammar

Present real conditional

If Clause	Result Clause
If you have direct deposit,	you get a free checking account.
If you open a new account,	you can get a $50 reward.

Result Clause	If Clause
You get a free checking account	**if** you have direct deposit.
You can get a $50 reward	**if** you open a new account.

Grammar Watch

- When the *if* clause comes first, use a comma between the clauses.
- Use the simple present in the *if* clause.
- Use *can, should,* or *must* in the result clause.
- Use an imperative in the result clause. (*If you want a free checking account, open an account with Zenith.*)

A **INVESTIGATE.** Circle the *if* clauses. Underline the result clauses.

Do you have a debit card? A debit card is similar to a credit card, but the money comes directly from your checking account. You will need to create a personal identification number, or PIN, to use your debit card. Do not share this number with anyone. If someone has your PIN, he or she can withdraw money from your checking account. If someone has your PIN, call your bank or go online to change it. If you lose your debit card, call your bank immediately to cancel the card. You can use your debit card to make purchases at a store or withdraw money from an ATM. Always check your bank account balance before you make purchases with your debit card. If you spend more money than you have, the bank may charge an overdraft fee.

PIN (personal identification number): a secret number password you type into an ATM to use it

B **PRACTICE.** Write one sentence. Use *if.*

1. you can hurt your credit / you write bad checks

   If you write bad checks, you can hurt your credit.

2. you want to buy a house / you need good credit

3. it's difficult to get a loan / you have bad credit

4. you can download an app / you want to use mobile banking

5. you lose your checks / you need to call the bank

Grammar

C **APPLY.** Combine the sentences. Use *if*.

1. You can use it to buy things at stores. You have a debit card.

   If you have a debit card, you can use it to buy things at stores.

2. You do a transaction at an ATM. You need to type in a secret PIN.

   _____

3. You need to tell the bank as soon as possible. You lose your debit card.

   _____

4. Someone steals your debit card. They can take money out of your bank account.

   _____

5. Call the credit card company immediately. Your credit card is missing.

   _____

Show what you know!

1. **COLLABORATE.** Discuss the following situations. How can you keep your personal information safe? What should you do?

   Your credit card expires.
   You lose your debit card.
   You have old bank statements.
   You are alone late at night at an ATM.

2. **WRITE.** Imagine you get an email that says you need to send your personal information so your bank account will be up-to-date. Explain what you should do in this situation. Use present real conditional.

   If I get an email that asks for my personal information, I should . . .

I can use present real conditional. ■   I need more practice. ■

For more practice, go to MyEnglishLab.

Lesson 4

Read about credit card debt

1 BEFORE YOU READ

DISCUSS. What is a credit card? Do you have a credit card? When do you use it?

2 READ

▶ Listen and read.

Academic Skill: Identify author's purpose

Writers have a purpose (or reason) for writing. Their purpose can be to give information, make an argument, or entertain. Sometimes a writer has more than one purpose.

Credit Card Debt

In the U.S., the average household has $16,000 in credit card debt. The amount has risen 10 percent since 2013. It's very easy to get into credit card debt. However, you can avoid it. You just have to be careful.

5 How do so many people get into credit card debt? You can buy almost anything with a credit card. It's easy to forget how much money you are spending. When you use a credit card, you are borrowing money from the credit card company. Most credit card companies don't require

10 you to pay the full amount you owe each month. Instead, you can just pay a part of it—the minimum. But then you have to pay interest to the credit card company. Sometimes the interest rate is 24 percent or higher!

This interest makes things cost more. Let's say you buy a

15 TV for $1,000. Your interest rate is 24 percent. You pay only the minimum each month. It could take six years to pay for the TV. It will cost you twice as much! $1,000 for the TV, and another $1,000 for interest. In the end, you

pay a lot of extra money. It's no wonder many people can't

20 pay off their credit card bills every month.

How can you use credit cards wisely? Try these tips:

1. Don't use more than one or two credit cards.

2. Pay in cash when you shop. Leave your credit card at home. Use credit cards only for big purchases.

25 **3.** Don't pay your credit card bill late. Late payments mean penalties. For example, you might pay a fee of $50. Always pay at least the minimum on time.

Credit card debt is a big problem these days. However, if you follow these tips, you can protect yourself from credit

30 card debt.

Who has the most credit card debt?

People between the ages of 35 and 54 have the most credit card debt. Why? Middle-aged people usually have families. They need to spend more money than young or elderly people do.

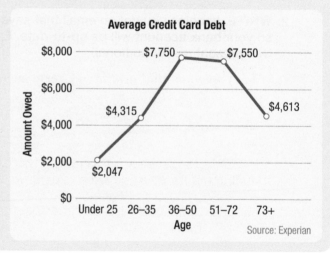

Average Credit Card Debt

Amount Owed

$8,000 — $7,750 — $7,550
$6,000
$4,315
$4,000 — $4,613
$2,000
$2,047
$0

Under 25 26–35 36–50 51–72 73+

Age

Source: Experian

3 CLOSE READING

A IDENTIFY. What is the main idea of the article?

a. It's easy to get into credit card debt, but you can avoid it if you're careful.
b. Most credit card companies don't require you to pay the full amount you owe each month.
c. Interest is the reason many people can't pay off their credit card bills every month.

B CITE EVIDENCE. Complete the sentences. Where is the information? Write the line numbers.

Lines

1. Credit card companies require you to pay _____ every month.
   a. the minimum   b. the interest   c. the full amount   _____

2. You should use credit cards to buy _____.
   a. everything   b. small purchases   c. big purchases   _____

3. You have to pay a penalty when _____.
   a. you pay only   b. you pay the full   c. you pay your   _____
      the minimum   amount due   bill late

4. The author's purpose is to _____.
   a. convince people   b. help people avoid   c. explain how credit   _____
      not to use   credit card debt   cards work
      credit cards

C INTERPRET GRAPHICS. Complete the sentences about the line graph.

1. Americans with the most credit card debt are _____ years old.
   a. less than 25
   b. between 36 and 50
   c. between 51 and 72

2. For most Americans, credit card debt _____ until they are 36 years old.
   a. increases
   b. decreases
   c. stays the same

4 SUMMARIZE

What are the most important ideas in the article? Write three sentences in your notebook.

Show what you know!

1. **ANALYZE.** Do you know anyone who has credit card debt? Describe the person's spending habits. Has he or she experienced the situation described in the article? How so?

2. **WRITE.** Summarize the issue of credit card debt. How do people get into debt, and how can they avoid it?

People get into credit card debt when they buy too much with credit cards . . .

I can identify author's purpose while reading. ☐   I need more practice. ☐

To read more, go to MyEnglishLab.

1 STUDY THE MODEL

ANALYZE. Read the model and Writing Skill. Then answer the questions.

Save on Your Electricity Bill

Electricity is a big expense, but there are many ways to save. You can turn off equipment when you are not using it. For example, turn off your television at night. You can use special products, such as energy-saving light bulbs. You can also cook more efficiently. For instance, use a microwave to boil water instead of an electric stove. It's more efficient. We all want to save money, and using electricity wisely can help you save.

Writing Skill: Add specific examples

Add specific examples to help the reader understand your ideas. Begin your examples with the words *for example, such as,* or *for instance.*

1. What are three ways to save money on electricity?
2. What are examples of each of these ways?

2 PLAN YOUR WRITING

Ⓐ **BRAINSTORM. Ask and answer the questions.**

What is another big expense? How can you save money on that expense?

Ⓑ **OUTLINE. Include examples of how to save money.**

Topic Sentence: _____

First Way: _____   Example: _____

Second Way: _____   Example: _____

Third Way: _____   Example: _____

Concluding Sentence: _____

3 WRITE

EXPLAIN. Write about how to save money on an expense. Give examples. Use the model, the Writing Skill, and your ideas from Exercise 2 to help you.

4 CHECK YOUR WRITING

COLLABORATE. Read the checklist. Read your writing together. Revise your writing.

WRITING CHECKLIST

☐ Does the paragraph include different ways to save money?

☐ Does the paragraph include specific examples?

☐ Do the examples begin with *for example, such as,* or *for instance*?

I can add specific examples. ■   I need more practice. ■

For more practice, go to MyEnglishLab.

Listening and Speaking

Budget expenses

1 BEFORE YOU LISTEN

IDENTIFY. Look at this budget for a married couple. How much money did they make last month before and after taxes? Circle the amounts. Then add up their expenses. Write their total expenses. How much money was left over?

2 LISTEN

This is a podcast about financial planning.

A ▶ **LISTEN FOR MAIN IDEA.** Circle the answer.

What is the topic of this conversation?
a. People don't like to budget.
b. People need to change their spending habits.
c. People need to budget for their future.

B ▶ **LISTEN FOR DETAILS.** Circle the answers.

1. What percentage of Americans don't budget?
   a. 6
   b. 60
   c. 16

2. What does the host say people need to budget for?
   a. emergencies
   b. financial goals
   c. both a and b

C ▶ **EXPAND.** Listen. Put the steps in the correct order.

_____ Figure out your expenses.

_____ Write down your net income.

_____ Check to see if your budget is realistic.

_____ Build savings into your budget.

January

Income		
	Gross income	3,300.00
	Taxes	380.00
	Net income	2,920.00
Savings	—	—
Expenses		
Housing	Rent	1,275
Food	Groceries	350
Transportation	Car insurance	300
	Car loan	200
	Gas and repairs	250
Utilities	Electric	150
	Cell phone	120
Children's	Clothing	10
Medical	Pharmacy	25
Entertainment	TV	90
	Miscellaneous	30
Total Expenses		

I can budget expenses. ■   I need more practice. ■

For more practice, go to MyEnglishLab.

Grammar

Future real conditional

If Clause	Result Clause
If you save some money each month,	you will be ready for an emergency.
If you pay your credit card bills on time,	you will save a lot of money on late fees.

Result Clause	*If* Clause
You will be ready for an emergency	**if** you save money each month.
You will save a lot of money on late fees	**if** you pay your credit card bills on time.

Grammar Watch

- Use the simple present in the *if* clause.
- Use *will* or *might* before a main verb in the result clause.

A INVESTIGATE. Circle the *if* clauses. Underline the main clauses.

WOMEN | MEN | HOME | ACTIVE 🔍

The Furniture Guy

In Seattle, Washington, Lloyd Evans helps people save money on furniture for their apartments. He finds and gives away used furniture to refugees from war-torn countries. If Lloyd learns of a family who needs help, he will spend extra time to meet their personal needs. Lloyd keeps extra furniture in a storage space until he finds someone who wants it. If people want furniture and visit Lloyd's storage space, they will find three rooms of sofas, beds, tables, chairs, cribs, TVs, and other furniture.

The refugees are very thankful to Lloyd. If you visit Lloyd's house, you will see African drums and Kurdish paintings. These are some of the gifts from the families Lloyd has helped.

B CHOOSE. Cross out the incorrect verbs.

1. If you **carpool / ~~will carpool~~**, you'll spend less money on transportation.
2. If you **will get / get** a monthly bus pass, you'll save on bus fare.
3. Your car will last longer if you **change / will change** the oil regularly.
4. You might save money on repairs if you **fix / might fix** your car.
5. If you **will take / take** good care of your car, it will last longer.
6. You will pay less in gas if you **don't drive / won't drive** too fast.

Grammar

C **COMPLETE.** Make future real conditionals with the verbs in parentheses. More than one answer is sometimes possible.

1. If you _____read_____ the supermarket's ads, you _____will know_____ which items are on sale.
   (read)   (know)

2. If you _____ coupons, you _____ less.
   (use)   (pay)

3. You _____ only the things you need if you _____ a shopping list.
   (buy)   (use)

4. If you _____ at a farmers' market, you _____ fresher fruit.
   (shop)   (get)

5. You _____ less for some items if you _____ the store brand.
   (pay)   (buy)

6. If you _____ supermarket prices, you _____ if you're getting a good deal.
   (compare)   (know)

Show what you know!

1. **COLLABORATE.** Look at the categories below. What are some ways you can save money on these things?

   appliances   children's clothing and shoes   furniture   transportation

   A: If you look for online coupons, you'll save a lot of money on appliances.
   B: You might save money on children's clothing if you shop at secondhand stores.

2. **WRITE.** Make a list of five things you can do to save money this year. Use future real conditional.

   1. I will save money if I _____
   2. If _____
   3. _____
   4. _____
   5. _____

I can use future real conditional. ☐   I need more practice. ☐

Lesson 8

Workplace, Life, and Community Skills

Read a utility bill and save money on utilities

1 READ A UTILITY BILL

A **DISCUSS.** Which utilities do you pay for? Gas? Electric? Water?

B **READ.** Look at the electric bill. Circle the amount due this month.

Your Account Number
987 654 320 3
Roberto Salazar
1801 E. South Street
Long Beach, CA 90805

24-Hour Service and info
(800) 427-2000

SunCal Energy
PO Box A
Monterey Park, CA 91755
www.suncalenergy.com

Billing Period	**Meter number**	Next meter reading date on or about 09/06/19
From 07/09/19 to 08/09/19	06076856	

Previous Charges	**Account Balance**
Total Amount Due at Last Billing	185.01
Payment – Jul 16 2019 Thank you	185.01 CR
Previous Balance	.00

Current Charges	**Amount**
Customer Charge 30 Days	4.93
Electricity Charges	180.07
Taxes and Fees	15.34
Total Electric Charges including Taxes and Fees	200.34
Total Amount Due	**200.34**

Current Amount Past Due if not paid by Aug 31, 2019.
A late charge of $5.00 may apply.

Your Energy Use Pattern

Energy Tip: We measure energy by the kilowatt-hour (kWh). When you read your utility bill, kWh shows how much energy you used.

Special Discount *You may be eligible for California Alternate Rates for Energy (CARE) program. For more information and to request an application, please call (800) 772-5050.*

C EVALUATE. Look at the bill again. Write *T* (true) or *F* (false).

_____ **1.** Last month's bill was $185.01.

_____ **2.** Last month's bill was for the same amount as this month's bill.

_____ **3.** This month's bill is due July 16.

_____ **4.** Last month's bill was paid, and there is no balance due.

_____ **5.** It is possible to apply for a special plan to pay less money for energy.

_____ **6.** If the bill is paid late, there is no fee.

D INTERPRET. Look at the graph on the bill. Circle the answers.

1. What does the graph show?
   a. energy use each week   **b.** energy use each month

2. When was the least electricity used?
   a. July and August   **b.** April and October

3. What does kWh represent?
   a. money spent on energy   **b.** energy used each hour

4. When was the most electricity used?
   a. August   **b.** January

2 SAVE MONEY ON UTILITIES

A APPLY. Check (✓) the things you do to save money on utilities.

☐ I turn off the lights when I leave a room.

☐ I turn off the air conditioner or heater when I leave home.

☐ I use fans instead of an air conditioner.

☐ I _____.

B DISCUSS. What are some other ways you can save money on utilities?

C GO ONLINE. Find other ways you can save energy.

I can read a utility bill and save money on utilities. ■   I need more practice. ■

Listening and Speaking

Ask about appliances and utilities

1 BEFORE YOU LISTEN

A **READ.** When people look for an apartment, they often look at classified ads. Write the abbreviations next to the words.

A

Oak Street
2 BR/1 BA
in 2 family house
New refrig., elec. stove
Cable TV incl.
H/HW incl.
$1,000/month
Avail. now
Call 555-817-2847

B

Argos Boulevard
Lg 2 BR/2 BA
Sunny EIK, laundry in
basement
Quiet neighborhood w/
good schools
$1100/month
No sec. dep. req.
Call 555-801-2709

C

Tremont Street
2 BR/1 BA
$1,200/month
Close to freeways
Lg LR, EIK
Elec. stove incl., Gas incl.
street pkg.
Liam_Caroll@yahoo.com

D

Cabela Ave.
2 BR/2 BA
gas, elec. & water
incl.
gas stove incl.
Near downtown
$1,100/month
Sec. dep. = $500
Call 555-310-3110

_____ available   _____ bathroom   _____ bedroom

_____ eat-in kitchen   _____ electric/electricity   _____ heat/hot water

_____ included   _____ large   _____ living room

_____ parking   _____ security deposit required   _____ with

B **DISCUSS.** Which things are most important to you in an apartment?

2 LISTEN

Roberto is calling a rental agent about an apartment.

A ▶ **LISTEN FOR MAIN IDEA.** Which apartment is Roberto calling about?

B ▶ **LISTEN FOR DETAILS.** Circle the answers.

1. What appliances are included?
   a. refrigerator and gas stove   **b.** electric stove   **c.** refrigerator and electric stove

2. What utilities are included?
   a. heat and hot water   **b.** gas   **c.** gas, electric, and water

3. When will Roberto meet the rental agent?
   a. at 3:00   **b.** at 3:30   **c.** at 4:00

3 PRONUNCIATION

A ▶ PRACTICE. Listen. Then listen and repeat.

I'd like to find an apartment in a good school district.
How much do you want to spend?
We need to live close to downtown.
I'd like to come see it.

B ▶ APPLY. Listen. Write the missing words.

1. We _____ live close to work.

2. I'd _____ make an appointment for this afternoon.

3. They _____ eat Chinese food for lunch.

4. Do you _____ meet at the new apartment?

4 CONVERSATION

A ▶ LISTEN AND READ. Then practice the conversation with a partner.

A: Hello. W&M Management Company.
B: Hi. I'm looking for a two-bedroom apartment.
A: OK, sure. How much do you want to spend?
B: No more than $1,200. And we need to live close to downtown.
A: Let me see. Hmm. I've got a great two-bedroom apartment on Cabela Avenue.
B: Does it come with appliances?
A: Yes, a refrigerator and a gas stove.
B: How much is the rent?
A: $1,100.
B: Are utilities included?
A: Yes, gas, electric, and water.
B: That's sounds good! I'd like to come see it.

Roberto

B ROLE-PLAY. Make a similar conversation. Use the ads on page 220.

C MAKE CONNECTIONS. Have you had trouble finding housing? Do you have trouble with your appliances or utilities?

I can ask about appliances and utilities. ■   I need more practice. ■

For more practice, go to MyEnglishLab.

Lesson 10

Grammar

Gerunds and infinitives as objects

Verb + Gerund	Verb + Infinitive
I **don't mind living** in an apartment.	I **need to live** close to the city.
We **finished packing** last night.	We **plan to move** next month.
I **prefer living** close to a shopping center.	I **prefer to live** close to a shopping center.

A **INVESTIGATE.** Underline the infinitives. Circle the gerunds.

My husband and I plan to rent an apartment in Long Beach. We plan to sign a lease tomorrow. The lease is for one year. The rent is $1,200 a month. The lease says the landlord promises to pay for heat, water, and gas. We need to pay electric and trash. The landlord is nice, and he offered to pay for new locks. We appreciated getting the help. I'm sure we'll enjoy living there, but if we want to move, we need to give the landlord one month's notice. If we don't, we lose our security deposit.

lease: a contract that allows someone to live in an apartment or house for a specific time period in exchange for rent

Grammar Watch

- Some verbs are used only with a gerund (*mind, feel like, finish*).
- Some verbs are used only with an infinitive (*afford, agree, hope, intend, mean, need, offer, plan, promise, wait, want*).
- Some verbs are used with both gerunds and infinitives (*like, love, prefer, start*).
- See page 263 for more information.

B **CHOOSE.** Cross out the incorrect form of the verbs.

1. We don't mind ~~to live~~ / **living** in an apartment, as long as the neighbors are quiet.
2. We hope **to get / getting** an apartment in a neighborhood with a good school.
3. I want **to find / finding** an apartment that has all utilities included.
4. Would you mind **to wait / waiting** for a few minutes? The landlord is on his way.
5. We need **to save / saving** money for the security deposit.
6. Do you plan **to move / moving** in next week?

Grammar

C **COMPLETE.** Write the correct form of the verbs in parentheses.

1. **A:** Do we need _____to pay_____ both the first month's rent and the security deposit?
   (pay)

   B: Just the first month's rent—I can wait _____ the security deposit.
   (get)

2. **A:** When do you plan _____ in?
   (move)

   B: As soon as we finish _____. Maybe on Friday?
   (pack)

   A: OK, that's fine. I don't mean _____ you. We'd just like _____
   (hurry)   (know)

   when you're coming. And remember, no one is allowed _____ in after 5:00 p.m.
   (move)

3. **A:** Do you plan _____ cable?
   (get)

   B: How much is it?

   A: The apartment is cable ready. So if you feel like _____ it, call the cable company.
   (get)

   The cable packages start at $85 a month.

   B: I don't think we can afford _____ it right now.
   (get)

Show what you know!

1. **COLLABORATE.** Talk about the kind of housing you want or need. Use the words below and your own ideas.

   | can afford / can't afford | don't mind | hope | like / don't like |
   | need / don't need | plan / don't plan | prefer | want / don't want |

   I don't want to live on the first floor because my neighborhood is not that safe.

   I don't mind living on a high floor even if I have to climb a lot of stairs.

2. **WRITE.** Describe the kind of housing you want or need in the future.

   I want to live . . .

   I need . . .

I can use gerunds and infinitives as objects. ■   I need more practice. ■

For more practice, go to MyEnglishLab.

Soft Skills at Work

Think critically

1 MEET JIN

Read about one of his workplace skills.

I think critically. I am able to consider many points of view. For example, I get feedback from several different people before I make a decision.

2 JIN'S PROBLEM

A READ. Write *T* (true) or *F* (false).

Jin works at Trust Bank. He has been employed there for the past four years. Recently, the bank updated its website, but there are some problems with it. It is difficult to use. Bank customers have problems getting to their accounts. Employees can't access information easily.

Jin's manager discussed the issues with him in detail. He gave Jin specific instructions about how to make the website more user-friendly. Jin has other ideas about how to solve the problems.

_____ **1.** The problems with the website are Jin's fault.

_____ **2.** The website can't be fixed.

_____ **3.** Jin disagrees with his manager's ideas.

B ANALYZE. What is Jin's problem? Write your response in your notebook.

3 JIN'S SOLUTION

A COLLABORATE. Jin thinks critically. He knows how to use resources to solve problems effectively. What should he do? Explain your answer.

1. Jin disagrees with his manager but follows his instructions. He doesn't want to cause trouble.
2. Jin disagrees with his manager but politely explains his idea and asks to do things differently.
3. Jin disagrees with his manager but asks to collect ideas from other employees and customers. He then suggests a different way to fix the website.
4. Jin _____.

B ROLE-PLAY. Act out Jin's solution with your partner.

Show what you know!

1. **REFLECT.** Have you ever had to think critically and consider many points of view at work? Give an example.

2. **WRITE.** Now write your example in your Skills Log.

   I can think critically. I use resources to help me think differently. For example, I worked with my co-workers to come up with a better way to ask for time off work.

3. **PRESENT.** Give a short presentation to show how you think critically.

I can give an example of how I think critically at work. ☐

Unit Review: Go back to page 205. Which unit goals can you check off?

12 Visiting Washington, D.C.

PREVIEW

Washington, D.C., is the capital of the U.S. The U.S. government is located there. What do you know about it?

UNIT GOALS

- [ ] Recognize places in or near Washington, D.C.
- [ ] Identify and discuss favorite places
- [ ] Read a subway map
- [ ] Ask for and give directions
- [ ] Talk about the U.S. government

- [ ] Identify famous places in Washington, D.C.
- [ ] **Academic skill:** Summarize
- [ ] **Writing skill:** Use sensory words to describe
- [ ] **Workplace soft skill:** Locate information

Vocabulary

Washington, D.C.

A **PREDICT.** Look at the pictures. They show places of interest in or near Washington, D.C. Which places do you know?

B ▶ **LISTEN AND POINT.** Then listen and repeat.

Vocabulary

Washington, D.C.

1. White House
2. Supreme Court
3. Capitol Building
4. Jefferson Memorial
5. Washington Monument
6. Lincoln Memorial
7. U.S. Treasury
8. Smithsonian Institution
9. Pentagon

Study Tip

Translate

Make cards for the words *memorial*, *court*, *monument*, *treasury*, and *national*. Write these words on the front of five cards. Write each word in your native language on the back.

C IDENTIFY. Look at the pictures on page 226. Write the names of the places.

1. There are famous works of art here.

   _____

2. Judges explain the law here.

   _____

3. The president lives and works here.

   _____

4. This department makes sure the U.S. economy is strong.

   _____

5. The Department of Defense works here to keep the U.S. safe.

   _____

6. In this building, the Senate and the House of Representatives write laws.

   _____

7. There are large statues of former presidents at these two places.

   _____

Show what you know!

1. **DISCUSS.** Which places in Washington, D.C., would you like to visit? Why?

   I love art and history, so I want to visit the Smithsonian Institution.
   I'd like to visit the White House to see where the president lives.

2. **WRITE.** Imagine you are taking a trip to Washington, D.C. Identify the places you will visit.

   If I take a trip to Washington, D.C., I want to visit . . .

I can recognize places in or near Washington, D.C. ■   I need more practice. ■

For more practice, go to MyEnglishLab.

Identify and discuss favorite places

1 BEFORE YOU LISTEN

DISCUSS. Have you ever taken a tour of a city? Where did you go? What did you see? Would you recommend it to a friend?

tour: a short trip through a place to see it

2 LISTEN

Tao and Lin are discussing their favorite places to visit in Washington, D.C.

A ▶ **LISTEN FOR MAIN IDEA.** Circle the answer.

What is the relationship between the two people?
  a. strangers
  b. relatives
  c. friends

B ▶ **LISTEN FOR DETAILS.** Write *T* (true) or *F* (false).

_____ **1.** Tao went to Washington, D.C., a few months ago.

_____ **2.** The Red Room is a room in the White House.

_____ **3.** The Blue Room is a room at the Supreme Court.

_____ **4.** You can see rockets at the National Air and Space Museum.

_____ **5.** Lin will probably visit Washington, D.C., again.

_____ **6.** Lin is not interested in seeing the National Air and Space Museum.

3 PRONUNCIATION

A ▶ PRACTICE. Listen. Then listen and repeat.

did you ("didja")   Where did you go?
Did you go to Washington?
What did you see?
What did you like the most?

Did you

In conversation, the words *did you* are often pronounced "didja." The words are joined together and pronounced as one word.

B ▶ APPLY. Listen. Cross out the incorrect word.

1. Where **do / did** you live?

2. What **do / did** you like the best?

3. **Do / Did** you like the museum?

4. Where **do / did** you go for vacation?

5. What **do / did** you like to do?

4 CONVERSATION

A ▶ LISTEN AND READ. Then practice the conversation with a partner.

A: So, what did you like seeing the most in Washington?

B: Hmm. Well, I really enjoyed the White House, and my parents did, too. We went on a tour of the rooms inside. I especially liked the Red Room and the Blue Room. What was your favorite place?

A: I liked the White House, but my favorite places were the museums. There are so many to choose from! The National Museum of American History has a lot of interesting things, and the National Air and Space Museum does, too. Those were probably my two favorite museums.

B: We went to the National Museum of American History but not the National Air and Space Museum. My dad didn't want to go there, and my mom didn't, either. We didn't have enough time.

The Oval Office in the White House

B MAKE CONNECTIONS. Talk about a city you know well. What is the best time of year to visit the city? What is the best thing to see or do?

I can identify and discuss favorite places. ■   I need more practice. ■

For more practice, go to MyEnglishLab.

Grammar

Simple present and simple past: Additions

Affirmative					Negative				
She loves traveling,		I you we they	**do, too.**		He doesn't travel often,		I you we they	**don't, either.**	
I live in Denver,	and	he she	**does, too.**		I don't live in Miami,	and	he she	**doesn't, either.**	
They took a trip,		I you we he she	**did, too.**		He didn't go there,		I you we he she	**didn't, either.**	

A **INVESTIGATE. Underline the sentences that have additions.**

<u>Japan has beautiful cherry trees, and Washington, D.C., does, too.</u> Actually, in 1912, Japan gave 3,000 cherry trees as a gift to the city of Washington, D.C. The gift honors the friendship between the U.S. and Japan. It was a wonderful gift! Today, residents enjoy seeing the cherry trees blossom in April, and tourists do, too. Visitors from all around the world come to see the famous cherry blossoms. The Cherry Blossom Festival is one of the most popular events of the year. However, residents don't like the crowds and long lines, and tourists don't, either. If you want to enjoy the Cherry Blossom Festival, get up early to avoid the crowds. I had a great time at the festival last spring, and my parents did, too.

Grammar Watch

- Use *too* for affirmative sentences.
- Use *not* and *either* for negative sentences.
- Use a comma before *too* and *either*.

Washington Monument and cherry blossoms

Grammar

B MATCH. Complete the sentences.

1. I went to Washington, D.C., and my sister ___c___.

2. New York has a lot of great restaurants, and Washington _____.

3. My parents didn't like the long lines, and I _____.

4. They like to travel, and we _____.

5. I don't know much about the Smithsonian, and my wife _____.

    a. does, too.

    b. do, too.

    c. did, too.

    d. doesn't, either.

    e. didn't, either

C COMPLETE. Use the words in the box to complete the sentences.

Hope Diamond

did   didn't   ~~do~~   does   doesn't

1. I want to visit the Smithsonian Institution, and my parents _____do_____, too.

2. The National Air and Space Museum has an interesting collection, and the National Museum of Natural History _____, too.

3. I saw the Hope Diamond at the National Museum of Natural History, and my neighbor _____, too.

4. The National Museum of American History has some of the dresses worn by First Ladies. I didn't see that exhibit, and my husband _____, either.

5. The National Gallery of Art doesn't allow flash photography, and the National Museum of American History _____, either.

Show what you know!

1. **DISCUSS.** Talk about a city you have visited. What did you like about the city? What famous places are there?

2. **WRITE.** Compare the city you visited with the city where you live now. Use affirmative and negative additions.

    Mexico City has a lot of big shopping centers, and Dallas does, too.

I can use additions. ■

I need more practice. ■

For more practice, go to MyEnglishLab.

Lesson 4

Read a subway map and ask for and give directions

1 READ A SUBWAY MAP

A **EVALUATE.** Look at the map. It shows part of the subway system in Washington, D.C.

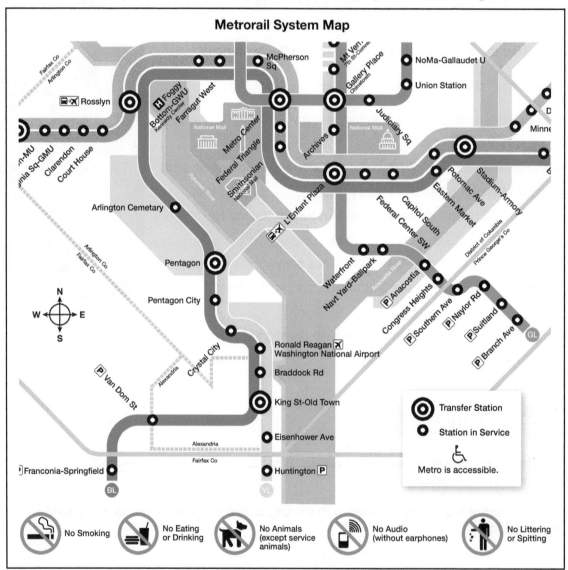

Metrorail System Map

B **COLLABORATE.** Discuss the questions.

1. What is the difference between the symbols **O** and **◎**?
2. What does *Metro is accessible* mean?
3. How many different subway lines are there?
4. You are at Metro Center and want to go to Union Station. Should you go east or west?

C INTERPRET. Answer the questions.

1. If you are on the green line at Gallery Place going to L'Enfant Plaza, are you going north, south, east, or west? _____

2. Which three lines stop at Smithsonian station? _____

3. You're at Dupont Circle on the red line and want to go to Smithsonian station. Where should you transfer? _____

4. Which lines go to Ronald Reagan Washington National airport? _____

5. You're at Stadium-Armory. How can you get to Waterfront? _____

2 ASK FOR AND GIVE DIRECTIONS

A COLLABORATE. Read and practice the conversation.

A: I'm trying to get to Ronald Reagan Washington National Airport, but I'm not sure how to get there. Do I have to change lines?

B: Yes. This stop is Judiciary Square. You need to go one more stop on the red line. Get off at Gallery Place. Then change to the yellow line.

A: The yellow line?

B: Yes. It will say Huntington.

A: When I get to the airport station, do I need to catch a bus?

B: No, the airport is right there.

B ROLE-PLAY. Make similar conversations.

A: You want to visit the Pentagon. You're at Metro Center.

B: Give directions. Then change roles. You want to go to Stadium-Armory station. You're at Smithsonian station.

A: Give directions.

C GO ONLINE. Find an app for the Washington, D.C., Metro System. Is there a subway system where you live? If so, find an app for it.

I can read a subway map and ask for and give directions. ■   I need more practice. ■

For more practice, go to MyEnglishLab.

Talk about the U.S. government

1 BEFORE YOU LISTEN

MAKE CONNECTIONS. What would you like to know about the U.S. government? If you could ask questions to a tour guide, what would you ask?

Tour guides show tourists a city. They ride on buses with the tourists, and they talk about and visit buildings.

Tour bus at Union Station, Washington, D.C.

2 LISTEN

A tour guide is leading a group of tourists around Washington, D.C.

A ▶ **LISTEN FOR MAIN IDEA.** Write the three places the tourists are going to see:

_____   _____   _____

B ▶ **LISTEN FOR DETAILS.** Write *T* (true) or *F* (false).

_____ **1.** The president works in the White House, but his family lives somewhere else.

_____ **2.** The Capitol is where Congress makes laws.

_____ **3.** Senators work in the House of Representatives.

_____ **4.** The Supreme Court is the highest court in the U.S.

_____ **5.** The Supreme Court makes laws.

_____ **6.** All the laws need to follow the U.S. Constitution.

Listening and Speaking

3 PRONUNCIATION

A ▶ PRACTICE. Listen. Then listen and repeat.

White House   **book** bag   **rest**room   **vis**itor center

B ▶ APPLY. Listen. Underline the compound noun in each sentence. Mark (•) the stressed syllable.

1. We visited the White House in Washington.

2. I had to check my handbag and camera.

3. My favorite room was the Blue Room.

4. We saw rocket ships at the museum.

5. I left my cell phone in the car.

> **Compound Nouns**
>
> A compound noun is made up of two words used together as a noun. Some compound nouns are one word, and some are two. We usually stress the first word or syllable in a compound noun.

4 CONVERSATION

A ▶ LISTEN AND READ. Then practice the conversation with a partner.

A: We are about to enter the White House. And please don't forget: No handbags, book bags, food and beverages, cameras, strollers, or video recorders are allowed inside the White House.

B: But I have a baby. Can't I take the baby in the stroller?

A: I'm sorry, strollers are prohibited.

B: Is there a place where I can store the stroller?

A: I'm sorry. We don't have any storage. But you can leave it outside.

C: Excuse me. Where are the restrooms?

A: The closest restrooms are in the White House Visitor Center.

B MAKE CONNECTIONS. Have you ever visited a famous place? What was it? Where was it located? Who were you with?

I can talk about the U.S. government. ■   I need more practice. ■

For more practice, go to MyEnglishLab.

Grammar

Simple present passive

Subject	be	Past Participle		
The White House	is	located		at 1600 Pennsylvania Avenue.
The White House and its gardens	are	visited	by 6,000 tourists	every day.

A INVESTIGATE. Underline the simple present passive.

In the U.S., power <u>is shared</u> between federal and state governments. The federal government is separated into three branches.

- The first branch is the Legislature. It's called Congress. It makes new laws that are signed by the president. Congress is made up of two parts—the Senate and the House of Representatives.
- The second branch is the Executive. It is headed by the president. The president controls many things, such as foreign affairs and the armed forces. The president also enforces the laws. Many important decisions are made by the president, but he or she does not make the laws.
- The third branch is the Judiciary. This branch includes the Supreme Court. The Supreme Court is the highest court in the U.S. It decides if laws follow the U.S. Constitution.

Grammar Watch

- We usually do not use the passive voice. We use the passive voice when
  - we don't know who did an action, or
  - the person or thing who did an action is not important.

B PRACTICE. Complete the paragraph. Use the simple present passive of the verbs in parentheses.

The White House ____*is located*____ at 1600 Pennsylvania Avenue in Washington, D.C. It
(locate)

_____ by 6,000 people every day! Why is it so popular? One reason is that it has
(visit)

many famous rooms. The Oval Office is a famous room that _____ by the president.
(use)

Important decisions _____ in the Cabinet Room. There are also beautiful rooms
(make)

that _____ after colors. These rooms _____ the Blue Room, the Red
(name)   (call)

Room, and the Green Room. Big parties _____ in the Red Room. Beautiful flowers
(hold)

_____ in the Blue Room. Guests _____ in the Green Room. Many
(display)   (entertain)

important leaders of other countries _____ there.
(welcome)

Grammar

C **COMPLETE.** Use the simple present passive forms of the verb in parentheses.

1. Veterans Day and Memorial Day ____*are observed*____ every year to remember our soldiers.
   (observe)

2. Martin Luther King, Jr. _____ in January on Martin Luther King, Jr. Day.
   (remember)

3. Independence Day _____ on the Fourth of July.
   (celebrate)

4. On President's Day, Presidents Washington and Lincoln _____.
   (honor)

Show what you know!

1. **COLLABORATE.** Discuss different U.S. holidays. When are they celebrated? How are they celebrated? Why are they celebrated?

   A: Independence Day is celebrated in July. Parades are held in many cities.
   B: Martin Luther King, Jr. Day honors the famous civil rights leader.

2. **WRITE.** Write a paragraph describing a U.S. holiday.

   Thanksgiving Day is celebrated in November. It is a day for giving thanks. People often take time off work to be with family. Some traditional Thanksgiving foods are turkey, mashed potatoes, corn, green beans, and cranberry sauce.

I can use the simple present passive. ■   I need more practice. ■

For more practice, go to MyEnglishLab.

Read about rights and freedoms

1 BEFORE YOU READ

BRAINSTORM. The Constitution is the highest law of the U.S. It gives many rights to U.S. citizens. What are some rights and freedoms people have in the U.S.?

2 READ

▶ Listen and read.

> **Academic Skill: Summarize**
>
> When you summarize a text, you state or write the most important ideas or information in the text. Summarizing helps you check your understanding and remember what you read.

Freedom of Religion and the Separation of Church and State

The U.S. guarantees certain rights and freedoms. One of these rights is the freedom of religion. Another is the separation of church and state. The government guarantees these rights in the First Amendment to the U.S. Constitution.
5 What do these ideas mean? Why are they important?

Freedom of Religion
Freedom of religion means that people can practice any religion. In the U.S., people worship at churches. They also worship at synagogues, mosques, temples, and many other
10 places. In fact, the U.S. may have more religions than any other country. Not everyone in the U.S. practices a religion. The Constitution protects this right, too.

Separation of Church and State
What about the separation of church and state? Religious
15 leaders are the "church." The government is "the state." Religious leaders cannot tell the government what to do. The government also cannot tell religious leaders what to do. The separation of church and state keeps religion out of government. It also keeps government out
20 of religion. There is no official religion of the U.S. The government cannot support one religion over another.

What does this mean for people in the U.S.? All government institutions must obey the First Amendment. Courthouses and public schools can't teach the beliefs of a certain
25 religion. They can't make people pray. At the same time, there is freedom of religion. People can usually practice their own religion in public.

In some countries, people are not allowed to practice different religions. Religious leaders control the
30 government. Freedom of religion and the separation of church and state are important. They make the U.S. different from many other countries. They are one reason that many immigrants choose to come to the U.S.

3 CLOSE READING

A IDENTIFY. What is the main idea of the article?

a. The government guarantees certain rights in the First Amendment to the Constitution.
b. Government institutions in the U.S. can't support or teach the beliefs of a certain religion.
c. People in the U.S. can practice any religion, and religious leaders and the government cannot tell each other what to do.

Reading

B CITE EVIDENCE. Answer the questions. Where is the information? Write the line numbers.

Lines

1. What does the government guarantee in the First Amendment to the Constitution?

   _____   _____

2. What is freedom of religion?

   _____   _____

3. What is the separation of church and state?

   _____   _____

4. In the U.S., which institutions have to obey the First Amendment?

   _____   _____

5. Why do freedom of religion and the separation of church and state make the U.S. different from some other countries?

   _____   _____

C INTERPRET VOCABULARY. Complete the sentences.

1. The word *guarantees* in line 1 means _____.
   a. promises **b.** discusses **c.** suggests

2. The word *worship* in line 8 means _____.
   a. live **b.** work **c.** practice a religion

3. The word *separation* in line 14 means _____.
   a. working **b.** bringing together **c.** keeping apart

4. The word *institutions* in line 23 means _____.
   a. ideas **b.** organizations **c.** workers

5. The word *obey* in line 23 means _____.
   a. make rules **b.** follow rules **c.** refuse to follow rules

4 SUMMARIZE

What are the most important ideas in the article? Write three sentences in your notebook.

Show what you know!

1. **REPORT.** Is there freedom of religion and a separation of church and state in your native country? What about other countries you have visited? Compare them to the U.S.

2. **WRITE.** Summarize the ideas of freedom of religion and the separation of church and state in the U.S.

   Freedom of religion means that people can practice any religion . . .

I can summarize while reading. ☐   I need more practice. ☐

To read more, go to MyEnglishLab.

Listening and Speaking

Identify famous places in Washington, D.C.

1 BEFORE YOU LISTEN

READ. Learn more about President Abraham Lincoln and the Civil War.

Abraham Lincoln was president during the U.S. Civil War. The U.S. Civil War was a war between the northern and southern states. It took place from 1861 to 1865. One of the causes of the war was slavery. The South wanted slavery and the North did not. The North won the war. In 1865, slavery became illegal in all of the states.

2 LISTEN

The tour guide continues guiding visitors around Washington, D.C. They are visiting the National Mall.

Abraham Lincoln

A  **LISTEN FOR MAIN IDEA.** Circle the answer.

What is the tour guide talking about?
   a. Abraham Lincoln's home
   b. the Lincoln Memorial
   c. the White House

B ▶ **LISTEN FOR DETAILS.** Write *T* (true) or *F* (false).

_____ **1.** Abraham Lincoln was the sixth president of the U.S.

_____ **2.** Lincoln was born in Illinois.

_____ **3.** Lincoln came from a poor family.

_____ **4.** Lincoln taught himself law and was a lawyer before he was president.

_____ **5.** Lincoln was president at the time of the Revolutionary War.

_____ **6.** Lincoln freed the slaves in the rebel states in 1863.

_____ **7.** Lincoln shot someone.

Listening and Speaking

3 CONVERSATION

A ▶ **LISTEN AND READ.** Then practice the conversation with a partner.

A: So, what do you want to do after the tour?
B: Well, we could go shopping or go back to the National Mall.
A: We've already been to the museums at the Mall.
B: I know, but I like walking around outside on the Mall. And we haven't visited any of the monuments or memorials yet.
A: Which ones do you want to see?
B: The Jefferson Memorial, the Lincoln Memorial, the Washington Monument, the Martin Luther King, Jr. Memorial. Let's see. I'm forgetting some of them.
A: Do you really want to see *all* of them? That's a lot of walking!
B: Come on! It will be fun. We'll walk slowly and stop a lot to take pictures.
A: OK, let's do it. I'm glad I wore comfortable shoes!

The National Mall

B **ROLE-PLAY.** Make conversations about places to see in Washington, D.C.

The National Zoo is free and has more than 1,500 animals, giant pandas, a bird house, a butterfly room, and several elephants.

Chinatown is downtown and has many Chinese and other Asian restaurants, nightlife, entertainment, and shopping.

I can identify famous places in Washington, D.C. ■   I need more practice. ☐

For more practice, go to MyEnglishLab.

Grammar

Past passive

Subject	*be*	Past Participle	
Abraham Lincoln	was		president in 1861.
		elected	
Abraham Lincoln and George Washington	were		for two terms.

A **INVESTIGATE. Underline the past participles.**

George Washington <u>was born</u> in 1732. He had very little school education, but he taught himself many things, such as how to read maps. He was chosen as the head of the Colonial Army in 1776. Washington was a hero and an excellent commander. His army fought to be free from the British in the Revolutionary War. Washington's army won. The British were defeated and went back to Britain. America had won its freedom.

B **COMPLETE. Use past passives.**

In 1789, George Washington ____was elected____ as the
                              (elect)
first president of the U.S. He _____ in 1792.
                               (reelect)
Washington did not want to be president a third time and went

back to his home. After his death, the city of Washington, D.C.,

_____ after him in his memory. George Washington's
  (name)
picture _____ on the U.S. one dollar bill to honor him.
        (print)
George Washington is known as the Father of Our Country.

George Washington

Show what you know!

1. **COLLABORATE. Research a U.S. president on the internet. Answer the following questions. Then share what you learn.**

   When was this person president? What was this president known for?
   Where was this president from? How many terms did this president serve?

2. **WRITE. Write a short report about the president you researched.**

I can use the past passive. ■   I need more practice. ■

For more practice, go to MyEnglishLab.

1 STUDY THE MODEL

ANALYZE. Read the model and Writing Skill. Then answer the questions.

A Special Place to Visit

Constitution Gardens is in Washington, D.C. Visitors to this special place can see fresh green grass, tall trees, and a beautiful blue pond. They can hear the cheerful sound of birds chirping, and they can feel the gentle wind. They can smell sweet flowers in the spring and summer. Constitution Gardens is not the most popular tourist attraction in Washington, D.C., but I love it.

Writing Skill: Use sensory words to describe

Use sensory words to describe a place. Sensory words are often adjectives. They describe things we notice when we use our senses, such as sight, hearing, touch, taste, and smell.

1. What place is described in the paragraph?
2. Which sensory words are used to describe the place?

2 PLAN YOUR WRITING

A **BRAINSTORM. Ask and answer the questions.**

What is a place you recently visited? What can you see there? What are sounds you can hear there? What does the place smell like?

B **OUTLINE. Include sensory words to describe what people would notice about the place.**

Place: _____

Sight: _____

Sound: _____

Touch: _____

Smell: _____

3 WRITE

DESCRIBE. Write about a place. Use the model, the Writing Skill, and your ideas from Exercise 2 to help you.

4 CHECK YOUR WRITING

COLLABORATE. Read the checklist. Read your writing together. Revise your writing.

WRITING CHECKLIST

☐ Does the paragraph describe a place?

☐ Does the paragraph use sensory words to describe the place?

I can use sensory words to describe. ■   I need more practice. ☐

For more practice, go to MyEnglishLab.

11 Soft Skills at Work

Locate information

1 MEET MAYA

Read about one of her workplace skills.

I know how to locate information. I am resourceful. For example, if I don't know the answer to a question, I know where to find the answer.

2 MAYA'S PROBLEM

A READ. Write *T* (true) or *F* (false).

Maya works for a travel company in New York City. She's had this job for five years and is efficient at dealing with any issue that comes up. An important business client from China is arriving soon. He has never been to Washington, D.C., and he would like to travel there while he is in the U.S.

Maya must organize the trip for him, but she has never been to Washington, D.C. She does not know anything about the area.

_____ **1.** Maya works in Washington, D.C.
_____ **2.** The client is visiting the U.S. from China.
_____ **3.** Maya has never been to Washington, D.C.

B ANALYZE. What is Maya's problem? Write your response in your notebook.

3 MAYA'S SOLUTION

A COLLABORATE. Maya can locate information. She is resourceful. What should she do? Explain your answer.

1. Maya tells her manager she cannot do the task since she's never been to Washington, D.C.
2. Maya contacts a travel agency in Washington, D.C., to plan the trip.
3. Maya goes online to research Washington, D.C. She makes a list of sites to see and places to go.
4. Maya _____.

B ROLE-PLAY. Act out Maya's solution with your partner.

Show what you know!

1. **REFLECT.** Have you ever needed to locate important information at work? Give an example.

2. **WRITE.** Now write your example in your Skills Log.

   I am resourceful. I can locate information I need. For example, if I don't know how to do something, I ask friends or co-workers who do know how.

3. **PRESENT.** Give a short presentation to show how you locate information.

I can give an example of how I locate information at work. ■

Unit Review: Go back to page 225. Which unit goals can you check off?

MY SOFT SKILLS LOG

This is a list of my soft skills. They are skills I use every day. They are important for work, school, and home. In a job interview, I can talk about my soft skills. I can give these examples from my life.

Unit 1: I'm inclusive.

For example, _____

_____

_____

_____

Unit 2: I take responsibility for professional growth.

For example, _____

_____

_____

_____

Unit 3: I separate work life and family life.

For example, _____

_____

_____

_____

Unit 4: I'm positive.

For example, _____

_____

_____

_____

Unit 5: I find creative solutions.

For example, _____

_____

_____

_____

Unit 6: I respond to customer needs.

For example, _____

_____

_____

_____

Unit 7: I'm flexible.

For example, _____

_____

_____

_____

Unit 8: I take initiative.

For example, _____

_____

_____

_____

Unit 9: I listen actively.

For example, _____

_____

_____

_____

Unit 10: I prioritize.

For example, _____

_____

_____

_____

Unit 11: I think critically.

For example, _____

_____

_____

_____

Unit 12: I locate information.

For example, _____

_____

_____

_____

GRAMMAR REVIEW

A Complete the conversation. Use the simple present form of the verbs in parentheses.

A: _____ you _____ around here?
                                         (live)

B: Yes, I _____. I _____ with my sister. She _____ an
                                  (live)   (have)

apartment on Oak Street. What about you?

A: I _____ around here, but I _____ nearby at Bloom's. My son
           (not / live)   (work)

_____ classes at the community center. Actually, I _____ to move,
       (take)   (need)

and this _____ like a nice neighborhood.
              (seem)

B: It is. When _____ you _____ to move?
                                           (want)

A: As soon as possible.

B: Let me call my sister. She _____ this neighborhood well. Maybe she can help you.
                                        (know)

B Complete the paragraph. Cross out the incorrect words.

Last November, our neighbors invited us to our first Thanksgiving dinner. It was **a lot of / many** fun.
We had **some / any** turkey, **a few / a little** sweet potatoes, **any / a lot of** rice, and a delicious
salad with **a little / a lot of** nuts. My husband tried **a little / a few** cranberry sauce, but I didn't try
any / some. I brought **much / some** homemade cupcakes and a cake for dessert. I think everyone
liked my desserts because by the end of the meal, there weren't **any / much** cupcakes and there
wasn't **many / much** cake left.

C Complete the paragraph. Use *used to* and verbs from the word box.

eat	go	have	see

I came to the U.S. from Brazil six years ago. My life here is different. In Brazil, I _____
my grandparents every weekend. Now, I only see them once a year. I _____ to the
beach and play volleyball or soccer on weekends. Now, I work most Saturdays, and on Sundays I
relax at home. In Brazil, my friends and I _____ all sorts of Brazilian specialties, like
fejoada. But here I only have those foods on special occasions. In Brazil, I never _____
steady work. But here I have a good job and many opportunities. All in all, I'm happy that I'm here. I
have a good future.

GRAMMAR REVIEW

UNIT 2

A Complete the conversation. Cross out the incorrect words.

A: Maria is thinking about going back to school.

B: When?

A: **She'll probably start / She'll start probably** this spring.

B: **Will she go / Might she go** to Bronx Community College?

A: No, **she won't / she might**. **She'll go / She goes** to Lehman College. It's closer to her home.

B: How many classes **will she take / she will take**?

A: She's not sure. She **might take / will take** one or two.

B: That's great. Maria's smart, and I'm sure **she'll do / she might do** well.

B Complete the conversation. Use the correct form of *be + going to* + the verb in parentheses.

A: My job will end next week. I _____ look for a new job.
  (have to)

B: Where _____ you _____?
  (look)

A: First I'll try online. Then I _____ the newspapers.
  (check)

B: Did you ask around? You have a big family. Maybe they can help.

A: Good idea. I _____ everyone next weekend at my cousin's wedding. I'll ask around.
  (see)

C Look at Tony's calendar for next week. Write questions and short answers. Use the present continuous.

1. When / Tony / register / for an English class?

   _____

2. What / Tony / do / on Tuesday?

   _____

3. Tony / buy books / on Thursday?

   _____

4. What day / Tony / start her class?

   _____

Monday	Tuesday
register for English class	take the English Placement Test

Wednesday	Thursday
buy books for class	English class begins

UNIT 3

A Complete the sentences. Use the correct form of the words in parentheses.

1. I want to go to a four-year college. _____ four years of English?
   (I / have to / take)

2. _____ any special tests for that college?
   (he / have to / take)

3. When _____ for City College?
   (he / should / apply)

4. Your application _____ in by March 30 of this year.
   (have to / be)

5. The test starts at 8:00. _____ in the room by 7:55.
   (you / have to / be)

6. _____ late for the test.
   (you / should / not / come)

B Complete the conversations. Build sentences with the words in the word boxes.

It's easy	for you	to always come on time
It's a good idea	for me	to make a mistake
It's hard	for us	to dress well
It's difficult	for him	to understand him

1. **A:** I have a job interview tomorrow. How should I dress?

   B: _____

2. **A:** My boss speaks very quickly. _____

   B: Ask him to speak more slowly.

3. **A:** Why do you and Hans always count the money twice?

   B: _____

4. **A:** Your friend Ivan is late for work again. Tell him I'm not happy about it.

   B: I'm sorry, Larry. The bus runs late sometimes. _____

C Complete the conversation. Use the simple past form of the verb in parentheses.

A: How _____ school?
   (be)

B: Great. We _____ to the museum.
   (go)

A: Which museum _____ you _____ to?
   (go)

B: The science museum.

A: What _____ you _____?
   (see)

B: We _____ the Leonardo da Vinci exhibit.
   (see)

A: I _____ he _____ an artist.
   (think)   (be)

B: He _____, but he _____ also a scientist. He _____ many talents.
   (be)   (be)   (have)

GRAMMAR REVIEW

UNIT 4

A Complete the conversations. Use the present perfect or the simple past form of the verb in parentheses. Use *for* or *since* where necessary.

1. **A:** _____ you ever _____ nights?
   (work)

   B: Yes, I _____. I _____ the night shift _____ three
   (work)

   months in 2018.

2. **A:** _____ you ever _____ to a technical school?
   (go)

   B: Yes, I _____. I _____ to ACME last year.
   (go)

3. **A:** _____ that store _____ closed for a long time?
   (be)

   B: It _____ closed _____ last year.
   (be)

4. **A:** How long _____ you _____ your own business?
   (have)

   B: I _____ my own business _____ over three years.
   (have)

5. **A:** What _____ you _____ before that?
   (do)

   B: Before that I _____ for The Wrap.
   (work)

B Rewrite each sentence with *used to.*

1. She lived in Cairo.

   _____

2. He worked at Lulu Products.

   _____

3. They shopped at Village Supermarket.

   _____

4. We played basketball at Green Park.

   _____

5. I took cooking classes.

   _____

UNIT 5

A Complete the conversations. Cross out the incorrect words or sentences.

1. **A:** Excuse me. Could we eat on the bus?

   B: Yes, you can. / Yes, you could.

2. **A: May you please / Would you please** fasten your seat belt?

   B: Oh, sure. Sorry about that.

3. **A:** There's a small carry-on bag in that corner. Is it yours?

   B: No, **mine / my** bag is on the bus. I think it's **her / hers**.

4. **A:** My grandfather needs a new ticket. He left **his / hers** at home.

   B: No problem. Just give me his name and address.

5. **A:** Could you **put / to put** your bags under the seat in front of you?

   B: Yes, of course. / Yes, I could.

6. **A:** We **won't be able to / couldn't** leave until they clean the plane.

   B: How long will that take?

7. **A:** We **won't be able to / couldn't** leave until the other train passed.

   B: How long did that take?

8. **A: May I / Will I** help you?

   B: Thanks. How much is a return ticket to Miami?

B Read the situations. Write polite requests. More than one answer is sometimes possible.

1. Someone's bag is on an empty seat on the bus. Ask the person to move his bag.

   _____

2. Ask someone if it's OK to use a cell phone on the bus.

   _____

3. You are taking a train trip. Ask a friend to drive you to the train station.

   _____

4. There's a storm. Ask if your bus will be able to leave on time.

   _____

GRAMMAR REVIEW

UNIT 6

A Compare the two refrigerators. Use the words in parentheses.

Brand	Price	Ease of use	Energy Efficient	Noise
W	$600	◑	◯	◯
X	$550	◯	◑	◑

◑ very good
◯ good
◑ bad

1. (noisy)

   _____

2. (expensive)

   _____

3. (quiet)

   _____

4. (cheap)

   _____

5. (efficient)

   _____

6. (easy to use)

   _____

B Complete each sentence with a verb and an *as . . . as* phrase. Use the adjective in parentheses.

Tina's Restaurant just opened up in my neighborhood. It's across the street from my favorite

place to eat, Bo's Diner. The good news is that Tina's _____ Bo's! I
                                                         (good)

love the chicken sandwich at Bo's, and Tina's chicken sandwich _____
                                                                  (tasty)

Bo's. I'm so happy. The service at Tina's _____ Bo's, and the staff
                                             (fast)

_____ the people who work at Bo's. Both are great places to eat. However,
   (polite)

Tina's is very popular right now. The wait at Bo's _____ it is at Tina's. Also,
                                                       (not / long)

Bo's prices _____ Tina's. For now, I think I'll continue going to Bo's Diner.
               (not / expensive)

A Complete the conversation. Write *a, an,* or *the.*

A: How's Bob?

B: Fine. He's looking for _____ new car. He had _____ old truck, but it used too much gas.

A: What kind does he want?

B: I'm not sure. I know he wants _____ smaller car.

A: Well, I saw _____ ad for a Honda Civic at _____ community center on River Avenue. I'll tell him about _____ ad. It looked like _____ good deal.

B Complete the conversation. Use the past continuous form of the verb in parentheses.

A: What caused the accident?

B: The driver _____ the road. He _____ at a map
                  (not / watch)   (look)
and _____ on his phone.
      (talk)

A: Where were you?

B: I _____ next to the bus stop. I could see everything from there.
   (stand)

C Combine the sentences into one sentence. Begin the new sentence with *when.*

1. It rains. Use the windshield wipers and turn on the headlights.

   _____

2. He has problems with his car. He goes to the repair shop on Oak Avenue.

   _____

3. You buy a car. You need to get car insurance.

   _____

4. You speed. You use more gas.

   _____

5. She sees stop lights or stop signs. She always comes to a complete stop.

   _____

GRAMMAR REVIEW

A Complete the sentences. Use the superlative form of the word in italics.

1. I went to a very *large* school. It's the _____ school in the city.

2. Do you have any *cheap* options for lunch? What's the _____ dish on the menu?

3. We've been trying to eat more *healthy* foods. What's the _____ food you have at this restaurant?

4. I think soccer is a *frustrating* game. What's the _____ game you've played?

B Complete the conversations. Use gerunds and the correct form of the verbs in parentheses.

1. **A:** When I get very hungry, I eat too much.

   B: _____ healthy snacks between meals.

(try / eat)

2. **A:** My husband has high blood pressure. What should he do?

   B: Tell him to _____ salty foods.

(avoid / eat)

3. **A:** I'd like my children to eat more vegetables, but they don't like them.

   B: Have you ever _____ vegetables to dishes they like?

(think about /add)

4. **A:** I started to diet five weeks ago, but I'm now only four pounds lighter.

   B: That's terrific. _____ what you're doing. It's better to lose weight

(keep / do)

   slowly. That way you keep it off.

C Rewrite each sentence. Start with a gerund.

1. It's good for your health to eat a lot of fresh fruits and vegetables.

   _____

2. It's hard to lose weight.

   _____

3. It's fun to cook.

   _____

4. It can be difficult to change your eating habits.

   _____

UNIT 9

A Read the conversation. Replace the nouns with *one* or *ones* whenever possible.

A: Excuse me. Are those computers on sale?

B: Which computers?

A: The computers over there. The small computers.

B: Yes, they are. They're all discounted.

A: Thanks. How much is this computer?

B: This computer is only $800 plus tax.

A: And that computer?

B: That computer is more. It's $1,400.

B Read the conversation between Joe and his manager, Steve. Then use the words in parentheses to complete the sentences.

Steve: Joe, please order some more supplies.
Joe: OK. What do we need?
Steve: Check the supply room. I know we're running low on paper.
Joe: OK. Anything else?
Steve: Yes. Answer the phone while Bill is away. He's out of the office all afternoon. And before you leave, don't forget to hand in your time sheet.

1. (order / Steve / Joe / ask)

   _____ some supplies.

2. (Steve / tell / check / Joe)

   _____ the supply room.

3. (watch / Joe / Steve / want)

   _____ the front desk.

4. (Joe / Steve / tell / not / forget / hand in)

   _____ his time sheet.

GRAMMAR REVIEW

UNIT 10

A Cross out the incorrect word.

1. I'm **interested / interesting** in what the doctor has to say.
2. The child was **frightened / frightening** by the hospital.
3. It's **embarrassed / embarrassing** to answer these questions in front of everyone in the waiting room.
4. He was **confused / confusing**. That's why he took too much medicine.
5. She was **frustrated / frustrating** that the doctor wouldn't see her that day.

B Complete the conversation. Use the present perfect continuous and the verbs in the word box.

eat	not / eat	exercise	feel	take	watch

A: So, Mr. Valdez, how _____ you _____? Any better?

B: A little. I _____ the pills, and I _____, but I still feel tired all the time.

A: What about your diet? _____ you _____ your diet?

B: Yes, a little. We _____ out as much, and I _____ healthier meals at home.

A: Good. A healthy diet is important. Let me take your blood pressure and see how that is.

C Complete the conversations. Use the gerund form of the verbs in the word box.

answer	be	bring	explain	feel	get	miss

1. **A:** John is worried about _____ an MRI.
   B: Is he afraid of _____ in a small space?
2. **A:** I plan on _____ a list of questions to ask Dr. Lee. He's helpful.
   B: Yes. Dr. Lee is good at _____ questions and _____ things clearly.
3. **A:** My friend complains about _____ weak and dizzy. She won't see a doctor because she's afraid of _____ work.
   B: Explain to your friend that her health is more important than any job.

UNIT 11

A Combine the two sentences into one sentence. Use the present real conditional.

1. I bank online. I can save money.

   _____

2. You can save money. You open a savings account.

   _____

3. We use direct deposit. We can get a cash bonus.

   _____

4. You don't have to pay right away. You use a credit card.

   _____

5. You pay interest. You don't pay your entire balance on a credit card bill.

   _____

B Complete the sentences. Cross out the incorrect words.

1. If you **pay / will pay** your bill late, you will pay a penalty.
2. If you **won't have / don't have** good credit, you will have trouble borrowing money for a house or car.
3. It **takes / will take** him five years to pay off his loan if he pays $100 a month.
4. She **isn't / won't have** trouble budgeting if she gives up her car.
5. If you **remember / will remember** your financial goals, it will be easier to save money.

C Complete the sentences. Cross out the incorrect words.

1. I hope **to find / finding** a cheap apartment near my job.
2. I keep **to look / looking** at ads in the paper and on the bulletin board at the community center.
3. Before we move, we need **to give / giving** our landlord two months' notice.
4. We don't mind **to fix / fixing** things ourselves if it means paying less rent.
5. We can't afford **to pay / paying** more than $1,000 a month.
6. We need **to live / living** near a subway station.

GRAMMAR REVIEW

UNIT 12

A Complete the sentences. Use words in the word box.

do	does	don't	didn't

1. I study English on Tuesdays, and my friend _____, too.
2. Marco didn't see the new movie, and Susan _____, either.
3. We don't like to eat seafood, and they _____, either.
4. She wants to visit New York, and I _____, too.

B Write questions in the simple present passive. Use the words in parentheses.

1. (What / the president's office / call)

   _____?

2. (Where / the National Air and Space Museum / locate)

   _____?

3. (When / Thanksgiving / celebrate)

   _____?

4. (What U.S. holiday / celebrate / on July 4)

   _____?

C Complete the paragraph. Use the past passive form of the verbs in the word box.

break	cancel	fill	take	wake

My brothers and I went to Washington, D.C. last week. We had some problems during our trip.
First, our flight _____. We got onto a different flight and arrived very late. We went
to our hotel. The nonsmoking rooms _____, so we got a smoking room. The room
_____ with a smoky smell. We tried to watch TV, but the TV _____. We
went to sleep. In the morning, we _____ by a noisy family in the next room.

GRAMMAR REFERENCE

Unit 1, Lesson 9, page 22

Common non-count nouns
Groups of similar items: baggage, clothing, equipment, furniture, garbage, money, cash, change, traffic
Drinks and fluids: water, coffee, tea, milk, oil, soda, soup, gasoline, blood
Foods: beef, bread, butter, cheese, chicken, chocolate, ice cream, lettuce, meat, pasta, rice, salad, sugar
Materials: glass, gold, paper, wood
Gases: air, oxygen, smoke, pollution
Concepts: advice, fun, health, homework, love, information, music, news, violence, work
Languages: Arabic, Chinese, English, Spanish
Fields of study: art, computer science, engineering
Entertainment: baseball, basketball, soccer, tai chi
Activities: driving, studying, swimming, walking
Nature: weather, fog, heat, humidity, lightning, rain, snow, thunder, wind, light, darkness, sunshine, electricity, fire

Measure words*	
a bit of salt	**a loaf of** bread
a bottle of juice	**a package of** cookies
a box of cereal	**a piece of** pie
a bowl of soup	**a pinch of** salt
a can of soda	**a pound of** rice
a carton of eggs	**a slice of** bread
a cup of sugar	**a stick of** butter
a gallon of gasoline	**a tablespoon of** oil
a jar of jam	**a teaspoon of** sugar
a quart of milk	

Measure words are usually used with non-count nouns so we can count the nouns.

GRAMMAR REFERENCE

Unit 2, Lesson 3, page 30

Contractions with *will*	
I will = I'll you will = you'll he will = he'll she will = she'll	it will = it'll we will = we'll they will = they'll

Unit 3, Lesson 10, page 62

Simple past: irregular verbs			
Base form	**Simple past**	**Base form**	**Simple past**
be	was	make	made
become	became	meet	met
buy	bought	pay	paid
catch	caught	put	put
come	came	read	read
cost	cost	ride	rode
cry	cried	run	ran
cut	cut	say	said
do	did	see	saw
drink	drank	sell	sold
drive	drove	send	sent
eat	ate	sit	sat
feel	felt	sleep	slept
find	found	speak	spoke
fly	flew	spend	spent
forget	forgot	stand	stood
get	got	steal	stole
give	gave	swim	swam
go	went	take	took
have	had	teach	taught
hear	heard	think	thought
hit	hit	try	tried
hold	held	wake	woke
hurt	hurt	wear	wore
know	knew	win	won
leave	left	write	wrote
lose	lost		

Present perfect: irregular verbs

Base form	Past participle	Base form	Past participle
be	been	make	made
become	become	meet	met
buy	bought	pay	paid
catch	caught	put	put
come	came	read	read
cost	cost	ride	ridden
cry	cried	run	run
cut	cut	say	said
do	done	see	seen
drink	drunk	sell	sold
drive	driven	send	sent
eat	eaten	sit	sat
feel	felt	sleep	slept
find	found	speak	spoken
fly	flown	spend	spent
forget	forgotten	stand	stood
get	gotten	steal	stolen
give	given	swim	swum
go	gone	take	taken
have	had	teach	taught
hear	heard	think	thought
hit	hit	try	tried
hold	held	wake	woken
hurt	hurt	wear	worn
know	known	win	won
leave	left	write	written
lose	lost		

GRAMMAR REFERENCE

Unit 6, Lesson 6, page 116

Comparative spelling rules
Add –er + *than* to most adjectives with one syllable. For example: **cheap** —➤ **cheaper than**
For adjectives ending with –y, change the –y to –ie and add –er. For example: **happy** —➤ **happier than**
For adjectives ending with –e, add –r. For example: **nice** —➤ **nicer than**
For adjectives that end in a consonant + a vowel + a consonant, double the consonant and add –er. For example: **big** —➤ **bigger than**
For adjectives with more than two syllables, add *more* before the adjective. For example: **expensive** —➤ **more expensive than**

Unit 8, Lesson 3, page 150

Superlative spelling rules
Add –est + *than* to most adjectives with one syllable. For example: **cheap** —➤ **cheapest**
For adjectives ending with –y, change the –y to –ie and add –est. For example: **happy** —➤ **happiest**
For adjectives ending with –e, add –st. For example: **nice** —➤ **nicest**
For adjectives that end in a consonant + a vowel + a consonant, double the consonant and add –est. For example: **big** —➤ **biggest**
For adjectives with more than two syllables, add *the most* before the adjective. For example: **expensive** —➤ **the most expensive**

Unit 10, Lesson 3, page 190

Common participial adjectives	
bored	boring
confused	confusing
embarrassed	embarrassing
excited	exciting
exhausted	exhausting
frightened	frightening
frustrated	frustrating
interested	interesting
overwhelmed	overwhelming
relaxed	relaxing
shocked	shocking
surprised	surprising
tired	tiring

Unit 11, Lesson 10, page 222

Verb + gerund		
admit	enjoy	mind
appreciate	escape	miss
avoid	explain	practice
can't help	feel like	quit
consider	finish	recommend
delay	forgive	regret
discuss	give up (stop)	risk
dislike	keep (continue)	suggest

Gerunds after prepositions		
agree with	believe in	depend on
approve of	care about	disapprove of
argue with	complain about	
ask about	decide on	

WORD LIST

UNIT 1

Countries
Brazil, 6
Cambodia, 6
China, 6
Colombia, 6
Ecuador, 6
El Salvador, 6
Ethiopia, 6
Laos, 6
Mexico, 6
Peru, 6

the Philippines, 6
Poland, 6
Russia, 6
Somalia, 6
South Korea, 6
Sudan, 6
Syria, 6
Ukraine, 6
Vietnam, 6

café, 14
celebrations, 20
city, 12
countryside, 12
go to a park, 8
hair salon, 14
holidays, 20
immigrants, 12
movie theater, 14
pharmacy, 14
population, 12

post office, 14
refugees, 12
rural areas, 12
shopping mall, 14
supermarket, 14
take an exercise class, 8
urban areas, 12
walk a dog, 8
watch a soccer game, 8

UNIT 2

achieve a goal, 32
apply for financial aid, 27
associate's degree, 28
automotive service
    excellence (ASE)
    certificate, 28
community center, 41
community services, 41
entrepreneurs, 32

equipment, 33
food and clothing drive, 41
get a certificate, 27
get a college degree, 27
get a high school diploma,
    27
get a promotion, 27
healthcare service, 41
job fair, 35

job listing, 34
license, 34
native-born, 32
neighborhood
    improvement, 41
obstacles, 38
reality, 33
set a goal, 38

Small business
    administration, 32
social media site, 34
state license, 28
supports, 38
take citizenship classes, 27
take responsibility, 44

UNIT 3

concept, 52
do research, 47
drop out, 47
effective, 52
electives, 50
fall behind, 48
figure out an answer, 47

go online, 47
go over homework, 47
go to a parent-teacher
    conference, 47
graduate, 57
hand in homework, 47
help someone out, 47

keep up with, 48
look up a word in a
    dictionary, 47
make personal
    connections, 52
make up a test, 47
memorize, 52

method, 52
report card, 58
self-test, 52
spaced repetition, 52
take time off, 55

UNIT 4

applicant, 78
cooperative, 66
dependable, 66
discriminate, 78
efficient, 66

employment history, 73
equipment, 69
flexible, 66
hardworking, 66
interview, 78

job application, 72
letter of recommendation,
    67
motivated, 66
organized, 66

pleasant, 66
punctual, 66
qualifications, 78
résumé, 72

UNIT 5

arrivals and departures
    display, 87
baggage screening, 98
bins, 87
board, 88
boarding pass, 87
car rental, 93
carry-on bag, 87

check in, 88
e-ticket, 87
electronic ticket, 87
gate, 87
kiosk, 87
lost and found, 93
luggage tags, 87
luggage, 87

mechanical problem, 88
metal detector, 87
passenger screening, 98
passenger, 87
public transportation, 84
screen, 98
secure, 98
security agent, 87

security screening, 98
threat, 87
ticket agent, 87
ticket booth, 93
Transportation Security
    Administration (TSA), 98
X-ray machine, 87

UNIT 6

appliances, 112
bent, 106
broken, 106
cell phone, 112
change the filter, 109
clean the brush, 109
cover, 112
cracked, 106

damaged, 106
defective, 106
dented, 106
extended warranty, 112
included in, 112
incompatible, 106
leaking, 108
make an exchange, 120

manufacturer, 112
model number, 109
rebate, 118
repair, 112
scratched, 106
service agreement, 112
service contract, 112
treadmill, 108

unlimited data, 114
unlimited talk, 114
unlimited text, 114
vacuum cleaner, 108
warranty, 107

UNIT 7

accelerator/gas pedal, 133
brakes, 133
bumper, 132
collision, 138
construction, 127
dashboard, 132
dent, 128
engine, 132
entrance ramp/on ramp, 127
exit, 127

flat tire, 131
freeway/highway, 127
glove compartment, 132
GPS, 132
headlights, 132
hood, 132
horn, 132
jumper cables, 131
lane, 127
license plate, 132

mechanic, 128
oil change, 128
oil leak, 131
overpass, 127
rearview mirror, 132
registration, 135
replace the brakes, 128
rotate the tires, 128
shoulder, 127
sideview mirror, 132

spare tire, 131
steering wheel, 132
tires, 128
toll booth, 127
tow truck, 127
traffic jam, 127
trunk, 132
turn signal, 132
vehicle, 127
windshield, 132

UNIT 8

affordable, 158
be on a diet, 146
buy fresh fruits and
   vegetables, 146
buy frozen dinners, 146
buy junk food, 146
calories, 152
cavity, 160
complain, 158

cook homemade meals, 146
dental care, 162
dental hygiene, 161
drink sugary beverages, 146
eat fast food, 146
eat fatty foods, 146
eat out, 149
fiber, 150
floss, 160

food allergies, 152
food containers, 148
food storage bags, 148
get takeout, 146
gum disease, 160
have a snack, 146
healthy habit, 147
high-fiber food, 150
innovations, 158

nutritional labels, 152
nutritious, 158
objected, 158
overweight, 158
serving, 152
slow cooker, 148
snack, 153
unhealthy habit, 147
X-ray, 160

UNIT 9

advantages, 172
attend a training session,
   166
be part of a team, 166
be responsible for
   something, 166
complain, 167
deal with complaints, 166

disadvantages, 172
do inventory, 168
duty, 172
exhausted, 172
expectations on the job,
   175
follow instructions, 166
give instructions, 166

give someone feedback, 166
insomnia, 172
inventory, 169
job skills, 166
on duty, 172
quantity, 168
safety hazards, 178
safety procedures, 178

safety rules, 178
supplies, 168
train other employees, 166
vendor, 168
work the late shift, 172

UNIT 10

admissions, 187
cancel an appointment, 189
diseases, 198
emergency room (ER), 187
exemptions, 198
intensive care unit (ICU), 187
laboratory, 187

make an appointment, 189
maternity ward, 187
medical history form, 192
medical procedures, 201
medical receptionist, 188
nurse's station, 187
participate, 198

pediatrics, 187
physical therapy, 187
polio, 198
radiology/imaging, 187
requirements, 198
reschedule an appointment,
   189

surgery, 187
symptoms, 194
vaccinations, 198
vaccines, 198
weight loss, 195

UNIT 11

account balance, 207
appliances, 220
ATM withdrawal, 207
ATM/debit card, 207
balance, 207
bank account, 207
bank statement, 207
bank teller, 207

budget, 215
check, 207
checking account, 208
credit card, 207
debit card, 207
debt, 212
direct deposit, 208
expenses, 215

financial planning, 215
gross income, 215
interest rate, 212
minimum, 212
mobile app, 208
mobile banking, 208
net income, 215
pay off, 212

paycheck, 208
penalty, 212
PIN (personal identification
   number), 210
savings, 215
security deposit, 220

UNIT 12

Air and Space Museum, 228
Capitol Building, 227
Chinatown, 241
freedom of religion, 238
guarantees, 238
institutions, 238
Jefferson Memorial, 227
Lincoln Memorial, 227

Martin Luther King, Jr.
   Memorial, 241
National Gallery of Art, 231
National Mall, 240
National Museum of
   American History, 231
National Museum of Natural
   History, 231

National Zoo, 241
obey, 238
Pentagon, 227
rights and freedoms, 238
separation, 238
slavery, 240
Smithsonian Institution, 227
Supreme Court, 227

the Constitution, 238,
tour, 228
U.S. Treasury, 227
Washington Monument, 227
White House, 227
worship, 238

UNIT 1

Page 8, Listen, Exercises A and B

Marco: Great game. Is this the Atlas soccer league? I've heard about them.
Edwin: Yes. I love to come here and watch them.
Marco: Do they play every Saturday?
Edwin: Yes, unless it rains. By the way, my name is Edwin.
Marco: Hi, I'm Marco. Nice to meet you.
Edwin: Nice to meet you, too. Do you live around here?
Marco: Nearby. I live in Southside. I'm originally from Brazil.

Page 8, Listen, Exercise C

Edwin: Oh, yeah? There's a guy in the league from Brazil. He's over there, number 4.
Marco: Wait a minute, I know him! He's from my town, Corumba . . . Hey! Hector! It's me, Marco. Hi! Uh-oh. He lost the ball.

Page 14, Listen, Exercises A and B

Sara: Hi there, I'm Sara. I live next door. I wanted to welcome you and your family to the neighborhood.
Eden: Thanks, Sara! It's nice to meet you. Have you lived here long?
Sara: About five years. I really love it here. Do you have any questions about the neighborhood?
Eden: Yes, I have a few. Where do you usually shop for food?
Sara: There's a supermarket about two miles away. It's a 24-hour store, so it's always open. We also have an outdoor farmer's market on Saturdays. It's next to Miller Park.
Eden: Thanks! That's very helpful. I need to get some diapers for my baby. Do you think the supermarket is the best place to go?
Sara: Hmmm. I don't know. It's usually crowded on weekends. There's a pharmacy right around the corner. They sell diapers. You can walk there in five minutes.
Eden: That's great! Is the pharmacy open 24 hours?
Sara: No, it closes at 9:00.
Eden: OK. Thanks for the information. I also need to go to the post office this afternoon. Is there one nearby?
Sara: Yes, the post office is right next to the pharmacy, but it's not open on Saturday.
Eden: Oh, then I will go on Monday. How about places to eat? Are there any restaurants I can walk to?
Sara: No, not really. We have a lot of great restaurants, but you need to drive or take a bus. There's a small café down the street, but it's not open very often. It's open for breakfast only, and it's closed on Sundays. Hey, do you like shopping?
Eden: Of course! Doesn't everyone?
Sara: Yes, I guess so. There's a new mall just a few miles away. It has some great stores and a movie theater. I rarely go to the movies, but I hear it's really nice.
Eden: That sounds nice. Thanks! Oh, one last thing. Where is the closest hair salon?
Sara: There's a salon in the mall. Why? Do you need a haircut?
Eden: No, I need a job. I'm a hairdresser. Do *you* need a haircut?

Page 20, Listen, Exercises A and B

Roger: This is 101.9 Radio New York. We turn now to events for the weekend. Ellen, could you tell us about the West Indian-American Day parade?
Ellen: Certainly, Roger. The annual West Indian–American Day parade takes place this Labor Day weekend, on Monday, Labor Day. Thousands of people will dance in beautiful costumes down Eastern Parkway in Brooklyn, New York. The costumes make this an exciting event. And don't forget the free music. You will hear calypso, rap, and reggae music played on guitars and steel drums. Last but not least, don't miss the food. This parade has terrific Caribbean food at low prices. You might want to try some rice and peas, or a little curried chicken or goat.
Roger: So, Monday, Labor Day, head to Brooklyn! Enjoy the sights, sounds, and the tastes of the West Indian-American Day Parade!

UNIT 2

Page 28, Listen, Exercises A, B, and C

Gustavo: So, Carmen, what's going on with you?
Carmen: You'll never guess! I'm going back to school.
Gustavo: Really?
Carmen: Uh-huh. I'm going to take night classes this fall.
Gustavo: Yeah? Where?
Carmen: At Los Angeles City College.
Gustavo: That's great. What will you study?
Carmen: Well, I want to be a nurse. I'd like to get an associate's degree.
Gustavo: What classes do you have to take for that?
Carmen: Well, first I have to take basic classes, like biology. Then I can apply to the clinical program.
Gustavo: How long will that take?
Carmen: I'm going to go part time. If I work really hard, I might get the degree in three years.
Gustavo: Well, good luck. Here's an orange.
Carmen: An orange? Why an orange?
Gustavo: Don't you know? Student nurses have to practice giving shots. And they always start on an orange.
Carmen: Oh! Thanks.

Page 34, Listen, Exercises A and B

Sheng: Hi, Min! How are you? How's your new job?
Min: Oh, it's not really working out. I like the restaurant, but my manager is terrible. I don't understand his instructions, and he changes the schedule every week. I'm going to look for another job.
Sheng: I'm sorry to hear that. Hey, I'm going to a job fair on Friday. Do you want to come with me?
Min: Sure! What time are you going to go?
Sheng: I'm going to leave right after work, around 2:00.
Min: Why are you looking for a new job?
Sheng: I'm going to graduate with an associate's degree in nursing next month. I'm looking for a job as a nurse.

Min: Congratulations! Do you use careerlinks.com? It's a social media site with lots of job listings. I'm going to set up a profile tonight.

Sheng: Yes, I already have a Careerlinks account. Add me as a connection when you set up your profile.

Min: OK, I will.

Page 34, Listen, Exercise C

Sheng: Hey! I found a job listing for you on Careerlinks. Look. It's a job at a restaurant.

Min: Really? Is it a full-time job?

Sheng: Yes. It says, "Full-time job at a busy restaurant. Must be good with people. Great location. Flexible hours."

Min: Great! I think I'll apply. Does it list the address?

Sheng: Yes. It's at 512 Market Street.

Min: Oh, no! That's where I work. That listing must be for my job!

Page 41, Listen, Exercises A and B

And now some announcements from Long Beach Community Center.

Free classes in English and computers will start again on Wednesday, September 10. We're giving English placement tests on September 8 and 9 for new students. Space is limited, so come early. Classes are free, but you need to register in advance.

During the months of September and October, there will be a mural painting project at the corner of 5th Avenue and Dupont. This'll be a special group project for people of all ages to improve our neighborhood. We'll be painting the mural every weekend from 9 until 5. Volunteers are welcome. To sign up, please call extension 6 or just drop by.

Finally, on Saturday, October 1, we're starting a food and clothing drive. Please bring in any cans or packages of food or clean clothes you don't need. And if you have time, please sign up to help distribute the food and clothes on October 20.

If you have any questions, please visit us at 89 Main Street, call us at 555-1234, or email us at lbcc . . .

UNIT 3

Page 48, Listen, Exercises A and B

Counselor: Hello, Ms. Cruz. How are you?

Ms. Cruz: Fine, thank you.

Counselor: So, let's see, let me get Elena's file. Her grades were good this year, especially in math and science. She's a good student.

Ms. Cruz: Thank you. She works very hard.

Counselor: Well, she's going to finish high school soon, but what does she want to do after that? What would you like to see Elena do in the future?

Ms. Cruz: We really want her to go to a four-year college.

Counselor: Oh, that's great. Well, in that case, we have to make sure she takes the right courses.

Page 48, Listen, Exercise C

Counselor: Elena should take certain classes to prepare for a four-year college.

Ms. Cruz: OK. What classes should she take?

Counselor: Well, she has to take four years of English. She needs three years of social studies, math, and science. She also needs to take two years of a foreign language and a semester of computer science.

Ms. Cruz: Two years of a foreign language? But Elena is already fluent in Spanish. She can read it and write it.

Counselor: Well, if she passes a test in Spanish, she doesn't have to take a foreign language. She can take more math and science.

Page 55, Listen, Exercises A and B

Pilar: Hi, Dave. This is Pilar. I'm calling because my daughter is going to be in a school play tomorrow afternoon. Could I come in a couple hours late?

Dave: I'm sorry, Pilar, but that probably won't work. It will be hard to find someone to cover your shift. Nestor is taking the day off tomorrow because his son is very sick, and it's important for him to see a doctor.

Pilar: OK, I understand.

Dave: It's a good idea to tell me about school events as early as possible. That way, I can help you. It's easy to arrange the schedule when I know about it a week or two in advance. One day is usually not enough.

Pilar: Yes, that makes sense. I'm sorry for not telling you about the play sooner. Now that we're talking about it, I just remembered something. I have a parent-teacher conference next Friday at noon.

Dave: OK. I'll put it on the schedule now. You can come in at 2:00 that day. And listen, I'll call some other employees to see if anyone else can cover your shift tomorrow afternoon. If I find someone, I'll let you know.

Pilar: Thanks, Dave! I really appreciate it.

Page 60, Listen, Exercises A and B

Beatriz: Hey, Rafael. How was school?

Rafael: OK, I guess.

Beatriz: What's wrong? You look really upset. Was it that homework for Mr. Meltzer? Did you get it back?

Rafael: Yeah. I got an A on it. It's not that.

Beatriz: Then what happened at school?

Rafael: Nothing.

Beatriz: I know something happened. What is it?

Rafael: It's some boys in my grade . . . Tommy and Mark.

Beatriz: What did they do?

Rafael: They always call me stupid and make fun of my name. Then today they grabbed my backpack and threw it in the street. They laughed at me when I ran to get it.

Beatriz: That's really dangerous. When did that happen?

Rafael: When we were walking home from school. I hate school. I'm never going back there.

UNIT 4

Page 68, Listen, Exercises A and B

Have you ever thought about a career as a licensed technician? Things break every day. Licensed technicians are always needed to fix them. At ACME technical school, you'll learn the skills you need to become a licensed technician. We offer programs in air conditioning, refrigeration, electronics, and automotive and computer technology. Classes are held days, nights, and weekends. Study full time or part time in our state-of-the-art labs. We offer financial aid to those who qualify. And all programs come with free job placement services. Employers call us every day looking for you. So what are you waiting for? Apply online at acmefix.com. That's A-C-M-E-F-I-X-dot-com.

Page 74, Listen, Exercises A and B

James: It's nice to meet you, Luis.
Luis: Thank you. It's nice to meet you, too, James.
James: So, I'm looking for a chef. Emilio, the assistant manager, recommended you. Can you tell me about your restaurant experience?
Luis: Sure. I've been a line cook at El Norte restaurant for the last five years. I also owned my own café in Mexico City. And before that I worked in a couple of restaurants in Mexico for several years.
James: So why do you want to leave El Norte?
Luis: Well, I've worked there for five years. It's a very good restaurant, but I'm ready for a change. And your restaurant has a great reputation.

Page 74, Listen, Exercise C

James: Oh, so you've heard of the restaurant?
Luis: Of course. Everyone knows PJ's has great food.
James: Thank you. Now, tell me more about your experience. Have you ever planned menus or prepared meals for large groups of people?
Luis: Yes, I have. We serve a hundred people a night at El Norte.
James: And have you managed staff?
Luis: Sure, when I owned my café.

Page 81, Listen, Exercises A and B

Kathy: This is Spotlight on Jobs. I'm your host Kathy James. My guest today is a well-known chef. Sana Solano is the owner and head chef of Sana's Kitchen, a restaurant specializing in Latin and Asian cuisine. Welcome to our program, Sana!
Sana: Thanks for having me!
Kathy: So, tell us, what are the most important qualities for restaurant owners?
Sana: It's important to be flexible. You never know how many people are going to come to your restaurant each day. You also need to be organized and efficient.
Kathy: How did you first become interested in cooking?
Sana: Well, I'm not sure. I've always loved cooking. I used to cook with my grandmothers a lot when I was a young girl.
Kathy: What kind of food did you use to cook?

Sana: My mother is Japanese, so my grandmother on that side of the family taught me how to make popular Japanese dishes. We used to make sushi together every weekend. And my father is Mexican. His mother taught me how to make tacos, enchiladas, and stuff like that.
Kathy: Did you always mix the two styles of cooking?
Sana: No, not until I was a teenager. When I was younger, I followed both of my grandmothers' recipes exactly. Later, when I was in high school, I started mixing Japanese and Mexican flavors. I used to make Japanese-style fish tacos for my friends.
Kathy: Mmmmm! You have lucky friends.
Sana: Thanks.

Page 81, Listen, Exercise C

Sana: My fish tacos were very popular, so I tried other new combinations. I added salsa to tofu dishes and ginger to Spanish rice. After I graduated high school, I decided to go to culinary school so I could get a job as a chef. I loved it! Now I also teach classes there twice a week.
Kathy: Oh, I didn't know that! What classes do you teach?
Sana: Well, I used to teach classes on food safety, but now I'm teaching a class on how to make different desserts.
Kathy: You are such a hardworking chef! How do you have time to run a restaurant and teach at a culinary school?
Sana: It doesn't feel like work. It's easy to stay motivated when you love your job. For me, it's not just a job. It's also my favorite hobby.
Kathy: That's amazing. And now I'm hungry! I encourage all of our listeners to go to Sana's Kitchen. The staff is pleasant, and the food is delicious!

UNIT 5

Page 88, Listen, Exercises A and B

Announcement 1
Announcer: Flight number 385 leaving for Bogota will begin the boarding procedure at Gate 13A. Passengers with small children or needing special assistance may preboard now.
Mother: Carlos, take your bag. We can board now.
Announcement 2
Announcer: Attention passengers on flight number 289 to San Diego. Flight number 289 has been canceled.
Passenger A: Excuse me, I couldn't hear the announcement. Did you hear what they said?
Passenger B: Flight 289 was canceled.
Passenger A: They canceled a flight! Wait, that's our flight!
Passenger C: Oh no, we'll miss the wedding!
Announcement 3
Announcer: Attention passengers on flight number 870 to Caracas. The departure gate has changed. Flight number 870 will now be departing from gate 22.

Mother:	What are we going to do? Samara won't be able to walk that far. She's only 3.
Father:	Don't worry, I can carry her.

Announcement 4

Passenger A:	We're late!
Passenger B:	Wait, Julio. I can't run that fast!
Passenger A:	Keep running!
Announcer:	Attention passengers: Flight number 901 is experiencing a mechanical difficulty. Boarding has been delayed. Flight number 901 will board in approximately 30 minutes.
Passenger B:	You can stop running, Julio.

Page 94, Listen, Exercises A and B

Ken:	Hey, Amy. It's me, Ken. I'm on the subway. Sorry, I'm running late. There was a 30-minute delay. A train got stuck at 24th Street.
Amy:	That's too bad. So, what time are you arriving then?
Ken:	I think about 3:30. Which station should I get off at?
Amy:	Lake Merritt Station. Call me when you get there. My car isn't running, but my mom will let me borrow hers. I'll park and come meet you.
Ken:	Great. See you soon.

Page 94, Listen, Exercise C

Amy:	Hello?
Ken:	Hey, Amy. I'm here. Where are you?
Amy:	Over here, next to the taxi stand. How come I don't see you? Oh, there you are. You're wearing that shirt I gave you. It looks good.
Ken:	*It* looks good? I look good.
Amy:	OK, do you have all your bags?
Ken:	Yeah. Wait a minute. This bag isn't mine!

Page 101, Listen, Exercise A

Bus number 908 from Jacksonville to Miami has been canceled due to bad weather conditions. The next bus to Miami, bus number 918, will be leaving at 3:30 from gate number 24.

Page 101, Listen, Exercises B and C

Announcer:	Bus number 908 from Jacksonville to Miami has been canceled due to bad weather conditions. The next bus to Miami, bus number 918, will be leaving at 3:30 from gate number 24.
Mrs. Ramirez:	Hello?
Carlos:	Hi, Mom. It's me.
Mrs. Ramirez:	Carlos! We can't wait to see you!
Carlos:	Listen, Mom. I have bad news and good news. I can't take the 2:00 bus. I missed it. I'm taking a bus at 3:30.
Mrs. Ramirez:	Oh, Carlos. I made a big dinner, and everyone's coming. You won't be able to eat with us.
Carlos:	I know, Mom, but we'll still be able to spend the whole Christmas day together tomorrow. I've got good news, too . . . I'll be back next month for your 70th birthday.
Mrs. Ramirez:	You will? Oh, that's great. But Carlos, would you do me a little favor?
Carlos:	Sure, Mom.
Mrs. Ramirez:	Don't tell anyone it's my 70th birthday.
Carlos:	Of course not, Mom. Anyway, no one would believe you're 70.

UNIT 6

Page 108, Listen, Exercises A and B

Emilio:	Ana, stop the vacuum.
Ana:	What's the matter?
Emilio:	Something is wrong. The vacuum sounds strange, and it smells funny, too. Maybe we need to change the filter or clean the brush. What do you think?
Ana:	The filter isn't dirty, and the brush isn't, either. The vacuum always sounds like that. It's just old.
Emilio:	When did we buy it? Do you think it's still under warranty?
Ana:	No way. This thing is at least five years old.
Emilio:	I guess we'll have to buy a new one, then.
Ana:	Good. I never liked this vacuum anyway.

Page 114, Listen, Exercises A and B

Lucas:	Yonas, I've got a big problem.
Yonas:	What's wrong, Lucas?
Lucas:	I just got my phone bill today. It was $640!
Yonas:	What? How did that happen?
Lucas:	Last month, I switched to a new phone carrier. The plan was for unlimited talk, text, and data for $100 a month.
Yonas:	That sounds like a good deal.
Lucas:	I thought so, too. And best of all, the salesperson said I could make unlimited calls to Brazil. That's the main reason I switched carriers.

Page 114, Listen, Exercise C

Yonas:	So what happened?
Lucas:	Look at this bill. They charged me $2 a minute for calls to Brazil.
Yonas:	Did you call the company?
Lucas:	I did. But they said my contract doesn't include international calls. I looked at my contract today. There's nothing in there about international calls. Now there's nothing I can do.
Yonas:	Call them back, and tell them you won't pay.
Lucas:	But then they'll shut off my phone, and I'll get a bad credit record. What should I do?
Yonas:	Just pay the bill, and then cancel your plan immediately. Switch to Horizon. They have good international plans
Lucas:	OK. Thanks, Yonas.

Page 120, Listen, Exercises A and B

Store clerk:	May I help you?
Rahel:	Yes, I want to return this phone.
Store clerk:	We have a 15-day return policy. When did you purchase it?
Rahel:	Last week.
Store clerk:	OK, good. Did you open the box?
Rahel:	Yes, I did. I used it for a couple of days, but it isn't as fast as my old phone. It takes a long time to download pictures and refresh the Internet browser.
Store clerk:	There is a $35 restocking fee for opened boxes.

Rahel:	But the phone is very slow. Do I have to pay the fee if the phone is defective?
Store clerk:	Maybe. Can I see your receipt?
Rahel:	Sure. Here it is.
Store clerk:	I see you didn't purchase our protection plan, and the phone didn't come with a manufacturer's warranty. I'm sorry. You will have to pay the $35 fee. Do you still want to return it?
Rahel:	Yes. I need a better phone.
Store clerk:	Do you want a refund or an exchange?
Rahel:	I'd like an exchange, please. Can I exchange it for this Simsung?
Store clerk:	Sure, but that's $50 more. We have other models that aren't as expensive as that one.
Rahel:	How about this LTC phone?
Store clerk:	That one is on sale today. It isn't as expensive as the Simsung, but it has all the same features.
Rahel:	I'll take it.
Store clerk:	OK, but I recommend the protection plan this time. It's only $20.

UNIT 7

Page 128, Listen, Exercises A and B

Mechanic:	So, what can I do for you?
Li:	I'd like an oil change.
Mechanic:	No problem.
Li:	How much will that be?
Mechanic:	$29.95.
Li:	OK. How long will that take?
Mechanic:	About half an hour.
Li:	Good.
Mechanic:	But when was the last time you had your tires rotated?
Li:	Oh, I think about a year ago.
Mechanic:	A year? Then we should rotate the tires.
Li:	How long will it take?
Mechanic:	About 15 minutes longer.
Li:	OK.
Mechanic:	By the way, did you see there's a big dent in the back of your car?
Li:	Oh, yeah. I know. I keep it that way on purpose.
Mechanic:	What? Why?
Li:	Well, a lot of people drive Subarus, so it's easier for me to know it's my car. When I'm in a parking lot, I just look for the dent, and I know it's mine.
Mechanic:	Oh.

Page 134, Listen, Exercises B and C

Officer:	Are you hurt, sir?
Mr. Desmond:	My neck is sore.
Officer:	Do you need an ambulance?
Mr. Desmond:	Nah, I'm OK.
Officer:	OK. License, registration, and insurance, please. Mr. Desmond, can you tell me what happened?
Mr. Desmond:	Yeah, I was slowing down to make a right-hand turn onto Martine Avenue, and that car behind me was going too fast and hit me. I think he was talking on his cell phone.

Officer:	Thank you, Mr. Desmond. I've got to take a statement from the other driver . . . . Stay there until I finish writing the report . . . Are you hurt, sir?
Mr. Ortiz:	No, I'm all right, Officer.
Officer:	OK. May I see your license, registration, and insurance, please? . . . Well, Mr. Ortiz, can you explain what happened?
Mr. Ortiz:	Yes, Officer. I was driving in the right-hand lane. There was nothing in front of me. Suddenly this car came out of nowhere. I think it came from the left lane. It was slowing down in front of me to turn onto Martine Avenue. There wasn't time for me to stop.
Officer:	Were you talking on a cell phone?
Mr. Ortiz:	Err . . . . No . . .
Officer:	You realize that talking on a cell phone is against the law in California, right?
Mr. Ortiz:	Um, no, I didn't know that. But I wasn't talking on the phone.
Officer:	Hmmm. OK. I'm going to go fill out the accident report. Wait here.

Page 141, Listen, Exercises A and B

This is Tara O'Neil . . . with "Tips for Drivers." We don't like to think about car accidents, but it's important to be ready if one happens. Do you know what to do if you have a car accident? First, you must stop any time that you have an accident. This is for all kinds of accidents, with moving cars, parked cars, and pedestrians. If you hit something and don't stop, this is a serious felony called a hit-and-run. If you hit and run, you can go to jail or lose your driver's license.

So what do you do after an accident? First, this depends on whether you hit a parked car or a moving car.

If you hit a parked car, try to find the owner. If you can't, you must leave a note for them on their car. Write your name, telephone number, your address, and write an explanation of the accident.

If you hit another moving car, make sure everyone is OK. If someone is hurt, call 911 for an ambulance.

Now, what other details are you responsible for after an accident?

When you have a car accident, you need to get information for your insurance company. Write down the other driver's name, address, driver's license number, license plate number, and insurance information, and give them your information, too. Make sure you also call the police. They will come and do a report of the accident. You must wait for them.

Next, look carefully at your car. Has it been damaged? If you have a camera, take a photo of the damage.

When the police come, tell the officer what happened, and do as he tells you. You will need to show the officer your proof of auto insurance and your driver's license. If you don't have these things, you may have to pay a fine. You might also lose your driver's license.

When the police officer leaves, you can go. But ask him where you can get a copy of the traffic report. You might need it later to show your insurance company. Also, write down the officer's name.

After the accident, remember, you have to call your insurance company and report the accident.

Thank you. Listen again next week for "Tips for Drivers."

UNIT 8

Page 148, Listen, Exercises A and B

Hello, and welcome back to Healthy Habits. Today, we're going to talk about making healthy food choices while managing a busy schedule. If you work through lunch without even taking a break for a snack, your body is not getting the energy it needs. You might find it difficult to concentrate or finish important tasks. There are a few changes you can make. These changes will give you more energy and improve your health.

First, don't skip breakfast. I believe breakfast is the most important meal of the day, and many experts agree with this opinion. A healthy breakfast gives you the energy you need to start your day right. Plus, skipping breakfast has been linked to an increase in obesity and diabetes. The best breakfast choices include foods that are high in protein and fiber.

Next, prepare food in advance. Food from fast food restaurants and vending machines may seem like the easiest options, but they're also the least healthy. When you prepare homemade meals, you can use the healthiest ingredients, such as fresh fruit and vegetables. One of the best things you can do is prepare snacks and meals for your day before you leave in the morning. Perhaps the easiest way to do this is to use a slow cooker. If you don't have time to prepare food in the morning, you can set aside time during the weekend. Prepare snacks and meals for the week, and put them in storage bags or containers in the refrigerator or freezer.

It's OK to eat out sometimes, but avoid the saltiest, fattiest items on the menu. Unfortunately, those are often some of the most common restaurant items, especially at fast food places. Try to look for items that are baked or grilled instead of fried. Look for side dishes like soups, salads, and fruit, instead of chips, onion rings, or fries.

Finally, be sure to stay hydrated. All liquids help you stay hydrated, but water is usually the best choice. Take a water bottle to work and refill it often. Water keeps every part of your body working properly. Avoid drinking too much caffeine, such as coffee or caffeinated sodas, because these can make you more dehydrated.

Just a few simple changes can make a big difference!

Page 154, Listen, Exercises A, B, and C

Good afternoon. This is Bob Lyons, from Family Health Matters.

In the past 10 years, more children have become overweight. In a recent study, the government found that about 17 percent of children and adolescents age 2 to 19 in the United States are overweight. Being overweight can cause serious health problems, like heart problems and type 2 diabetes.

Why are so many children overweight? The answers are poor eating habits and not enough physical activity. So what can parents do to stop their children from becoming overweight or help them lose weight?

Here are some tips.

First, encourage healthy eating habits.

Give your children plenty of vegetables, fruits, and whole grain foods like whole wheat bread.

Make sure your children get plenty of low-fat dairy products and lean meats like chicken and fish.

Beans are also good for protein.

Make sure that meals are not too large.

Don't give your children too many drinks or desserts with a lot of sugar or saturated fat.

What else can you do to keep your children healthy?

The second important thing you can do is to increase your children's physical activity. Children and teens should get 60 minutes of physical activity most days of the week. Remember that your children will follow your example. Make sure that you are physically active and encourage your children to join you.

Here are examples of activities you can do with your children: take a walk, ride a bike, play soccer, or jump rope. Encourage your children to spend more time outside. Limit their time watching TV or on the computer.

For Family Health Matters, I'm Bob Lyons.

Page 160, Listen, Exercises A and B

Dentist: Well, David, I looked at your X-rays. Your teeth look pretty good, but when I cleaned them, your gums were bleeding a little bit. You probably need to floss more. Do you floss?

David: Well, not that much.

Dentist: Try flossing more. Flossing keeps your gums healthy.

David: Isn't brushing my teeth enough?

Dentist: Brushing after every meal is important, too. But you can't always get your teeth clean unless you floss. If you don't get all the food off your teeth, it will turn to plaque and cause cavities. And you can also get gum disease.

David: What is gum disease?

Dentist: If you have too much bacteria in your mouth, your gums get red and swollen. Look . . . This is a picture of gum disease.

David: Ugh.

Dentist: OK, I think we're done. Let me give you a toothbrush to take home.

David: Thanks. Do you also give away dental floss?

Dentist: Sure, here you go. And here is your free toothbrush. Is your toothbrush at home soft or hard?

David: I think it's a hard toothbrush . . . why?

Dentist: A soft one is better. It's easier on your teeth. OK, See you next time. And make sure to floss.

David: Definitely!

UNIT 9

Page 168, Listen, Exercises A and B

Margo: OK, you need to be sure there are enough supplies in the kitchen. First, you do inventory. Start with the things on the counter. See if there are enough paper cups and paper towels. If something is missing, check in the cabinets and drawers.

Jason: OK.

Margo: If we don't have enough, you need to order more.

Jason: How do I do that?

Margo: You fill out an inventory sheet. Write down what you need under "item." Then, write quantity or amount.

Jason: Which box shows quantity?

Margo: This one.

Jason: OK. Then what do I do?

Margo: Call Anthony. He's our vendor. He sells us our supplies. We give the order over the phone. Now, be careful. Sometimes, people order the wrong amount. Make sure you get the right quantity. Always check how many come in a box. But the most important thing is, make sure we always have enough coffee. The employees here are very unhappy without their coffee.

Jason: Yes, Margo. I know what you mean.

Page 175, Listen, Exercises B and C

Bill: Carl, Tony is out of the office for a while, and he didn't have time to finish a job. I need you to do it for him.

Carl: No problem. What is it?

Bill: I need you to look at a building . . . a condominium. I want you to take photos and finish the report for Tony. I'll check it. The bank wants the report by Friday, so we have to work quickly.

Carl: Is there anything else?

Bill: No, that's all. Oh . . . you asked to see me earlier today.

Carl: Yes, um . . . I was wondering if I could leave early next Friday. My son is graduating from high school. We want to be there for the graduation.

Bill: Sure. I don't see why not. Congratulations, by the way.

Carl: Thanks, Bill.

Page 180, Listen, Exercises A and B

Margo: Jason, Mr. Yang just called me. He said that the copy machine next to his office isn't working.

Jason: It isn't?

Margo: That's right. Did you check all the copy machines and printers this morning?

Jason: Well, I checked almost all of them, but maybe I forgot about that one. I'm sorry.

Margo: OK, Jason. I know you're new here, but remember: You need to check all of the copy machines and printers first thing when you come in. We need to make sure they're working. If there's a problem, we need to fix it. If we can't fix it, we have to call service repair.

Jason: I understand, Margo. I'll make sure it doesn't happen again.

Margo: OK, very good.

UNIT 10

Page 188, Listen, Exercise A

Office Assistant: Hello. Westside Health Center.

Yao: Hi. This is Yao Chen. I have an appointment with Dr. Barnes for today at 4:00, but I need to cancel.

Office Assistant: OK, Mr. Chen. Would you like to reschedule?

Yao: Yes, I would. Can I come in next Thursday at 3:00?

Office Assistant: Sorry, we're all booked. How about Friday at 3?

Yao: I think that's OK. But let me call you back. I have to check with my boss.

Office Assistant: Alright. Bye.

Page 188, Listen, Exercise B

Office Assistant: Hello. Westside Health Center.

Alvia: Hi, I'd like to make an appointment with Dr. Barnes.

Office Assistant: Who's calling, please?

Alvia: Alvia Ledesma.

Office Assistant: Are you a new patient?

Alvia: No, I'm not.

Office Assistant: What's the problem, Ms. Ledesma?

Alvia: I'm tired all the time, but I can't sleep. I feel awful, and I don't know what to do.

Office Assistant: Well, we've just had a cancellation. Can you come here today at 4?

Alvia: Is it possible to come at 5?

Office Assistant: I'm sorry, I don't have anything for 5.

Alvia: OK, I'll take the 4:00 appointment.

Office Assistant: OK, great. See you this afternoon.

Page 194, Listen, Exercises A and B

Dr. Barnes: Good afternoon, Ms. Ledesma. What seems to be the problem?

Alvia: I feel terrible. I haven't been sleeping well. I fall asleep, and I wake up after a couple of hours.

Dr. Barnes: Hmm. Anything else?

Alvia: Well, I've been trying to lose weight like you said, but I can't. I come home exhausted, and I eat too much.

Dr. Barnes: Is anything bothering you?

Alvia: My job. They fired two people last month, so the rest of us have been working twice as hard.

Dr. Barnes: Hmm. You do have a lot on your mind. Well, let me examine you. Please step on the scale.

Alvia: The scale? Do I have to?

Page 194, Listen, Exercise C

Dr. Barnes: Ms. Ledesma, your blood pressure is high, and you've gained a few pounds. I'll give you some medication for high blood pressure, but you really have to watch what you eat and do more exercise. Then you might not need the medicine, and you might even sleep better. Now do you do any exercise?

Alvia: Not much. In the evenings, I like to watch TV. That's how I relax.

Dr. Barnes: Well, try to get some exercise. Dancing, even doing housework faster will help. Here's some information on healthy eating.

Alvia: What about sleeping pills or pills to lose weight?

Dr. Barnes: Let's hold off on the pills. I don't like to prescribe pills unless they're really necessary.

Page 201, Listen, Exercises A, B, and C

Mrs. Garcia: Doctor, I'm worried about next week.

Dr. Finkel: Don't worry, Mrs. Garcia. I've done many gall bladder operations. And you'll feel a lot better afterwards.

Mrs. Garcia: Oh, I'm not so worried about having the operation. I'm worried about being away from home. My husband is not used to taking care of the children. And I'm worried about missing a month of work.

Dr. Finkel: I see. Maybe you could ask a relative or a friend to help out.

Mrs. Garcia: I was thinking about asking my niece, but she's very busy. She has four children. Maybe I could call Maria, my cousin. She doesn't have a job right now, so she could probably come over to the house.

UNIT 11

Page 208, Listen, Exercises A and B

Are you tired of paying fees for your checking account? Well, if you want a free checking account, come to Zenith Bank! At Zenith, we offer a free checking account when you have direct deposit or enroll in mobile banking. Our mobile banking app allows you to securely check your balance, transfer money, pay bills, and make deposits. Banking has never been so easy! And if you open an account by April 3, you get a $50 cash bonus. So hurry! Come to your nearest Zenith branch or go to zenithbank.com.

Page 215, Listen, Exercises A, B, and C

I'm Adelyn Juste with Money Matters. Today, we're talking about budgets. Now, most people don't like to think about budgets. In fact, 60% of Americans don't have a budget and spend more than they have. They might live this way for a while, but what happens in an emergency, such as a car accident? If you don't have a budget, you may not have money for an emergency. You'll also have trouble reaching your financial goals. So, if you want to create a budget, how do you get started? There are four steps you need to take.

First, you need to know your net income. In other words, your take-home pay. Write down how much you make each month after taxes.

Second, figure out your expenses. Write down all of the things you spend your money on each month— for example, rent, food, car payments, and utilities. Sometimes, you'll have to make a guess. For example, you may not know for sure how much you spend on gas each month.

The third step is to build savings into your budget. You have to plan to save every month for emergencies and for your long-term goals, like buying a house. Otherwise, you might not save anything, or you might not save enough. Before you decide how much you can save, look at your total expenses.

The last step is to check to see if your budget is realistic. At the end of the month, compare what you actually spent to the expenses you wrote in your budget. If you spent more than you budgeted for, you may need to spend less.

Remember, think about the big picture. What do you want for yourself and your family? What can you do to reach your goals? If you remember your reasons for saving, you'll be more motivated to keep your budget.

For Money Matters, I'm Adelyn Juste.

Page 220, Listen, Exercises A and B

Valeria: Hello. W & M Management Company.

Roberto: Hi. I'm looking for a two-bedroom apartment.

Valeria: Ok, sure. How much do you want to spend?

Roberto: No more than $1,200. And we need to live close to downtown.

Valeria: Let me see. Hmmm. I've got a great two-bedroom apartment on Cabela Avenue.

Roberto: Does it come with appliances?

Valeria: Yes, a refrigerator and a gas stove.

Roberto: How much is the rent?

Valeria: $1,100.

Roberto: Are utilities included?

Valeria: Yes, gas, electric, and water.

Roberto: That sounds good! I'd like to come see it.

Valeria: Fine. Our rental office is open from 9:00 to 5:00. What time is good for you?

Roberto: How about 3:30?

Valeria: Hmmm. I have an appointment at 4:00. Can you be here by 3:00?

Roberto: Yes, I can.

Valeria: Great. The office is at 10 Bryant Street on the first floor.

Roberto: Great. See you then.

UNIT 12

Page 228, Listen, Exercises A and B

Tao: Hi, Lin.

Lin: Hi, Tao! How are you? It's been a while since I ran into you.

Tao: I just came back from a trip to Washington, D.C.

Lin: Oh, that's funny. I went there a couple of months ago, and Sue did, too.

Tao: Did you and Sue go there together?

Lin: No, I went with my parents. They've always wanted to tour Washington. Sue was there for a job interview. What about you? What were you doing there?

Tao: I was visiting my cousin. He showed me all around the city. So, what did you like seeing the most in Washington?

Lin: Hmmm. Well, I really enjoyed the White House, and my parents did, too. We went on a tour of the rooms inside. I especially liked the Red Room and the Blue Room. What was your favorite place?

Tao: I liked the White House, but my favorite places were the museums. There are so many to choose from! The National Museum of American History has a lot of interesting things, and the National Air and Space Museum does, too. Those were probably my two favorite museums.

Lin: We went to the National Museum of American History but not the National Air and Space Museum. My dad didn't want to go there, and my mom didn't, either. We didn't have enough time.

Tao: It's amazing. They've got rockets, rocks from the moon, and lots of airplanes. It has one of the largest collection of planes in the world!

Lin: Wow, I'm sorry I missed it. I'll have to go there next time.

AUDIO SCRIPT

Page 234, Listen, Exercises A and B

Guide: Hello. I'm Sandy Wheeler, your guide for today. Welcome, everyone, to Washington, D.C., our nation's capital. This morning we're going to visit three places. First, we're going to see the White House.

Child: That's where the president and his family live.

Guide: Um, right. We will arrive at the White House in just a few minutes. We'll go inside and visit the famous rooms. Then, after we leave the White House, our next stop will be the Capitol. That's where Congress meets to make laws.

1st tourist: Is that where the senators work?

Guide: Yes, the senators work there, in the Senate. Congress is made up of two parts, the Senate and the House of Representatives. You might see some senators or some members of the House when we visit.

2nd tourist: What time is lunch?

Guide: We'll have lunch after we visit Congress. Then, after lunch, we'll walk over to the Supreme Court. Now, any questions?

3rd Tourist: Can you explain . . . What exactly does the Supreme Court do?

Guide: Good question. The Supreme Court is the highest court of our land. There are many courts in the U.S., but the Supreme Court is above all the other courts. The judges there are called justices. They interpret the laws and decide if the laws follow the Constitution. Any more questions?

2nd tourist: Yes, is the restaurant where we're eating any good?

Page 240, Listen, Exercises A and B

Guide: Now, on your right you can see the Lincoln Memorial. It was built as a memorial for Abraham Lincoln, the 16th President of the United States. Lincoln was one of our most loved presidents.

Tourist: Could you tell us about his life?

Guide: Sure. He was born in Kentucky in 1809. He came from a very poor family and had to work hard his entire life. He taught himself law and became a lawyer. He was known for his honesty.

Tourist: When was he elected president?

Guide: Lincoln was elected president in 1860. The Civil War started soon after when the Southern states separated from the country. At that time, slaves worked in the South on big farms called plantations. The Northern states wanted to end slavery. In 1863, Lincoln gave orders to free the slaves in the rebel states. In 1864, he was re-elected president. Unfortunately, in 1865, Lincoln was shot and killed. Many Americans were upset and saddened by his death. He was mourned by many people.

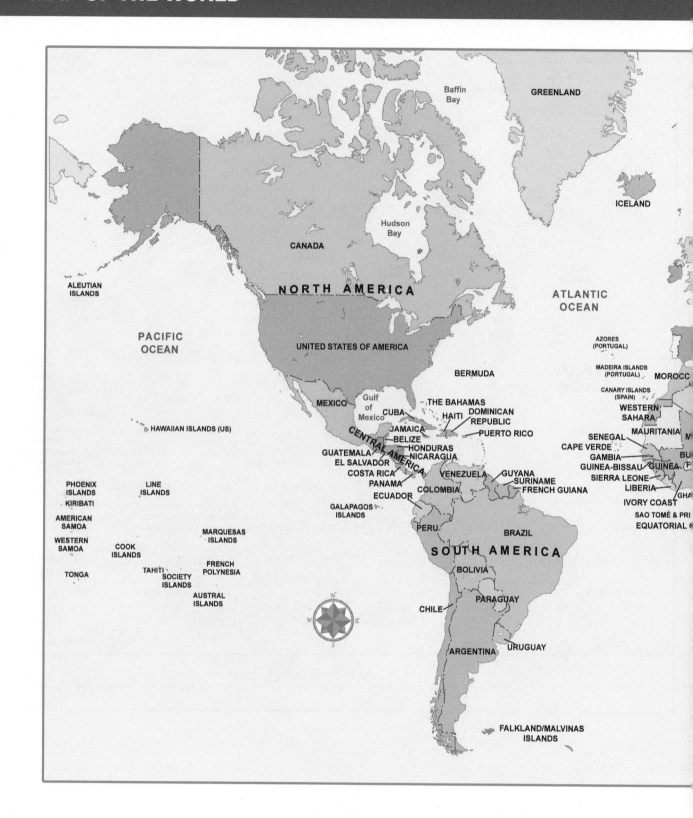

ARCTIC OCEAN

Barents Sea

RUSSIA

Bering Sea

Sea of Okhotsk

EUROPE

ASIA

KAZAKHSTAN

MONGOLIA

PACIFIC OCEAN

Black Sea
GEORGIA
ARMENIA
AZERBAIJAN
Caspian Sea
UZBEKISTAN
KYRGYZSTAN
TAJIKISTAN
TURKMENISTAN

NORTH KOREA
Sea of Japan
SOUTH KOREA
JAPAN

TURKEY

CHINA

Mediterranean Sea
CYPRUS
LEBANON
ISRAEL
SYRIA
IRAQ
JORDAN
IRAN
AFGHANISTAN
KUWAIT
BAHRAIN

East China Sea

TUNISIA

PAKISTAN

BHUTAN

NEPAL

LIBYA
EGYPT

QATAR
SAUDI ARABIA
UNITED ARAB EMIRATES

INDIA

MYANMAR BURMA
LAOS

TAIWAN

WAKE ISLAND (US)

AFRICA

NIGER
CHAD
ERITREA
YEMEN
OMAN
DJIBOUTI
SOCOTRA (YEMEN)

Arabian Sea

BANGLADESH
THAILAND
VIETNAM

PHILIPPINES

NORTHERN MARIANA ISLANDS

GUAM

SUDAN

CAMBODIA

South China Sea

MARSHALL ISLANDS

NIGERIA
CENTRAL AFRICAN REPUBLIC
SOUTH SUDAN
ETHIOPIA

SRI LANKA

BRUNEI
MALAYSIA
SINGAPORE

YAP
PALAU

FEDERATED STATES OF MICRONESIA

NAURU

CAMEROON
BENIN
GABON
CONGO
DEMOCRATIC REPUBLIC OF CONGO
SOMALIA
UGANDA
KENYA
RWANDA
BURUNDI
MALAWI
COMOROS
TANZANIA

INDIAN OCEAN

INDONESIA
EAST TIMOR

PAPUA NEW GUINEA

SOLOMON ISLANDS

TUVALU

ANGOLA
ZAMBIA
ZIMBABWE

MADAGASCAR

MAURITIUS
REUNION (FRANCE)

Coral Sea

VANUATU

FIJI

NAMIBIA
BOTSWANA
MOZAMBIQUE
SWAZILAND
LESOTHO
REPUBLIC OF SOUTH AFRICA

AUSTRALIA

NEW CALEDONIA

ATLANTIC OCEAN

FAROE ISLANDS

ICELAND

SHETLAND ISLANDS

TASMANIA (Australia)

NEW ZEALAND

NORWAY
SWEDEN
Gulf of Bothnia
FINLAND

UNITED KINGDOM
SCOTLAND
North Sea
DENMARK

ESTONIA

NORTHERN IRELAND

Baltic Sea
LATVIA
LITHUANIA

RUSSIA

REPUBLIC OF IRELAND
ENGLAND

NETHERLANDS
LUXEMBURG
BELGIUM

GERMANY
POLAND

BELARUS

EUROPE

FRANCE

CZECH REPUBLIC
LIECHTENSTEIN
AUSTRIA
SLOVENIA
CROATIA
BOSNIA-H.

SLOVAKIA
HUNGARY
ROMANIA

UKRAINE

MOLDOVA

G. Gascogne

MONACO
ITALY

SERBIA & MONTENEGRO
MACEDONIA
ALBANIA

BULGARIA

ANDORRA
PORTUGAL
SPAIN

SWITZERLAND

GREECE

TURKEY

MALTA

INDEX

CREDITS

Photos:

Front Cover: (front, center): Golero/E+/Getty Images; (back, left): Ariel Skelley/Digital Vision/Getty Images; (back, right): Sam Edwards/Caiaimage/Getty Images

Frontmatter
Page vi (cell phone): Tele52/Shutterstock; vi (front cover): Golero/E+/Getty Images, Ariel Skelley/Digital Vision/Getty Images, Sam Edwards/Caiaimage/Getty Images; vi (MyEnglishLab screenshot): Pearson Education; p. vi (ActiveTeach screenshot): Pearson Education; vi (CCRS page, bottom, left): Wavebreakmedia/Shutterstock; vi (CCRS page, top, right): Illustration Forest/Shutterstock;

Unit Tour
Page vii: Wavebreakmedia/Shutterstock; viii (1): Obencem/123RF; viii (2): Erik Isakson/Getty Images; viii (3): Jacob Lund/Shutterstock; viii (4): Sunti/Shutterstock; viii (5): Purestock/Getty Images; viii (6): Andor Bujdoso/123RF; viii (7): Qaphotos.com/Alamy Stock Photo; viii (8): Dynamic Graphics/Creatas/Getty Images; viii (9): Denis Ismagilov/123RF; ix (A): Peter Steffen/dpa picture alliance/Alamy Stock Photo; ix (B): Imagenavi/Getty Images; ix (C): Rob Judges/Pearson Education Ltd.; ix (D): Dolgachov/123RF; x (jumper cables): Marietjie Opperman/123RF; x (oil leak): Itman_47/Shutterstock; x (flat tire): PA©ter Gudella/123RF; x (spare tire): Charles Knowles/Shutterstock; xiii: Image Source/Photodisc/Getty Images; xxii: Courtesy of Sarah Lynn; xxii: Courtesy of Ronna Magy; xxii: Courtesy of Federico Salas Isnardi.

Pre-Unit: Getting Started
Page 4: Tele52/Shutterstock.

Unit 1
Page 5: Monkey Business Images/Shutterstock; 8 (A): Peter Steffen/dpa picture alliance/Alamy Stock Photo, (B): Imagenavi/Getty Images, (C): Rob Judges/Pearson Education Ltd., (D): Dolgachov/123RF; 10: Neil McAllister/Alamy Stock Photo; 14 (A): Ariel Skelley/DigitalVision/Getty Images, (B): Trong Nguyen, (C): Wavebreakmedia/Shutterstock, (D): Dmitriy Shironosov/123RF, (E): Monkey Business Images/Shutterstock, (F): Ferenc Szelepcsenyi/Shutterstock, (G): PaylessImages/123RF; 16: Ashley Corbin-Teich/Image Source/Getty Images; 19 (lettuce): Naila Ruechel/DigitalVision/Getty images, (carrot): Nonwarit Pruetisirirot/123RF, (turkey): Belchonock/123RF, (refrigerator): Sirtravelalot/Shutterstock; 20: Ingolf Pompe 31/Alamy Stock Photo; 21: Fotos593/Shutterstock; 22: Volanthevist/Moment/Getty Images; 24: Fizkes/Shuttestock.

Unit 2
Page 25: Moodboard/123RF; 28 (A): Gelpi/Shutterstock, (B): Sudheer Sakthan, Shutterstock, (C) Goodluz/Shutterstock; 28 (center, right): Rido/Shutterstock; 29 (1): SasinTipchai/Shutterstock, (2): Fuse/Corbis/Getty Images, (3): Wavebreak Media Ltd/123RF; 30: Dragon Images/Shutterstock; 32: Iakov Filimonov/123RF; 34 (top, left): Tele52/Shutterstock, (top, right): Scott Keeler/Tampa Bay Times/ZUMA Press Inc/Alamy Stock Photo, (center, right): Kawee Wateesatogkij/123RF; 36: Hero Images Inc./Alamy Stock Photo; 39: Tanya Constantine/Blend Images/Getty Images; 41: Stephen Simpson Inc/Tetra Images, LLC/Alamy Stock Photo; 42: Marmaduke St. John/Alamy Stock Photo; 44: Juice Images/Alamy Stock Photo.

Unit 3
Page 45: Ariel Skelley/Digital Vision/Getty images; 46 (1): Jupiterimages/Brand X Pictures/Stockbyte/Getty Images, (2): Kdonmuang/Shutterstock, (3): Ian Shaw/Alamy Stock Photo, (4): Fuse/Corbis/Getty Images, (5): Hill Street Studios LLC/Digital Vision/Getty Images, (6): Simone van den Berg/Shutterstock, (7): Dennis MacDonald/Age Fotostock/Alamy Stock Photo, (8): Rabia Elif Aksoy/123RF, (9): Fuse/Corbis/Getty Images; 48: Stockbroker/MBI/Alamy Stock Photo; 55 (left): Monkey Business Images/Shutterstock, (right): Monkey Business Images/Shutterstock; 57: JGI/Jamie Grill/Getty Images; 60 (top): Jules Selmes/Pearson Education Ltd, (bottom): Monkey Business Images/Shutterstock; 64: Leungchopan/Shutterstock.

Unit 4
Page 65: Wavebreakmedia/Shutterstock; 66 (1): Obencem/123RF, (2): Erik Isakson/Getty Images, (3): Jacob Lund/Shutterstock, (4): Sunti/Shutterstock, (5): Purestock/Getty Images, (6): Andor Bujdoso/123RF, (7): Qaphotos.com/Alamy Stock Photo, (8): Dynamic Graphics/Creatas/Getty Images, (9): Denis Ismagilov/123RF; 74: Hero Creative/Cultura Creative/Alamy Stock Photo; 81 (top): Noel Hendrickson/Digital Vision/Getty Images; 81 (bottom): Mint Images/REX/Shutterstock; 82: Sergey Nivens/123RF; 84: Image Source/Photodisc/Getty Images.

Unit 5
Page 85: Amble Design/Shutterstock; 89 (left): Design56/123RF, (center): Marc Dietrich/Shutterstock, (right): George Tsartsianidis/123RF; 94 (left): Blue Jean Images/Alamy Stock Photo, (right): Artemisphoto/Shutterstock; 98: Evgeniy Shkolenko/123RF; 101 (left): Blvdone/Shutterstock, (right): TVP Inc/Digital Vision/Getty Images; 102: Subman/E+/Getty Images; 104: Andriy Popov/123RF.

Unit 6
Page 105: Gary Kious/Hill Street Studios/Tetra Images LLC/Alamy Stock Photo; 106 (1): Jerome Wilson/Alamy Stock Photo; (2): Gustavo Andrade/123RF; (3): Sotnichenko/123RF; (4): Tom Grill/Getty images; (5): Bumbim Pensinee/Shutterstock; (6): Andriy Popov/123RF; (7): Santi Nanta/Shutterstock; (8): RuslanDashinsky/iStock/Getty Images; (9): Antonio Gravante/123RF; 108 (vacuum): Monticello/123RF, (car seat): Alexander Mitrofanov/123RF, (treadmill): Vereshchagin Dmitry/123RF, (coffee maker): Cristi Dangeorge/Shutterstock;

108 (bottom, right): LightField Studios/Shuttersock; 110: Monkey Business Images/Shutterstock; 114: Yellow Dog Productions/DigitalVision/Getty images; 116: Tele52/Shutterstock; 117 (LED TV): Africa Studio/Shutterstock, (monitor): Chakrapong Worathat/123RF, (vacuum, left): I studio/Alamy Stock Photo; (vacuum, right): Hurst Photo/Shutterstock; 119: Pro3DArtt/Shutterstock; 120: Stokkete/Shutterstock; 124 Cathy Yeulet/123RF.

Unit 7
Page 125: Pixel_Pig/E+/Getty Images; 128 (A): MonkeyApple/Greatstock/Alamy Stock Photo, (B): Jacek Bilski/imageBROKER/Alamy Stock Photo, (C): Wavebreak Media Ltd/123RF; 128 (bottom, right): ViewStock/Getty Images; 129 (left): Maksym yemelyanov/123RF, (center): Francisco Turnes/Shutterstock, (right): Alejandro duran/123RF; 131 (jumper cables): Marietjie Opperman/123RF, (oil leak): Itman__47/Shutterstock, (flat tire): PA©ter Gudella/123RF, (spare tire): Charles Knowles/Shutterstock; 132: Alex Maxim/123RF; 133: Algre/123RF, (dashboard icons): A Aleksii/Shutterstock; 134 (top, left): Tommaso Altamura/123RF, top, center left): Andrey Armyagov/Shutterstock, (top, center right): Africa Studio/Shutterstock, (top right): Antonio Diaz/123RF, 134 (center, right): Dmac/Alamy Stock Photo; 141: Tommaso79/Shutterstock; 144: Cathy Yeulet/123RF.

Unit 8
Page 145: Leo Lintang/Shutterstock; 146 (1): Dinodia Photos/Alamy Stock Photo, (2): Radius Images/Alamy Stock Photo, (3): Jack Hollingsworth/Photodisc/Getty Images, (4): Angela Hampton Picture Library/Alamy Stock Photo, (5): Jasmin Merdan/Moment/Getty Images, (6): Greg Vaughn/Alamy Stock Photo, (7): Monkey Business Images/Shutterstock, (8): David L. Moore-UK/Alamy Stock Photo, (9): Ferli/123RF, (10): Mark Edward Atkinson/Blend Images/Getty Images; 148 (left): Devrim PINAR/123RF, (center): Tooga/Photodisc/Getty Images, (right): Bravissimos/123RF; 150: Alinamd/123RF; 154: ESB Professional/Shutterstock; 155 (top, left): Yupiramos/123RF, (top, right): Baiba Opule/123RF, (bottom, left): MJ Photography/Alamy Stock Photo, (bottom right): Kriang phromphim/Shutterstock; 156: FatCamera/E+/Getty Images; 158 (top): Jamie Grill/Tetra Images/Alamy Stock Photo; (bottom): Wavebreakmedia/Shutterstock; 160 Echo/Juice Images/Getty Images; 164: Yellow Dog Productions/The Image Bank/Getty Images.

Unit 9
Page 165: Flairmicro/123RF; 166 (1): ShaunL/E+/Getty Images, (2): BassittART/E+/Getty Images, (3): Image Source/Stockbyte/Getty Images, (4): Wavebreak Media Ltd/123RF, (5): Qaphotos.com/Alamy Stock photo, (6): Thinkstock Images/Stockbyte/Getty Images, (7): Colorblind/Stone/Getty Images, (8): Colorblind Images LLC/DigitalVision/Getty Images, (9): Jack Hollingsworth/Digital Vision/Getty images; 168: Jeff Weber/Alamy Stock Photo; 170: Adriana Adinandra/123RF; 172 (left): Darryl Estrine/Uppercut Images/Getty Images, (center): Aila Images/Shutterstock; (right): Wavebreakmedia/Shutterstock; 175: Cathy Yeulet/123RF; 177: wavebreakmedia/Shutterstrock; 180: Ryan McVay/Photodisc/Getty Images; 184: Chris Sattlberger/Getty Images.

Unit 10
Page 185: Dinis Tolipov/123RF; 186 (1): ER Productions Limited/DigitalVision/Getty Images, (2): Levent Konuk/Shutterstock, (3): Cathy Yeulet/123RF, (4): Tyler Olson/123RF, (5): S4svisuals/Shutterstock, (6): Africa Studio/Shutterstock, (7): Fuse/Corbis/Getty Images, (8): Thomas Northcut/DigitalVision/Getty Images, (9): Photo Researchers/Science Source/Getty Images, (10): BSIP/Universal Images Group/Getty Images; 188: Wavebreakmedia/Shuttertstock; 193: Thinkstock/Stockbyte/Getty Images; 194: Rocketclips, Inc./Shutterstock; 196: Sturti/E+/Getty Images; 198: PT Images/Shutterstock; 201: GoGo Images Corporation/Alamy Stock Photo; 204: PhotoAlto/Odilon Dimier/PhotoAlto Agency RF Collections/Getty Images.

Unit 11
Page 205: Ferli/123RF; 206 (1): Sanjagrujic/Shutterstock, (2): ESB Basic/Shutterstock, (3): Ganna Zubkova/123RF, (5): Yin Yang/E+/Getty Images, (6): Tele52/Shutterstock; 209: Simonkr/E+/Getty Images; 216: PCJones/Alamy Stock Photo; 221 (left): Nicolasmenijes/123RF; 221 (right): Imtmphoto/123RF; 224: LDWYTN/Shutterstock.

Unit 12
Page 225: Mary Terriberry/Shutterstock; 226 (1): Orhan Cam/Shutterstock, (2): Orhan Cam/Shutterstock, (3): Travel Bug/Shutterstock, (4): MDOGAN/Shutterstock, (5): LittlenySTOCK/Shutterstock, (6): Orhan Cam/Shutterstock, (7): Michael G Smith/Shutterstock, (8): DavidNNP/Shutterstock, (9): Ivan Cholakov/Shutterstock; 228: BJI/Blue Jean Images/Getty Images; 229: Brooks Kraft LLC/Corbis Premium Historical/Getty Images; 230: Steve Heap/Shutterstock; 231: Jim Engelbrecht/DanitaDelimont/Alamy Stock Photo; 234: Kumar Sriskandan/Alamy Stock Photo; 238 (background): Orhan Cam/Shutterstock, 238 (left): Ksenia Ragozina/123RF, 238 (center): B Christopher/Alamy Stock Photo, 238 (right): Russell Kord/Alamy Stock Photo; 240: Stock Montage/Archive Photos/Getty Images; 241 (Washington Monument): IDP eastern USA collection/Alamy Stock Photo, (panda): Hoberman Collection/Universal Images Group/Getty Images, (Chinatown gate): 4kclips/Shutterstock; 242: IanDagnall Computing/Alamy Stock Photo; 244: Hongqi Zhang/123RF.

Illustrations: Steve Attoe, pp. 190; Luis Briseño, pp. 160; Deborah Crowle, pp. 6, 14; Electra Graphics, pp. 18, 24, 26, 34, 43, 44, 52, 58, 64, 68, 72, 73, 84, 86 (bottom), 92, 93, 98, 104, 117, 118, 119, 124, 144, 152, pp. 179 (row 2, center, right), 184, 224, 232, 244, 275-277; Brian Hughes, pp. 51; Stephen MacEachern, pp. 178; Luis Montiel, pp. 86 (top), 126; Allan Moon, pp. 179 (row 1, left, center, right; row 2, left); Steve Schulman, pp. 3; Anna Veltfort, pp. 2